To Barry,

with much love

on your birthday,

Love from Mary Louise xxxx.

# NME ROCK'N'ROLL
# DECADES
## THE SIXTIES

# NME NEW MUSICAL EXPRESS ROCK'N'ROLL

# DECADES

**60**

## THE SIXTIES

WHSMITH
EXCLUSIVE · BOOKS ·

# THE SIXTIES

Consultant Editor: John Tobler

Contributors: Roy Carr, Barry Lazell, Dave McAleer, David Sandison.

Editor: David Heslam
Assistant Editor: Mike Evans

Designed by Christopher Matthews

# CONTENTS

The publishers wish to thank the New Musical Express (NME) for their kind assistance and access to archive material without which this project would not have been possible. All American chart information is © 1955-1992 BPI Communications Inc. and appears courtesy of Billboard magazine.

This edition produced exclusively for WH Smith

Published by Octopus Illustrated Publishing
Michelin House, 81 Fulham Road, London SW3 6RB
part of Reed International Books Limited.

# THE SIXTIES

Elvis and Nancy Sinatra

In terms of popular music, the 1960s is regarded as the benchmark to which all other decades are compared, despite the fact that very little of enduring note occurred in the decade's first three years. The Twist? A passing phenomenon, and symptomatic of the way the established music industry encouraged obsolescence. It could be seen in the careers of America and Britain's rock icons, Elvis Presley and Cliff Richard, who were clearly being steered away from rock 'n' roll and towards what was termed 'family entertainment'.

At the end of 1962, The Beatles arrived, and conquered Britain. It would take over a year with three flop singles and a dormant album before the USA would capitulate to the Liverpudlian charmers with the pudding basin haircuts, but when Beatlemania gripped America, it heralded the longest period of world rock music influence that Britain has yet experienced. And at the same time, it fundamentally changed the nature of popular music, or the way it was perceived, from that of a fun/leisure activity to that of 'culture' and even 'art'. Nevertheless, what didn't change in the way that some hoped was the fact that the vast profits involved were still in the hands of a few major record companies.

Initially, the revolution began when The Beatles and The Rolling Stones independently began to find a fast growing audience for their enthusiastic live performances of songs by Chuck Berry. American music – blues, rock 'n' roll, R&B – was what they played before they started writing their own songs. Between 1964 and 1966, dozens of British groups made fortunes in the States, some, like the Dave Clark Five and Freddie & The Dreamers, doing better in the USA rather than their homeland.

Some young American groups, like The Byrds, tried to look British – on their first single, they were known as The Beefeaters – and a trio of unrelated young Americans, The Walker Brothers, used Britain as a springboard to launch American success. Neither would be as enduring as the quintessential Californian group, The Beach Boys, whose more clean-cut image would help them to commercial pay-dirt at first, but whose leading light, Brian Wilson, was pressured into illness in his efforts to progress, both commercially and artistically. Phil Spector – the visionary with a Wagnerian complex – was producing unique classics with exotic artists like The Ronettes, The Righteous Brothers and finally Ike and Tina Turner, and when he went off the boil commercially, The Monkees, three young Americans and an actor from England, became the teeny-bop sensation of 1967, not least because they were also TV stars.

Black music made as notable an emergence as Merseybeat, although it had always been around, but without the focus it acquired via Atlantic and Motown, which remain the best-loved soul labels today, largely because of what they achieved in the 1960s. Between them, they had all the early soul stars of note, including The Drifters, Aretha Franklin, Otis Redding, The Supremes, The Four Tops, Little Stevie Wonder (who first topped the US chart when he was 13 years old), Ray Charles, The Temptations and Marvin Gaye. They were worshipped by The Beatles and The Stones, which both launched them onto a wider (white) public and guaranteed their long-term success on both sides of the Atlantic.

In 1967, everything was poured into a melting pot and the result was music designed as the perfect soundtrack for drug-induced hallucination, a state discovered by stars and audiences alike – psychedelia was personified by Jimi Hendrix, a black American who emerged internationally from Britain, Jefferson

The Kinks

The Beach Boys

The Flowerpot Men

The Beatles

The Supremes

Airplane, Quicksilver Messenger Service, Moby Grape and many more. It was the era of bell-bottom jeans and tie-dye T-shirts, anti-war sentiments and counter culture, far-out lyrics and music that had few rules and sometimes less form, names like The Grateful Dead, Country Joe & The Fish and The Doors, hedonism . . . and drugs. Soon the drugs led to deaths, and a decade which produced more innovation than any other fell flat on its face as it forgot the meaning of moderation.

Yet rock music's most enduring acts – who are revered in the 1990s (even though they rarely have new hit records) – first appeared in the 1960s. Such artists as The Stones, The Who, The Beach Boys and Bob Dylan. Then there were the later developers like Pink Floyd, whose original inspiration, Syd Barrett, became too unreliable for his colleagues. They quickly replaced him with Dave Gilmour, Roger Waters assumed songwriting chores, and they became far bigger than anyone expected. Many members of 1960s groups moved into solo work – Eric Clapton (The Yardbirds, then The Bluesbreakers), Rod Stewart (The Jeff Beck Group), Diana Ross (The Supremes), Smokey Robinson (The Miracles), Elton John (Bluesology), Neil Young (Buffalo Springfield) and of course ex-Beatle Paul McCartney – all became superstars, but many others died before their time: R.I.P. Jim Morrison (The Doors), Janis Joplin (Big Brother & The Holding Company), Brian Jones (The Rolling Stones), Keith Moon (The Who), Gram Parsons and Clarence White (The Byrds), Al Wilson and Bob Hite (Canned Heat), Dennis Wilson (The Beach Boys), Florence Ballard (The Supremes), plus far too many others, like Jimi Hendrix, Marvin Gaye, John Lennon – the list gets longer every year. They weren't all drug-related deaths, though self-destruction always grabbed the biggest headlines – traffic accidents, murders and drowning took their toll as well.

An apocryphal statement frequently quoted in the 1990s suggests that anyone who claims to remember the Sixties could not possibly have lived through the decade. This is plainly incorrect as Sixties influences in fashion and music are arguably even more prevalent today than they were in the innovative decade in which they first appeared. If it's not artists from the Sixties such as those named above, it's cover versions of Sixties hits by new artists, some of whom probably weren't even born when the original version of their chart-topping hit was first in the charts: examples range from Robert Palmer's recent cover of Bob Dylan's 'I'll Be Your Baby Tonight' to versions of Brian Hyland's early Sixties hits 'Sealed With A Kiss' and 'Itsy Bitsy Teenie Weenie Yellow Polka Dot Bikini' by Jason Donovan and Bombalurina respectively. It's not just the true classics of the swingin' decade that have been resurrected over the years.

A few Sixties stars survived, but clearly had lost their impetus, like head Beach Boy Brian Wilson, David Crosby of The Byrds and others. Innovation can demand a big price. Pete Townshend wrote the immortal line 'Hope I die before I get old' in his first eternal classic, 'My Generation'. Nobody thought he meant it, but there was certainly some truth in the fact that no one wanted the Sixties to end – and few regard the subsequent decades with such respect. The 1960s is the subject of minute scrutiny from every possible angle because it is the epitome of nostalgia both for the ageing hippies and rockers who lived it and the younger generations who tuned in to the sounds and identified with the images of the period.

## ELVIS: 'NO MORE HIGH LIVING!'

In Paris, on a five-day pass, the soon-to-be discharged Sgt Elvis Presley emerged from his £7-a-day suite in the capital's most expensive hotel (Prince of Wales) to offer his thoughts on how he intends to adapt to civilian life.

Said Elvis: 'Being in the Army, I've lost my love of high living. I've learned to relax and take things leisurely during my off-duty Army hours. Before, I was rushin' around 'case I missed somethin'!'

# COCHRAN SPILLS THE BEANS

*Bobby socks it to 'em*

In Britain to promote his latest recording – his version of Ray Charles' 'Hallelujah, I Love Her So' – Eddie Cochran answers a few personal questions.

Who has been the biggest influence on his career? 'Without a doubt, Ray Charles,' Eddie says. 'He's so good – one of the greatest blues singers I've ever heard. But I don't consciously try to copy him. I simply try to generate the same feeling that he produces when he sings.'

As to what has been the most significant break in his young career, Cochran reveals:

'Appearing in the film, *The Girl Can't Help It*. You see, I wasn't even a singer before I made the movie, and hadn't had any vocal discs at all.

'How'd it happen? Well, one day I was playing guitar on a session when up comes a guy, and asks, "How would you like to make a picture?"

'Well, the next day he called and asked if I could sing. I went along with the gag, said I could. Then he asked me to make a demonstration disc of a tune called "20 Flight Rock".

'I still thought it was a joke – let's face it, I didn't know if I could sing. Anyways, I made the record, he liked it, signed me for

the film, and that was the start of everything!'

Eddie went on to confirm rumours that on some of his hit records he not only sings but also plays *all* the instruments.

'On the "Summertime Blues" session, for example, I sang the solo voice, the bass voice that comes in now and again, and also wrote the song,' he explains.

'In addition, by using multi-recording techniques, I also played guitar, bass and drums. I also repeated the formula on "C'mon, Everybody".'

'On my latest disc, "Hallelujah, I Love Her So", I play piano, and I sit at the keyboard for quite a few of the tracks on my new album, which should be issued soon.'

### THE GRAPEVINE

■ Cliff Richard & The Shadows have been special UK guests on month-long 'Dick Clark's Caravan of Stars' US tour.

■ Dinah Washington & Brook Benton have been storming US charts with 'Baby (You've Got What It Takes)'; likewise Chuck Berry's 'Let It Rock'.

■ Adam Faith's new UK single is called 'Poor Me'.

*Charles: Eddie's inspiration*

*Brook's got what it takes*

# GOOD: 'NO CLIFF WITHOUT ELVIS'

Far left: Cliff Richard
Left: erotic Fury

## JESSE BELVIN KILLED – KKK TO BLAME?

Jack Good, who soared to fame as producer of the pioneering all-live rock'n'roll British TV show *Oh Boy!* (and is currently enjoying success with his latest TV presentation *Boy Meets Girls*) tells it as it is!

Asked if he thinks Cliff Richard would have been more successful or less successful had there never been an Elvis Presley, Good replies: 'I don't think Cliff would have existed at all as a singer without Elvis. He certainly wouldn't be the singer he is today. The initial impetus of Cliff's singing was entirely due to Elvis.'

Asked about public criticism of singer Billy Fury's erotic gyrations on *Boy Meets Girls*, Good stated his position: 'I fully agree that anything suggestive should be avoided – though of course, these things are partially in the minds of individual viewers.

'Frankly, there are one or two things that Billy Fury does that I would rather he didn't. I have, in fact, suggested so to Billy who does tend to get carried away by his performance.'

West Coast R&B star, Jesse Belvin (27), his wife Jo Anne and driver Charles Shackleford were among the five victims to perish when the rented Cadillac carrying Belvin's party suddenly swerved at great speed across the centre line of US Route 67, near Fairhope, Arkansas, to crash head on into an oncoming car.

Belvin was en route from a Little Rock concert he'd played with Jackie Wilson and Little Willie John to the next evening's appearance in Dallas, Texas.

Conjecture still surrounds the accident: rumours suggest that local Ku Klux Klansmen tampered with the wheel of the vehicle, but the more accepted theory is that Shackleford's abilities as a chauffeur were impaired through his use of heroin, and tiredness from the long journey. Previously, Shackleford had been fired by singer Ray Charles because of erratic driving.

A most influential ballad stylist – earning him the tag of 'Mr Easy' – Belvin proved something of a role model to his closest rival Sam Cooke, whom RCA attempted to style in Jesse's image.

Jesse Belvin will be best remembered as the composer of The Penguin's multi-million selling doo-wop anthem 'Earth Angel', and his own recording of 'Goodnight My Love', which became the signing-off song for dj Alan Freed's radio show.

*Peter Jay: a Meek triumph?*

## CHARTS

|  |  |
|---|---|
| US45 | Running Bear<br>*Johnny Preston* |
| USLP | Here We Go Again<br>*Kingston Trio* |
| UK45 | Why<br>*Anthony Newley* |
| UKLP | South Pacific<br>*Soundtrack* |

——— W E E K 2 ———

|  |  |
|---|---|
| US45 | Teen Angel<br>*Mark Dinning* |
| USLP | The Sound Of Music<br>*Original Cast* |
| UK45 | Why<br>*Anthony Newley* |
| UKLP | South Pacific<br>*Soundtrack* |

——— W E E K 3 ———

|  |  |
|---|---|
| US45 | Teen Angel<br>*Mark Dinning* |
| USLP | The Sound Of Music<br>*Original Cast* |
| UK45 | Why<br>*Anthony Newley* |
| UKLP | South Pacific<br>*Soundtrack* |

——— W E E K 4 ———

|  |  |
|---|---|
| US45 | Theme From 'A Summer Place'<br>*Percy Faith* |
| USLP | The Sound Of Music<br>*Original Cast* |
| UK45 | Why<br>*Anthony Newley* |
| UKLP | South Pacific<br>*Soundtrack* |

## THE GRAPEVINE

■ The John Barry Seven have released 'Hit and Miss', the theme from BBC-TV's *Juke Box Jury*.

■ Innovative British producer Joe Meek has launched his own Triumph label with 'Just Too Late' by drummer Peter Jay.

■ The Everly Brothers have left Cadence for the just-launched Warner Brothers label and debut with 'Cathy's Clown'.

■ Eddie Cochran and Gene Vincent have begun their mammoth 20-week British tour in Glasgow.

# 1960

Back on civvy street, Elvis faces the press as he says goodbye to US army

## CHARTS

| | |
|---|---|
| US45 | Theme From 'A Summer Place' *Percy Faith* |
| USLP | The Sound Of Music *Original Cast* |
| UK45 | Poor Me *Adam Faith* |
| UKLP | South Pacific *Soundtrack* |

—— WEEK 2 ——

| | |
|---|---|
| US45 | Theme from 'A Summer Place' *Percy Faith* |
| USLP | The Sound Of Music *Original Cast* |
| UK45 | Poor Me *Adam Faith* |
| UKLP | South Pacific *Soundtrack* |

—— WEEK 3 ——

| | |
|---|---|
| US45 | Theme From 'A Summer Place' *Percy Faith* |
| USLP | The Sound Of Music *Original Cast* |
| UK45 | Running Bear *Johnny Preston* |
| UKLP | South pacific *Soundtrack* |

—— WEEK 4 ——

| | |
|---|---|
| US45 | Theme From 'A Summer Place' *Percy Faith* |
| USLP | The Sound Of Music *Original Cast* |
| UK45 | My Old Man's A Dustman *Lonnie Donegan* |
| UKLP | South Pacific *Soundtrack* |

# ELVIS IS BACK!

Elvis Presley's demobilization from the US Army has proved to be just as big a media event as his induction.

It commenced at the Friedberg Barracks in West Germany where 'the most publicized soldier since General MacArthur' gave a 'farewell' press conference before leaving Europe. Said Elvis of his immediate future: 'I don't know if I shall manage to get on top again. I only wish I knew. I hear that trends have changed, so it might be pretty difficult for me. But, I'll tell you this . . . I'm sure gonna try hard.

'My attraction to rock'n'roll hasn't changed one bit, and I think it would be a mistake for me to change my style. The public will let me know in due course if they don't like it.'

Asked what he thinks of his new rivals – Fabian and Frankie Avalon – Elvis replies: 'I don't consider them rivals . . . there's room for everyone. And, if other people can make it, good luck to them.'

So, what souvenirs will Elvis be taking back to the USA?

Aside from personal luggage, two tons of fan mail stuffed into 12 large sacks, and a collection of 2,182 records, Elvis reveals: 'Two German guitars, one camera, but no girls!'

What about 16-year-old Priscilla Beaulieu, who has been his steady Army date?

'It's nothing serious,' insists Elvis. 'I can promise you, there's no big romance!'

A howlin' blizzard, singer Nancy Sinatra, 2,000 fans and a press battalion welcomed Elvis back Stateside when, on March 3, the military aircraft carrying his unit back from Germany touched down at McGuire Airbase, New Jersey. Two days later, Elvis was back on civvy street.

On March 20 and 21, he undertook his first post-Army recording date, at the RCA Studios in Nashville. Two of the titles cut, 'Stuck On You'/'Fame and Fortune' (RCA) went on sale in Nashville within 48 hours of having been taped.

The momentum continued: on March 26, Elvis's return to active public life via network telelvision occurred when he appeared as special guest on *The Frank Sinatra Timex Show*. In the show, Elvis performed both sides of his newest single, then duetted with Sinatra.

The King is back.

## EVERLY-CRICKETS TOUR

The Everly Brothers have ensured both banner headlines and a box-office stampede when they revealed that Buddy Holly's former band – The Crickets – will do the back-up honours on Don and Phil's UK tour scheduled to open on April 1.

In the meantime, there was standing room only at the opening night of a package show featuring three other hot US chart stars – Bobby Darin, Duane Eddy and Clyde McPhatter – at the Lewisham Odeon, London.

Emile Ford & The Checkmates supplied local interest.

*The Everlys: Cricket match*

*Twang man Duane*

# THE GRAPEVINE

■ Actor-singer Anthony Newley's latest movie *Jazzboat* has opened at London's New Victoria Cinema

■ A French singer named Johnny Halliday, of whom much is expected, has released his first single on the Vogue label – 'Laisse Les Filles'.

■ Soul singer Sam Cooke kicks off a tour of the West Indies.

# EDDIE COCHRAN KILLED, VINCENT INJURED IN TAXI CRASH

Following a concert at the Bristol Hippodrome, Eddie Cochran, Gene Vincent, Sharon Sheeley (Cochran's fiancée) and tour manager Patrick Thompkins set off for London in a Ford Consul taxi driven by a local 19-year old youth.

Cochran was in a hurry, as he was due to fly back to America from Heathrow Airport the next afternoon.

Averaging 70 mph, the taxi reached Chippenham, Wiltshire at midnight. However, the driver had lost his sense of direction and control of the vehicle. As he emerged from beneath a railway viaduct, the car hit the curb, careering 150-yards before crashing into a concrete lampstand.

The impact threw Cochran upwards against the car roof and then through the door and on to the road. Gene Vincent suffered a fractured collar bone and Sheeley back injuries, while Thompkins and the driver escaped unhurt.

At 4 p.m. Easter Sunday, 16 hours after the accident, Eddie Cochran died as a result of severe brain lacerations. He was buried at Forest Lawn Cemetery, Glendate, California, on April 25.

Born on October 30 1938 in Oklahoma City, Cochran was a most accomplished singer and guitarist best remembered for hits such as '20 Flight Rock', 'Summertime Blues', 'C'Mon Everybody', 'Somethin' Else' and 'Hallelujah, I Love Her So'.

He also made guest appearances in such movies as *The Girl Can't Help It*, *Go Johnny Go* and *Untamed Youth*.

A new single, with the sadly prophetic title 'Three Steps To Heaven' is being considered for release by London Records, his British label.

## CHARTS

| | |
|---|---|
| US45 | Theme From 'A Summer Place' *Percy Faith* |
| USLP | The Sound Of Music *Original Cast* |
| UK45 | My Old Man's A Dustman *Lonnie Donegan* |
| UKLP | South Pacific *Soundtrack* |

### WEEK 2

| | |
|---|---|
| US45 | Theme From 'A Summer Place' *Percy Faith* |
| USLP | The Sound Of Music *Original Cast* |
| UK45 | My Old Man's A Dustman *Lonnie Donegan* |
| UKLP | South Pacific *Soundtrack* |

### WEEK 3

| | |
|---|---|
| US45 | Theme From 'A Summer Place' *Percy Faith* |
| USLP | The Sound Of Music *Original Cast* |
| UK45 | My Old Man's A Dustman *Lonnie Donegan* |
| UKLP | South Pacific *Soundtrack* |

### WEEK 4

| | |
|---|---|
| US45 | Theme From 'A Summer Place' *Percy Faith* |
| USLP | The Sound Of Music *Original Cast* |
| UK45 | Do You Mind *Anthony Newley* |
| UKLP | South Pacific *Soundtrack* |

*Connie copies the Colonel in pop price stakes*

## ELVIS: THE PRICE RISES

In an effort to frighten off all but legitimately-interested parties, Colonel Tom Parker has set the non-negotiable price of $150,000 for any future Elvis Presley concert performances.

So far, this has proved even more effective than the Colonel anticipated: there are no takers!

The Colonel's price tag is understandable, given the news that Presley has been named America's best-selling recording artist at the first presentation of the NARM Awards — a new annual prize-giving ceremony instigated by the National Association of Record Merchants.

Connie Francis's manager may follow suit. His client was named top-selling female artist.

## WHAM UNVEILED

Direct from Manchester, ABC-TV screened the first edition of celebrated producer Jack *Oh Boy!* Good's new weekly rock'n'roll extravaganza, *Wham!* on April 23.

The first show featured Billy Fury, Joe Brown, Jess Conrad, Dickie Pride, Little Tony, Vince Taylor and Johnny Kidd & The Pirates.

Critics' response? A hit!

## THE GRAPEVINE

■ Elvis Presley has gone back in uniform on Paramount Pictures' Hollywood lot, to commence filming *G.I. Blues*.

■ UK chart newcomer Lance 'Be Mine' Fortune and US singer Jerry 'Here Comes Summer' Keller replaced the late Eddie Cochran on Gene Vincent's current UK tour.

■ Pye Records have released 'This Is Hancock', a collection of U.K. comedian Tony Hancock's best radio sketches.

*British cult favourite and comic genius Tony Hancock*

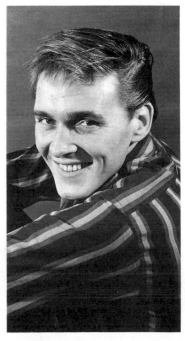

*Fury: Wham! star*

11

## CHARTS

US45 | Stuck On You
*Elvis Presley*
USLP | The Sound Of Music
*Original Cast*
UK45 | Cathy's Clown
*Everly Brothers*
UKLP | South Pacific
*Soundtrack*

——— W E E K 2 ———

US45 | Stuck On You
*Elvis Presley*
USLP | Sold Out
*Kingston Trio*
UK45 | Cathy's Clown
*Everly Brothers*
UKLP | South Pacific
*Soundtrack*

——— W E E K 3 ———

US45 | Stuck On You
*Elvis Presley*
USLP | Sold Out
*Kingston Trio*
UK45 | Cathy's Clown
*Everly Brothers*
UKLP | South Pacific
*Soundtrack*

——— W E E K 4 ———

US45 | Stuck On You
*Elvis Presley*
USLP | Sold Out
*Kingston Trio*
UK45 | Cathy's Clown
*Everly Brothers*
UKLP | South Pacific
*Soundtrack*

——— W E E K 5 ———

US45 | Cathy's Clown
*Everly Brothers*
USLP | Sold Out
*Kingston Trio*
UK45 | Cathy's Clown
*Everly Brothers*
UKLP | South Pacific
*Soundtrack*

## CAVERN GOES POP

After three years, Liverpool's popular Cavern Club, in Mathew Street, has moved with the times and finally 'recognized' rock music.

The club's previous jazz-only booking policy has been dropped. The first two local beat groups to benefit – Cass & The Casanovas and Rory Storme & The Hurricanes.

*Tallahassee, New Orleans, California – it's the UK next for Freddy Cannon*

# COCHRAN 'NOT DEAD', SAYS SHARON

'Eddie Cochran is not dead!' says his fiancée, Sharon Sheeley, the 20-year-old US songwriter, still recovering in a London hospital from multiple injuries she received in the auto smash that killed Cochran.

'Eddie is away on a long tour and it won't be long before I see him again soon. I don't need to find another lover. My love for Eddie is strong enough to last, and, I thank God for the three years He let me have with him.'

Their relationship began in 1957, when they were introduced by The Everly Brothers. 'It was, on my part, love at first sight, but Eddie paid no attention to me. We did not meet again for about nine months,' recalls Sharon.

'Eddie asked me for a date, but asked if I would first agree to go steady with him – I gladly con- sented. A month later, we be- came engaged.

'We planned to marry in America. We were due to fly back last month, and it was on the way to the airport that Eddie was killed. I can tell you that Eddie was singing "California, Here I Come", at the time – and we were both so happy that we were going home to be married.'

Miss Sheeley, who has flatly rejected offers from various US record companies to cut a 'tri- bute' disc about Eddie, insists that she's sickened by the attempts by certain individuals to make a profit from Cochran's death.

Does she treasure any particu- lar memories of her relationship with Eddie? 'No! our love and the times we had together is the deepest, dearest memory I pos- sess.'

## THE GRAPEVINE

■ Stateside, 'The Eddie Cochran Memorial Album' has been rush-released.

■ Conway Twitty, Freddy Cannon, Johnny Preston are trekking around the UK with locals Wee Willie Harris & Tony Crombie's Rockets.

■ Safe-As-Milk Elvis surrogate Tommy Sands has commenced a six-month stint with US Air Force.

■ Liverpool beat group, The Silver Beetles are touring Scotland as Johnny Gentle's backing band.

## PAYOLA: FREED FOR TRIAL

A Manhattan Grand Jury has in- dicted eight people – including America's most influential and popular disc jockey, KDAY's Alan Freed – for having received in excess of $30,000 in payola.

This illegal pay-for-play policy has run rampant through- out the US radio industry for many years, but in an effort to improve its poor image, Freed is believed to have been made something of a scapegoat.

Though he has pleaded not guilty as charged, Freed's trial has been set for September 19.

*Freed, free for the moment but prison a possibility*

## STAR QUOTE

### RICKY NELSON

*'Perhaps the most embarrasing moment in my career was when six girls tried to fling themselves under my car, and shouted to me to run over them. That sort of thing can be very frightening!'*

# WILLIAMS QUITS PLATTERS

Before Tony Williams abdicated this month from his position as lead singer with vocal group The Platters to embark upon a solo career, the stylish tenor – who sang on such evocative Mercury label hits as 'Only You', 'The Great Pretender' and 'Smoke Gets In Your Eyes' – generously and publicly introduced his replacement, Sammy Turner (21), on stage at the Copa Club, Newport, Kentucky. It was a gesture typical of the man and the group.

Whereas many similar vocal acts have only enjoyed short-lived fame, the secret of The Platters' prolonged success has been their avoidance of gimmicky doo-wop vocal tricks.

Instead, their preference is for straight-ahead beat ballads which, aside from the familiar piano triplets trade mark, are practically accappella.

A major contributory factor in their initial success was the dignity of their appearance in 'Rock Around The Clock' when they were filmed performing their perennial best-sellers, 'Only You' and 'The Great Pretender'.

## NEWLEY – NO IDOL ACTOR

Movie actor Anthony Newley – the Artful Dodger to Alec Guinness's memorable Fagin in *Oliver Twist*, who suddenly found himself a bona-fide chart-busting pop star after playing a rock'n'roll singer conscripted into the (British) Army in the hit comedy movie *Idle On Parade*, has adopted an entirely new image.

*Stop The World, I Want to Get Off*, the avant-garde stage musical he co-wrote with lyricist/

*Newley-launched musical bound for London opening*

composer Leslie Bricusse, and in which he stars, has been hailed an instant hit at its première at Manchester's Palace Theatre.

Plans are now afoot to bring the show, in which Newley plays a confused character called Littlechap, to London, and to record an album of material from the production.

## THE GRAPEVINE

■ The Hollywood Argyles' Kim Fowley produced 'Alley-Oop', which is chartbound in the USA.

■ BBC Radio's weekly celebrity check-list *Desert Island Disc* has celebrated its 500th edition.

■ Instrumental guitar combo, The Ventures have got their careers off to a quick start with 'Walk Don't Run'.

# JUNE 1960

## EMILE GOES GOLD

Pye recording stars Emile Ford & The Checkmates have joined the exclusive band of British artists to have sold in excess of one million copies of any single in the UK.

They have received a gold disc for 'What Do You Want To Make Those Eyes At Me For'.

## STAR QUOTE

### PAT BOONE

who married at 19, after a three-year courtship.

*'I receive many queries from young people who want to get married. I spend my time discouraging them!'*

*Nokie Edwards, Don Wilson, Howie Johnson and Bob Bogle make up The Venture*

# 1960

## DUANE: 'IT'S HARD WORK!'

Twangy guitar star Duane Eddy, currently enjoying world-wide success with his theme tune for the movie *Because They're Young*, has revealed a few trade secrets:

'A lot of people seem to think it's easy to gather round a studio mike and pluck guitar strings, play tenor sax and make all the other noises that come out on our disc,' he confided.

'How I wish I could make people see how much hard work the boys really put in. From The Rebels to the sound engineer, and from the extra musicians to the guys whose job it is to keep us supplied with coffee and hot dogs, we are all working to one end.'

## S T A R QUOTE

### FATS DOMINO

*'I don't care if my discs hit the top spot or if they are never seen in the charts, so long as the collectors who appreciate rhythm and blues buy them. When the real collectors lose interest, man, I'll retire.'*

*Twistin' time with Hank*

# NO KIDDING JOHNNY THE PIRATE!

Johnny Kidd & The Pirates have 'vibrated' into the UK charts with 'Shakin' All Over' – a record which many insist has come close to wiping away the memory of Cliff Richard's 'Move It' as the greatest-ever British-made rock'n'roll single.

Kidd's self-penned follow-up to his last year hit 'Please Don't Touch' again employs a 'shakin'' theme, but it's quite unlike any other record in the charts.

With an aggressive visual image as unmistakable as his R&B-rooted voice – black patch over his left eye, matching leather waistcoat and thighboots, plus a cutlass – Kidd stands apart from the numerous Elvis imitators who make up the British rock'n'roll scene.

Similarly, his guitarists steer away from Shadows-style 'tremeloing' and Duane Eddy elastic-band 'twang', preferring a hard-edged black blues sound.

For 'Shakin' All Over', top session guitar-picker Joe Moretti was responsible for that hackle-raising guitar lick.

Regarding who influenced Kidd's highly-personalized style, all he had to say was: 'I just open my mouth and sing – that's all there is to it!'

## ROLF'S NEW SOUND

A new decade – a new sound!!!!

The Wobble Board, invention of bearded Australian TV presenter and cartoonist Rolf Harris is the featured instrument on his new record 'Tie Me Kangaroo Down Sport', which has wobbled straight into the UK charts at No. 15.

How To Play The Wobble Board!

Step 1: Locate a piece of hardboard 3ft long by 18in wide.

Step 2: Grasp both ends of the board firmly in your hands.

Step 3: With a flick of the wrists bend the board up and down to produce a rhythmic 'Whoolp' and 'Beloop'.

Step 4: Immediately become rich and famous.

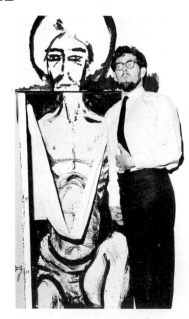

*Rolf wobbles into the chart*

## T H E GRAPEVINE

■ Widower Vernon Presley (Elvis' Dad) has married divorcee Dee Elliott.

■ Hank Ballard & The Midnighters launch 'The Twist'.

■ Bing Crosby has been presented with a platinum disc to commemorate record sales of 200 million.

■ Only six months after it commenced, Marty Wilde's two year, £100,000 contract with impresario Harold Fielding is to be terminated in September, by mutual agreement.

## CHARTS

| | | |
|---|---|---|
| US45 | Everybody's Somebody's Fool | *Connie Francis* |
| USLP | Sold Out | *Kingston Trio* |
| UK45 | Good Timin' | *Jimmy Jones* |
| UKLP | South Pacific | *Soundtrack* |
| **WEEK 2** | | |
| US45 | Everybody's Somebody's Fool | *Connie Francis* |
| USLP | Sold Out | *Kingston Trio* |
| UK45 | Good Timin' | *Jimmy Jones* |
| UKLP | South Pacific | *Soundtrack* |
| **WEEK 3** | | |
| US45 | Alley-Oop | *Hollywood Argyles* |
| USLP | Sold Out | *Kingston Trio* |
| UK45 | Good Timin' | *Jimmy Jones* |
| UKLP | Elvis Is Back | *Elvis Presley* |
| **WEEK 4** | | |
| US45 | I'm Sorry | *Brenda Lee* |
| USLP | The Button-Down Mind Of | *Bob Newhart* |
| UK45 | Please Don't Tease | *Cliff Richard* |
| UKLP | Elvis Is Back | *Elvis Presley* |
| **WEEK 5** | | |
| US45 | I'm Sorry | *Brenda Lee* |
| USLP | The Button-Down Mind Of | *Bobby Newhart* |
| UK45 | Please Don't Tease | *Cliff Richard* |
| UKLP | Elvis Is Back | *Elvis Presley* |

# WHICH CAME FIRST – SHADOWS OR BERT?

*Cliff 'n' the Shads*

Controversy has erupted as Cliff Richard's fancy-footwork backing group The Shadows enjoy chart-topping solo status with their instrumental hit, 'Apache'. The question on BBC disc jockeys lips is: was 'Apache' written for 'Play-Guitar-In-A-Day' personality Bert Weedon (the loser in the singles race), or was it penned for The Shadows?

So what does 'Apache' composer Jerry Lordan have to say?

'I don't write specifically for any artist – I've never really tried. I'm not like Lionel Bart – I wish I was!' he laughs.

'I gave no thought at all who should play it until it was completed,' he says, but lets slip that when 'Apache' was still in manuscript form, Bert Weedon was the first name that sprang to mind.

Nevertheless, while on tour together, The Shadows asked Lordan if he had any material that might be suitable for them.

'As I don't write exclusively for any artist, and I wasn't certain if Bert Weedon was even considering recording the tune, I suggested "Apache" to The Shadows,' Lordan says.

## VINCENT CHEWS THE FAT

Gene Vincent takes time out during his hectic UK schedule to chew the fat with the NME in a question-and-answer session:

Q: How does British TV compare with the US in terms of rock'n'roll presentation?

A: 'In Britain, they try to achieve perfection. In the States, they just put you in front of a camera, and tell you to sing!'

Q: How do you think UK rock artists would fare in the US?

A: 'I felt inferior compared to many British singers. Artists over here know all kinds of music – they discuss keys, arrangements and so on. Speaking for myself, somebody just gives me a chord and I sing. That's all I can do!'

Q: Have you thought about branching out into other fields of entertainment?

A: 'I'm a rock singer and I reckon that's the way I'll stay. I don't think that I could alter if I tried!'

## DECCA DITHER OVER DEATH DISC

He who hesitates is hitless!

Two British cover versions of American singer Ray Peterson's controversial *death-disc*, 'Tell Laura I Love Her' have been rushed-released.

And, as Ricky Valence and John Leyton competed for attention, Decca Records commenced the first of five high-level boardroom discussions to determine whether or not they should release the 'offending' Peterson original. In doing so, they lost valuable sales – and the No. 1 slot.

*Ricky tells Laura*

*Dustman Donegan cleans up with 'My Old Man's' million-seller*

## CHARTS

| | | |
|---|---|---|
| US45 | I'm Sorry | Brenda Lee |
| USLP | The Button-Down Mind Of | Bob Newhart |
| UK45 | Please Don't Tease | Cliff Richard |
| UKLP | Elvis Is Back | Elvis Presley |
| | **WEEK 2** | |
| US45 | Yellow Polka Dot Bikini | Brian Hyland |
| USLP | The Button-Down Mind Of | Bob Newhart |
| UK45 | Please Don't Tease | Cliff Richard |
| UKLP | Elvis Is Back | Elvis Presley |
| | **WEEK 3** | |
| US45 | It's Now Or Never | Elvis Presley |
| USLP | The Button-Down Mind Of | Bob Newhart |
| UK45 | Apache | Shadows |
| UKLP | Elvis Is Back | Elvis Presley |
| | **WEEK 4** | |
| US45 | It's Now Or Never | Elvis Presley |
| USLP | The Button-Down Mind Of | Bob Newhart |
| UK45 | Apache | Shadows |
| UKLP | Elvis Is Back | Elvis Presley |

15

## MORE COCHRAN

The Eddie Cochran memorial industry rolls on.

Liberty Records' President Al Bennett has issued a statement claiming the company is in possession of 40 unreleased studio and demo tapes by the late Eddie Cochran.

Enough, suggests Bennett, for at least four more posthumous singles, plus an album.

## BLACK BACK

Elvis Presley's former bassist, Bill Black – now a highly successful instrumental combo leader in his own right – has stormed back into the US charts with a personalized treatment of his ex-boss' hit, 'Don't Be Cruel'.

# IT'S TRAD, DAD!

*Acker Bilk (left) and Ken Colyer (below) both benefitting from the boom in trad jazz*

Will Dixieland kill rock? That's the latest topic circulating through the British music scene.

For the first time ever, jazz has become 'pop' music. And, in Britain, locally produced brash revivalist New Orleans-style trad jazz performed by the likes of Acker Bilk, Chris Barber, Kenny Ball, Terry Lightfoot and Ken Colyer, has spread out from the cellar clubs and art college Saturday night 'raves' and into the charts, where it now stands shoulder-to-shoulder with rock'n'roll.

Perhaps employing the theory of embrace one's enemy, or maybe staging a calculated take-the-money-and-run operation, impresario Larry Parnes and TV pop producer Jack Good have packaged together 15 British rock singers including Billy Fury, Joe Brown, Tommy Bruce, Dave Sampson, Dickie Pride, Duffy Power and Georgie Fame, and pushed them in front of a thundering 15-piece band led by show-drummer Jimmy Nicol for an extensive trek around the British Isles under a 'Rock And Trad' banner.

Jack Good commented about the production he has masterminded: 'I want the show to be fast-moving, but with a pronounced Dixieland theme . . . but don't get the idea that we are scrapping rock altogether.'

Does this mean that the package couldn't stand up purely as a rock'n'roll show?

'I can't really answer that!' was Good's final word on the subject.

## SHADOWS GO MOVIE

The Shadows have scored another first – starring in the very first 'video-disc': a technicolour promotional film made for use both on television and the specially designed video juke-boxes that have begun appearing in the bars of selected French and Italian coastal holiday resorts.

## MOTOWN IN UK

Motivated by the brisk import trade in American soul singles, Oriole Records has acquired the UK release rights to Detroit's Tamla-Motown label, and has celebrated the deal by releasing The Contours' 'Do You Love Me', Mary Wells' 'You Beat Me To The Punch' and The Marvelettes' 'Beechwood 4-5789'.

*Contours: UK release*

# POLL: PRESLEY AND CONNIE TRIUMPHANT

With thousands of votes cast, the NME Annual Reader's Poll shows that Elvis Presley's hold on fans' hearts has not diminished – nor has age dimmed Frank Sinatra's appeal!

On the distaff side, Connie Francis continues to reign supreme, although given a good run by Brenda Lee and Shirley Bassey.

The results in full:

## World Section

*Male Section*
1 Elvis Presley
2 Cliff Richard
3 Frank Sinatra

*Female Singer*
1 Connie Francis
2 Brenda Lee
3 Shirley Bassey

*Vocal Group*
1 The Everly Brothers

*Musical Personality*
1 Duane Eddy

## British Section

*Male Singer*
1 Cliff Richard
2 Adam Faith
3 Anthony Newley

*Female Singer*
1 Shirley Bassey
2 Alma Cogan
3 Petula Clark

*Vocal Group*
1 The King Brothers

*Vocal Personality*
1 Lonnie Donegan

*Large Band/Orchestra*
1 Ted Heath

*Small Group*
1 The Shadows

*New Disc or TV Singer*
1 Emile Ford

*Instrumental Personality*
1 Russ Conway

*Disc-Jockey*
1 David Jacobs

*British Disc of the Year*
1 The Shadows – 'Apache'

*Artist For Poll Concert*
1 Adam Faith

*Shirley shines in Poll*

## THE GRAPEVINE

- Dion & The Belmonts have split.
- Africa is the first stop for the US State Department's newly-inaugurated Jazz Ambassador – Louis Armstrong.
- With Frank Sinatra as best man, Sammy Davis Jr. defied racist death threats and has married Swedish blonde actress, Mai Britt.
- Youth exploitation flick, *Beat Girl*, starring Adam Faith and featuring a John Barry soundtrack, has opened in London.

## CHARTS

| | |
|---|---|
| US45 | My Heart Has A Mind Of Its Own — *Connie Francis* |
| USLP | String Along — *Kingston Trio* |
| UK45 | Tell Laura I Love Her — *Ricky Valance* |
| UKLP | Down Drury Lane To Memory Lane — *101 Strings* |

### WEEK 2

| | |
|---|---|
| US45 | Mr. Custer — *Larry Verne* |
| USLP | String Along — *Kingston Trio* |
| UK45 | Tell Laura I Love Her — *Ricky Valance* |
| UKLP | Down Drury Lane To Memory Lane — *101 Strings* |

### WEEK 3

| | |
|---|---|
| US45 | Mr. Custer — *Larry Verne* |
| USLP | String Along — *Kingston Trio* |
| UK45 | Only The Lonely — *Roy Orbison* |
| UKLP | South Pacific — *Soundtrack* |

### WEEK 4

| | |
|---|---|
| US45 | Save The Last Dance For Me — *Drifters* |
| USLP | Nice & Easy — *Frank Sinatra* |
| UK45 | Only The Lonely — *Roy Orbison* |
| UKLP | South Pacific — *Soundtrack* |

### WEEK 5

| | |
|---|---|
| US45 | I Want To Be Wanted — *Brenda Lee* |
| USLP | The Button-Down Mind Of — *Bob Newhart* |
| UK45 | Only The Lonely — *Roy Orbison* |
| UKLP | South Pacific — *Soundtrack* |

## STARS ON FANS

Connie Francis, Cliff Richard and Lonnie Donegan have spoken candidly about fan-power. The results are intriguing:

Connie Francis: 'I estimate that I receive 7,000 fan letters every week from all over the world. I have three offices dealing with them. Of these, I get to read about 250. I always make certain I see any special letters, or correspondence from servicemen.'

Cliff Richard: 'I must confess that I don't enjoy being mobbed, and it's rather a pity the fans don't realize that it's to their disadvantage. You see, if they weren't so fanatic, it would then be possible to stand among them and sign autographs.'

Lonnie Donegan: 'I don't like the idea of being looked up to as an idol – I'd much rather that my supporters were genuinely interested in the music!'

## SAM COOKE: NO BIZ, NO SHOW

Words of wisdom from Sam Cooke:

'Show business seems to be inhabited by two types of people - those who merely "show" and those who combine "show" with "business".

'During the past three years, I have devoted as much time as I could to the practical business side of the "show" end. Unemployment offices are full of "one shot" artists – performers who suddenly got "hot" with one recording, then completely faded from the scene.

'Why? Possibly because they had no real talent, and because they did not understand show business *is* a business.'

*Soul stylist Sam slams showbiz slackers*

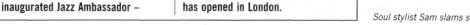

17

# NOVEMBER 1960

# JOHNNY HORTON KILLED

Texas-born country music star, Johnny Horton (33), who enjoyed worldwide crossover hit success with 'Battle Of New Orleans' and 'North To Alaska', was killed in an auto smash on November 5 after playing a date at The Skyline, Austin, Texas – the very same venue where Hank Williams gave his last-ever performance.

This wasn't the only bizarre similarity between the singers. Horton had been married to Williams' former wife, Billie Jean.

Discussing her most recent ex-husband, Billie Jean Williams Horton reveals: 'Johnny knew he was going to die – he talked about it constantly. It reached the point where he wouldn't fly any more because he was so certain he'd get killed in a plane crash.'

*I like Ike says Tina.*

# THE GRAPEVINE

- Pat Boone's second book, *Betwixt You and Me and the Gatepost* has been published with 75,000 advance orders.

- Tina Turner has celebrated her 21st birthday.

- The Shirelles have posed the eternal question, 'Will You Love Me Tomorrow'.

- One-time Devil's Advocate, Elvis Presley has recorded a Gospel LP, 'His Hand In Mine'.

*Left: The Shirelles*

## CHARTS

| | |
|---|---|
| US45 | Save The Last Dance For Me — Drifters |
| USLP | The Button-Down Mind Of Bob Newhart |
| UK45 | It's Now Or Never — Elvis Presley |
| UKLP | South Pacific — Soundtrack |

### WEEK 2

| | |
|---|---|
| US45 | Save The Last Dance For Me — Drifters |
| USLP | The Button-Down Mind Of Bob Newhart |
| UK45 | It's Now Or Never — Elvis Presley |
| UKLP | South Pacific — Soundtrack |

### WEEK 3

| | |
|---|---|
| US45 | Georgia On My Mind — Ray Charles |
| USLP | The Button-Down Mind Of Bob Newhart |
| UK45 | It's Now Or Never — Elvis Presley |
| UKLP | South Pacific — Soundtrack |

### WEEK 4

| | |
|---|---|
| US45 | Stay — Maurice Williams & The Zodiacs |
| USLP | The Button-Down Mind Of Bob Newhart |
| UK45 | It's Now Or Never — Elvis Presley |
| UKLP | South Pacific — Soundtrack |

# INSTRUMENTALS RULE UK, OK?

Silk-suited singers were given short-shrift in the NME's UK Top 30, for the week of November 4, as instrumental singles account for no fewer than *nine* positions!

These were:

5 Johnny & The' Hurricans: 'Rocking Goose' (London)

11 The John Barry Seven: 'Walk Don't Run' (Columbia)

12 The Piltdown Men: 'Macdonald's Cave' (Capitol)

18 The Ventures: 'Walk Don't Run' (Top Rank)

21 The Shadows: 'Apache' (Columbia)

22 Manuel: 'Never On A Sunday' (Columbia)

23 Don Costa: 'Never On A Sunday' (London)

28 Duane Eddy: 'Because They're Young' (London)

29 Bert Weedon: 'Sorry Robbie' (Top Rank)

Unlike some people in the music business who are spreading alarmist talk to the effect that pop singers are becoming a thing of the past, The Shadows' lead guitarist, Hank B. Marvin gave a realistic personal overview of the situation:

'It seems to me that we are returning to the situation of five or six years ago, when there was a considerable vogue for instrumentals – though of course, in those days it was mostly for big band material.

'Despite this, I don't think there's any slackening of interest in vocals.'

*Hank B. Marvin, of the tremelo guitar sound, defends vocals in the wake of the Shadows' solo success*

# SUCCESS AT LAST FOR ORBISON

Though Roy Orbison recorded for Sam Phillips' Sun label in Memphis at around the same time as Elvis, Jerry Lee Lewis, Carl Perkins and Johnny Cash, the success enjoyed by those stars has rubbed off belatedly on the introverted Texan.

A move to Monument Records in Nashville, and suddenly The Big 'O' has *three* tunes on the UK charts: there's his angst-ridden former No. 1, 'Only The Lonely' plus 'Blue Angel' (No. 21) and 'Today's Teardrops' (No. 28).

## STAR QUOTE

### THE EVERLY BROTHERS

*'We're not Grand Ole Opry . . . we're obviously not Perry Como . . . we're just pop music. But, you could call us an American skiffle group!'*

# ELVIS – HIT DISC, HIT MOVIE

Colonel Parker is in seventh heaven – it has taken just six weeks for ex-soldier Elvis Presley's 'It's Now or Never' to sell one million copies in Britain alone, thereby beating the previous 1957 sales record held by RCA-Victor label-mate Harry Belafonte's 'Mary's Boy Child'.

However, prior to its release (Aug 21), this record (a re-write of the Italian standard 'O Solo Mio') was the subject of long-winded UK copyright law entanglement.

At one point, RCA Records (UK) feared that it might take another seven years before the track was cleared for release.

Things are also buzzing for Elvis on the movie front. His *G.I. Blues* film is grossing an incredible $190,000 nightly in 22 prestigious US movie houses.

## THE GRAPEVINE

■ Station WNTA dj Clay Cole has replaced disgraced Alan Freed following the latter's conviction on payola charges, to host Brooklyn Paramount Theater's 'Christmas Rock'n'Roll Show' which featured Chubby Checker, Bobby Rydell, Dion, Neil Sedaka, Bo Diddley and The Drifters.

■ Bobby Darin has married movie actress Sandra Dee.

■ Cliff & The Shadows have begun a six-month London Palladium variety season.

## FAITH TO FACE

In a bid to be taken seriously, singer Adam Faith has appeared on Britain's most controversial interview programme, BBC-TV's *Face To Face*. For 30 minutes, host John Freeman subjected Faith to a relentless and probing cross-examination. Faith came through his trial-by-combat with flying colours.

## CLIFF BUYS BACK MOVIE DEAL

*Cliff clinches movie move*

In an unprecedented behind-the-scenes deal said to involve a five figure sum, Cliff Richard has bought back the option movie producer Mickey Delamar holds on his future services as a movie actor.

'It's all been settled very amicably,' insists the singer's manager, Tito Burns.

Though it was announced at the end of July that Delamar was about to star Cliff in an adaption of Margery Allingham's novel *Hide My Eyes*, Burns claims that Delamar had chosen to take a rest from a heavy work schedule.

'We had arranged for Cliff to begin work at the end of January on the first of the outstanding films,' Burns reveals. 'We did not want a further postponement because of our plans for next year,' Delamar realized that Cliff was being inundated with offers and was anxious not to stand in his way.'

The original Cliff Richard-Mickey Delamar contract was signed soon after the singer's success with 'Move It', and immediately resulted in Cliff winning a major role in the controversial movie 'Serious Charge.'

The contract called for Cliff to make two more movies at the option of Delamar. This option was initially waived, in 1959, to allow Cliff to star with Laurence Harvey in the box office hit *Expresso Bongo*.

## MGM BUY VERVE

MGM Records have purchased impresario/producer Norman Granz's famed Clef/Verve jazz label for $2.5 million.

The extensive catalogue includes numerous sessions by Ella Fitzgerald, Louis Armstrong, Billie Holiday, Charlie Parker, Dizzy Gillespie, Count Basie, Oscar Peterson, Art Tatum, Lester Young, Stan Getz, Buddy Rich and Gene Krupa, plus the entire Jazz At The Philharmonic concert recordings.

*Norman grants MGM deal*

## THE GRAPEVINE

- The Hollywood Women's Press Club have nominated Elvis 'the Least Co-Operative Actor of 1960.'

- UK Decca Records boss, Edward Lewis, received a knighthood in the Queen's New Year Honours List.

- Barry Mann (half of the successful songwriting team Mann & Weil) has screamed into the US charts with 'Who Put The Bomp (In The Bomp, Bomp, Bomp).

## CHARTS

| | |
|---|---|
| US45 | Are You Lonesome Tonight *Elvis Presley* |
| USLP | G.I. Blues *Elvis Presley* |
| UK45 | It's Now Or Never *Elvis Presley* |
| UKLP | G.I. Blues *Elvis Presley* |

— WEEK 2 —

| | |
|---|---|
| US45 | Are You Lonesome Tonight *Elvis Presley* |
| USLP | G.I. Blues *Elvis Presley* |
| UK45 | Poetry In Motion *Johnny Tillotson* |
| UKLP | G.I. Blues *Elvis Presley* |

— WEEK 3 —

| | |
|---|---|
| US45 | Wonderland By Night *Bert Kaempfert* |
| USLP | The Button-Down Mind Strikes Back *Bob Newhart* |
| UK45 | Poetry In Motion *Johnny Tillotson* |
| UKLP | G.I. Blues *Elvis Presley* |

— WEEK 4 —

| | |
|---|---|
| US45 | Wonderland By Night *Bert Kaempfert* |
| USLP | Wonderland By Night *Bert Kaempfert* |
| UK45 | Poetry In Motion *Johnny Tillotson* |
| UKLP | G.I. Blues *Elvis Presley* |

— WEEK 5 —

| | |
|---|---|
| US45 | Wonderland By Night *Bert Kaempfert* |
| USLP | Wonderland By Night *Bert Kaempfert* |
| UK45 | Are You Lonesome Tonight *Elvis Presley* |
| UKLP | G.I. Blues *Elvis Presley* |

# ADAM KEEPS THE FAITH

For his second shot at stardom, it's taken 20-year-old London-born singer Adam Faith just 12 hectic months and six top five singles (including 'What Do You Want?', 'Poor Me' and 'Someone Else's Baby') to transform himself from a has-been to Cliff Richard's closest rival as Britain's premier teenage idol.

A product of the Soho coffee bar skiffle craze, Adam Faith's initial attempt at stardom proved a dismal failure: a couple of flop 45s and forgettable TV appearances prompted a quick return to his old job as a messenger boy at Rank Screen Services. A year later, an appearance in the teen-flick *Beat Girl* and the offer from songwriter Johnny Worth of his composition, 'What Do You Want?' reversed his luck.

With a John Barry arrangement – stylistically, almost identical to Buddy Holly's 'It Doesn't Matter Anymore' – Faith's flat nasal hiccuping and a tendency to over-emphasize the word 'Bay-Bee', made 'What Do You Want?' the biggest hit of 1960 in the UK.

With advance orders for his next single 'This Is It' guaranteeing him another hit, Faith has been booked to headline the prestigious prime-time TV show, *Sunday Night At The London Palladium* and negotiations are underway for a four-movie deal.

Faith's ambition is to become an all-round entertainer.

*Sartorially splendid Marty Wilde*

## STAR QUOTE
### MARTY WILDE

*'I'm out to take Lonnie Donegan's crown as Britain's best-dressed pop singer. I doubt if I can do it this year, but I'm having a shot at the title for 1962.'*

# SINATRA ANNOUNCES OWN LABEL

Following much gossip column speculation, Frank Sinatra has announced the formation of his very own record label – Reprise – which he intends to launch in March with his new album, 'Ring A Ding Ding.'

Sinatra has also intimated that some of his notorious 'Rat-Pack' friends (such as Sammy Davis Jr) might be among the initial signings.

This eagerly-anticipated project is believed to have been partly bankrolled by Sinatra himself, as a result of a rumoured $15-million movie deal the singer has entered into with the United Artists' Studios.

*Frank Sinatra – label owner*

# MITCHELL TO GO SOLO?

Les Chaussettes Noire – the popular French rock group that features the explosive Eddy Mitchell – have just made their eagerly-awaited disc debut on the Paris-based Barclay label, with a four-track EP that contains French-language covers of Gene Vincent's 'Be-Bop-A-Lula' and Presley's 'Dirty Dirty Feeling'.

However, it's the slow 'Daniela' that has become the unexpected hit, prompting Mitchell (who is seen as a rival to Johnny Halliday) to seriously consider a solo career.

# JACKIE WILSON SHOT

Jackie Wilson, the 25-year-old R&B hitmaker of 'Reet Petite', 'Lonely Teardrops' and 'Doggin' Around', and on whom it is said that Elvis Presley first modelled both his singing style and extrovert stage antics, has been shot and seriously wounded at his New York apartment. His assailant was a female acquaintance, 28-year-old Juanita Jones.

Wilson, whose in-person appearances trigger off scenes of female mass hysteria, first came to fame by replacing Clyde McPhatter in Billy Ward's Dominoes when still only 17.

At the time of the shooting, Wilson had established his reputation as one of America's most visually exciting performers.

## STAR QUOTE

### JOHNNY BURNETTE

'My brother Dorsey and I first got to know Elvis Presley when he went to Humes High and we went to the Catholic High . . . Elvis would tote his guitar on his back when he rode past on his motor-cycle on his way to school. He would see us and always wave.'

Rock'n'roller Johnny Burnette

## PLATTERS SUE MERCURY

Platters – pictured during happier times

February 14: St Valentine's Day – but there's no love lost between The Platters and their record company, Mercury. Though Tony Williams left the act to go solo back in June of last year, he is at the root of a dispute that has escalated into litigation.

Because Mercury have chosen not to accept and release new Platters' tracks which don't feature ex-lead singer Williams, the group are taking legal action.

Their manager, Buck Ram, claims that The Platter's contract with Mercury doesn't stipulate that Williams has to be the featured solo voice. According to the group themselves, when Williams was a member of the act, it was common for any one of the other four singers to take over the lead.

## ELVIS LIVE AGAIN

Elvis Presley has made his first public appearance in four years, playing two 50-minute shows before 10,000 ecstatic fans at the Ellis Auditorium, Memphis, Tennessee.

The receipts of $51,612 were split between 27 local charities.

## CHARTS

| | | |
|---|---|---|
| US45 | Will You Love Me Tomorrow | *Shirelles* |
| USLP | Exodus | *Soundtrack* |
| UK45 | Are You Lonesome Tonight | *Elvis Presley* |
| UKLP | G.I. Blues | *Elvis Presley* |
| | **WEEK 2** | |
| US45 | Will You Love Me Tomorrow | *Shirelles* |
| USLP | Wonderland By Night | *Bert Kaempfert* |
| UK45 | Are You Lonesome Tonight | *Elvis Presley* |
| UKLP | G.I. Blues | *Elvis Presley* |
| | **WEEK 3** | |
| US45 | Calcutta | *Lawrence Welk* |
| USLP | Wonderland By Night | *Bert Kaempfert* |
| UK45 | Are You Lonesome Tonight | *Elvis Presley* |
| UKLP | G.I. Blues | *Elvis Presley* |
| | **WEEK 4** | |
| US45 | Calcutta | *Lawrence Welk* |
| USLP | Exodus | *Soundtrack* |
| UK45 | Are You Lonesome Tonight | *Elvis Presley* |
| UKLP | G.I. Blues | *Elvis Presley* |

## FEBRUARY 1961

## FRENCH FANS RIOT

The first of three *Festival du Rock* extravaganzas have been staged amid some of the wildest scenes ever experienced in the French capital, at the Palais des Sports de Paris.

Featured artists included Bobby Rydell (USA), Emile Ford & The Checkmates (UK), plus local top rockers Johnny Halliday, Frankie Jordan and Les Chaussettes Noires featuring Eddy Mitchell.

However, it was the concert headlined by Vince Taylor & The Playboys and Dick Rivers & Les Chats Sauvages which turned into a full-scale rock'n'roll riot, to which the local *gendarmerie* were called to give the more excited fans a practical display of modern police tactics!

## THE GRAPEVINE

■ Tamla Records has its first million-selling single with The Miracles' 'Shop Around'.

■ Frank Sinatra was the main event at President John F. Kennedy's Inaugural Ball in Washington.

■ The Shadows' new single is 'F.B.I.'

■ Matt Monro has won ITV's *British Song Contest* with 'My Kind Of Girl'.

■ Helen Shapiro – a mature-voiced 14-year-old London schoolgirl – has launched a successful disc career with 'Don't Treat Me Like A Child'.

Contest winner – Matt Monro

Mature of voice – Helen Shapiro

# 1961

Johnny & The Hurricanes, with leader Johnny Paris (right)

## ELVIS: NO MORE GIGS?

The 4,000-seat Bloch Arena, Pearl Harbor, Honolulu, was the location for what looks like becoming Elvis Presley's last concert appearance for some time.

Staged as a benefit for the USS *Arizona* Memorial Fund, the concert featured Elvis performing 'Heartbreak Hotel', 'All Shook Up', 'A Fool Such As I', 'I Got A Woman', 'Love Me', 'Such A Night', 'Reconsider Baby', 'I Need Your Love Tonight', 'That's All Right (Mama)', 'Don't Be Cruel', 'One Night', 'Are You Lonesome Tonight?', 'It's Now Or Never', 'Swing Down, Sweet Chariot' and 'Hound Dog'.

With film work seeming to take up all of Presley's energy and enthusiasm, concert appearances and tours seem likely to be a low priority in the foreseeable future.

## STAR QUOTE

### THE EVERLY BROTHERS

*'We're often asked whether the fact that we're brothers has ever been a handicap in our careers. The way they figure it is that most brothers quarrel, and in our case if there's no harmony behind the scenes, it's not very likely that there'll be much on stage.'*

# HURRICANES SCORE WITH GOLDEN OLDIES

All-American hot rockin' instrumental combo Johnny & The Hurricanes have just celebrated their sixth UK Top 20 hit in 14 months with 'Ja-Da'.

Firmly established as one of the most consistent transatlantic recording acts, The Hurricanes – led by 19-year-old tenorman Johnny Paris – specialize in 'modernizing' pre-rock era oldies.

Originally from Toledo, Ohio, their widespread appeal commenced when, after the Stateside-only success of 'Crossfire', they transformed the old Army bugle call into 'Reveille Rock', turned the country music weepie 'Red River Valley' into 'Red River Rock', rearranged the traditional folk song 'Blue Tail Fly'

as 'Beatnik Fly' and then turned their personal attention to 'Down Yonder' and now the old jazz standard 'Ja-Da'.

However, one of the group's biggest successes has been an original, 'Rockin' Goose' – a novelty number that relied for its gimmick appeal on a shrill squawking goose, made by the shrieking saxophone of Johnny Paris.

Johnny & The Hurricanes have the biggest sound around by having blended Paris's raucous tenor raspings to the piping hot Hammond organ of Paul Tesluk, while Butch Mattice powers the rhythm section with the wall-to-wall rumble produced by his mighty Dan Electro bass.

## THE GRAPEVINE

■ The Allisons' 'Are You Sure' was placed second in the *Song For Europe*

■ Cliff Richard & The Shadows

have opened their South African tour in Jo'burg.

■ Elvis has been recording the soundtrack for his *Blue Hawaii* movie.

■ Beatles' manager Alan Williams has secured a three month residency at Hamburg's Top Ten Club for the Liverpool group.

## NME POLL CONCERT

The major British pop event of the year the NME Annual Readers' Poll Winners Concert at Wembley Pool, London was held on March 5.

Among those appearing were The John Barry Seven, Alma Cogan, Russ Conway, Lonnie Donegan, Adam Faith, Emile Ford, Connie Francis, Billy Fury, Ted Heath & His Music, The King Brothers, Jerry Lordan, Bob Millar's Millermen, The Mudlarks, Cliff Richard & The Shadows, Bert Weedon and Mark Wynter.

Skiffle king Lonnie

## CHARTS

| US45 | Pony Time<br>*Chubby Checker* |
| USLP | Exodus<br>*Soundtrack* |
| UK45 | Walk Right Back<br>*Everly Brothers* |
| UKLP | G.I. Blues<br>*Elvis Presley* |

— WEEK 2 —

| US45 | Pony Time<br>*Chubby Checker* |
| USLP | Calcutta<br>*Lawrence Welk* |
| UK45 | Walk Right Back<br>*Everly Brothers* |
| UKLP | G.I. Blues<br>*Elvis Presley* |

— WEEK 3 —

| US45 | Pony Time<br>*Chubby Checker* |
| USLP | Calcutta<br>*Lawrence Welk* |
| UK45 | Walk Right Back<br>*Everly Brothers* |
| UKLP | G.I. Blues<br>*Elvis Presley* |

— WEEK 4 —

| US45 | Surrender<br>*Elvis Presley* |
| USLP | Calcutta<br>*Lawrence Welk* |
| UK45 | Wooden Heart<br>*Elvis Presley* |
| UKLP | G.I. Blues<br>*Elvis Presley* |

# GUITAR ACE SHIVERS DEAD

Wesley Clarence 'Charlie' Shivers, a 27-year-old rockabilly guitarist, died when a methane gas explosion destroyed his farmhouse near Scottsville, Kentucky on April 7.

Shivers was to rockabilly what Buddy Bolden was to jazz – a shadowy, yet influential player who never released any commercial recordings. The son of a wealthy civil engineer-turned-government diplomat, Charlie turned down major label offers from the likes of Norman Petty and Steve Sholes, preferring to work on family engineering projects in Panama's Canal Zone.

His prolific recording activities were confined almost exclusively to sessions he held in the private studio he built at the back of his farmhouse. It was here that many country and bluegrass music stars dropped by to enjoy his hospitality.

It is believed that over 200 privately recorded sides, said to include Johnny Burnette, Tennessee Ernie Ford, Ivory Joe Hunter, Hank Williams and Elvis Presley, perished with Shivers in the fire. The tracks featuring Elvis were thought to have originated from a session held in the studio of a small radio station at which Charlie guided the pre-Sun singer through a selection of recent pop and country jukebox favourites.

Said guitarist Scotty Moore, on hearing of Shivers' death: 'If Charlie had decided to give up building bridges and turn professional, we'd have all had to look for new jobs!'

## CHARTS

| | | |
|---|---|---|
| US45 | Surrender | *Elvis Presley* |
| USLP | Calcutta | *Lawrence Welk* |
| UK45 | Wooden Heart | *Elvis Presley* |
| UKLP | G.I. Blues | *Elvis Presley* |
| **WEEK 2** | | |
| US45 | Blue Moon | *Marcels* |
| USLP | G.I. Blues | *Elvis Presley* |
| UK45 | Are You Sure | *Allisons* |
| UKLP | G.I. Blues | *Elvis Presley* |
| **WEEK 3** | | |
| US45 | Blue Moon | *Marcels* |
| USLP | Calcutta | *Lawrence Welk* |
| UK45 | Wooden Heart | *Elvis Presley* |
| UKLP | G.I. Blues | *Elvis Presley* |
| **WEEK 4** | | |
| US45 | Blue Moon | *Marcels* |
| USLP | Calcutta | *Lawrence Welk* |
| UK45 | Are You Sure | *Allisons* |
| UKLP | G.I. Blues | *Elvis Presley* |
| **WEEK 5** | | |
| US45 | Runaway | *Del Shannon* |
| USLP | Calcutta | *Lawrence Welk* |
| UK45 | You're Driving Me Crazy | *Temperance Seven* |
| UKLP | G.I. Blues | *Elvis Presley* |

## CMA STAGE COUNTRY FESTIVAL

The first official Country Music Festival has been staged at the Jacksonville Coliseum, Florida by the new Country Music Association.

The all-star line-up included Webb Pierce, Faron Young, Patsy Cline, Porter Wagoner, Flatt & Scruggs, The Louvin Brothers, Mel Tillis, George Hamilton IV plus The Foggy Mountain Boys.

*(L to R) Bruce Welch, Cliff Richard, Hank B. Marvin*

## THE GRAPEVINE

- Pye Records UK have launched their Piccadilly subsidary with Joe Brown's 'Crazy Mixed-Up Kid'.
- New from Cliff Richard, 'Gee Whiz It's You'.
- Shirley Bassey has entered the London Clinic to have her tonsils removed.
- Actor/Singer Jess Conrad has released one of the all-time bad singles, 'This Pullover'.
- The Drifters' ex-lead singer, Ben E. King, has released 'Stand By Me'.

*Joe Brown as the 'Crazy Mixed-up Kid'*

*Shirley Bassey – throat problems cured?*

## FILMING STARTS ON NEW CLIFF MOVIE

When they shoot your movies in colour, then you've really hit the big time!

Following the success of *Expresso Bongo*, Cliff Richard & The Shadows have commenced filming a big budget movie, *The Young Ones*. Unlike the former, which was a black and white film, *The Young Ones* will be a full-colour extravaganza.

The basic plot concerns a rumour that the youth club attended by Cliff and his pals is about to be demolished by a big city corporation. £1,500 can save the building from possible destruction, so they decide to stage a show to raise the money. The cast will include Carole Gray as Cliff's love interest, and Robert Morley as his father.

The producers have said that *The Young Ones* will be ready for release in January 1962.

# 1961

# GUITAR GREATS SWAP NOTES

Bert Weedon reflects on fame . . . and make up!

The Twang's The Thang for Duane

## WILDE BIRDIE

Prior to switching to the prestigious Her Majesty's Theatre in London's West-End, the British production of the Elvis-spoof Broadway musical smash, *Bye Bye Birdie* has opened its provincial run at the Manchester Opera House, with pop idol Marty Wilde suitably cast in the title role.

When Britain's king-size-guitar man Bert Weedon recently dropped backstage to catch twangy guitar star Duane Eddy's UK tour, the two top players engaged in much mutual back-slapping.

During the course of the conversation, the very outgoing Weedon couldn't help remarking on the American performer's extremely inanimate low-profile before an audience.

Bert: 'Duane, I notice you usually don't use make-up on stage. Any reasons?'

Duane: 'Simply because I don't like it. Frankly, I usually have enough of a sun-tan to get by with.'

Bert: 'May I speak truthfully? I think your stage act with The Rebels is tremendous, but at the same time I'm sure it could do even better with more production. What do you think?'

Duane: 'If you mean movement and choreography, I'm not very keen on the idea. My plan is simply to go on and entertain without too many trimmings. I'd rather it be a spontaneous act than a too-well-planned one.'

## THE GRAPEVINE

■ Advance sales of 461,500 copies of Elvis's new UK release 'Surrender' qualified it as biggest ever UK pre-sale.

■ Lonnie Donegan has adapted traditional cocaine-snorter's anthem 'Have A Whiff On Me' into a cheery bar-room singalong 'Have A Drink On Me'.

■ Gene Vincent has become the first US star to feature on the UK ABC-TV's prestigious chart-slanted show, *Thank Your Lucky Stars.*

## STAR QUOTE

### ED 'KOOKIE' BYRNES
Actor/Singer

*'It's hard for some people to believe, but I only talk like Kookie in* 77 Sunset Strip *— never in private. But, I don't live the role 24 hours a day and that disappoints them!'*

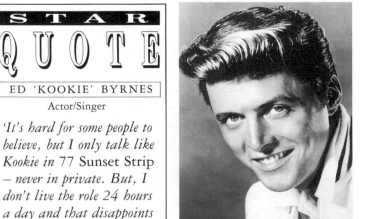

Ed Byrnes — not as 'Kookie' in reality

## BERRY-GO-ROUND!

Not one to squander his earnings from endlessly touring in support of such definitive rock hits as 'Sweet Little 16', 'Johnny B. Goode', 'Carol', 'Sweet Little Rock And Roller', 'Almost Grown', 'Little Queenie', 'Memphis Tennessee', 'Let It Rock' and a dozen more, Chuck Berry has realized a personal ambition and opened Berry Park – a 30-acre family amusement complex on the outskirts of his St Louis hometown.

Aside from the usual crowd-pulling attractions such as a Ferris Wheel, amusement rides, sideshows and a children's zoo, there's swimming, minature golf, picnic areas and barbecues.

For many, however, the real attraction is the possibility of catching the owner himself performing in the ballroom.

# FURY: 'I'M GROWING UP!'

'I recorded "Halfway To Paradise"', confessed Billy Fury, 'because I wanted people to think of me simply as a singer – and not, more specifically, as a rock singer!'

'I'm growing up, and I want to broaden my scope. I shall continue to sing rock songs, but at the same time my stage act isn't going to be as wild in the future,' he says.

And yet, Fury revealed, he was in something of a dilemma over one of the more creative aspects of his young talent. 'Because "Halfway To Paradise" isn't one of my own compositions,' (it was penned by Tony Orlando) 'several people have asked me if I've stopped writing songs. I certainly haven't, but I'm bound to admit that my style of writing has changed radically in recent times.

'The point is I just can't seem to write the rock stuff like I used to. Ideas don't seem to come to me any more.

'My aim now is to write catchy, easy-paced songs after the style of "You Made Me Love

You". . . I enjoy that kind of material very much. I'm also writing a lot of rhythm & blues stuff these days, but for the moment I'm having to shelve

*Billy Fury going for the adult audience*

these, because nobody seems to want to know about them as far as recording is concerned!'

## BOBBY VEE: 'I'M NO COPY-CAT!'

Bobby Vee – having been plagued by press and fan accusations over the similarity in style between his recent hits, 'Rubber Ball' and 'More Than I Can Say', to material recorded by Buddy Holly – has chosen to publicly rebuff such claims. 'I'm no copycat' has been his defence.

Despite such denials, the truth that his style has been derived from Holly's is further compounded by the fact that, while still an untried amateur, Bobby Vee & The Shadows (no relation to the British group) made their public debut in Minneapolis by filling in for Buddy Holly who (in the company of Richie Valens and The Big Bopper) had perished the previous evening in an air disaster.

## THE GRAPEVINE

■ DJ Alan Freed's new American road show features Brenda Lee, The Shirelles, Bobby Vee, Etta James, Gene McDaniels, The Ventures, Clarence 'Frogman' Henry, The Fleetwoods, The Innocents, Kathy Young and Jerry Lee Lewis.

■ Gene Vincent and The Shadows have headlined the latest U.K. to France 'Rock Across The Channel' cruise.

■ Adam Faith celebrated his 21st birthday this month.

## JUNE 1961

## ELVIS: MORE MOVIE NEWS

20th Century-Fox have released *Wild In The Country* – an implausible melodrama starring Elvis Presley (Glenn Tyler) with both Hope Lange and Tuesday Weld supplying the female interest.

At the same time, Colonel Tom Parker has announced that Elvis is to receive $600,000, plus a hefty percentage of the box office gross, as star of the movie *Pioneer Goes Home*.

The film's title has been changed – to *Follow That Dream*. The money, however, stays the same!

## CHARTS

| | | |
|---|---|---|
| US45 | Travelin' Man | *Ricky Nelson* |
| USLP | G.I. Blues | *Elvis Presley* |
| UK45 | Surrender | *Elvis Presley* |
| UKLP | G.I. Blues | *Elvis Presley* |
| | **WEEK 2** | |
| US45 | Running Scared | *Roy Orbison* |
| USLP | Camelot | *Original Cast* |
| UK45 | Surrender | *Elvis Presley* |
| UKLP | G.I. Blues | *Elvis Presley* |
| | **WEEK 3** | |
| US45 | Travelin' Man | *Ricky Nelson* |
| USLP | Camelot | *Original Cast* |
| UK45 | Surrender | *Elvis Presley* |
| UKLP | G.I. Blues | *Elvis Presley* |
| | **WEEK 4** | |
| US45 | Moody River | *Pat Boone* |
| USLP | Camelot | *Original Cast* |
| UK45 | Runaway | *Del Shannon* |
| UKLP | G.I. Blues | *Elvis Presley* |

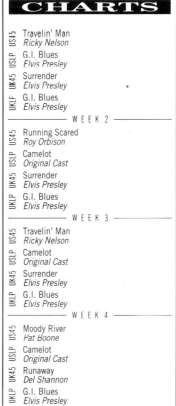

*Bobby Vee – dreamboat not coypcat!*

## HARRY'S MERSEY BEAT

Liverpool live-wire Bill Harry has published the first-ever edition of his alternative pop music paper, *Mersey Beat*.

Devoted almost entirely to the vast local pop scene, the debut edition features the article, 'Being a Short Diversion on the Dubious Origins of Beatles', accompanied by a 'translated from the John Lennon' by-line. Lennon is a member of The Beatles, one of Liverpool's most popular homegrown groups.

# RICKY – I'M NO TRAVELLIN' MAN

While busy developing the movie acting side of his career, 21-year-old Ricky Nelson has suddenly realized that because he never tours or appears on television outside the States, the progress of his singles is somewhat erratic.

Though both 'Hello Mary Lou' and 'Travellin' Man' have repeated their recent Stateside chart success in the UK, Ricky is confronted by the knowledge that he has yet to build up the kind of fan loyalty he enjoys at home.

'Maybe you've been wondering what has been happening to me during the past 18 months. The fact that my records haven't been doing any too well on your side of the Atlantic came as something of a disappointment to me, I must admit, bearing in mind the luck I had with several of my earlier releases'.

'A lot of people have suggested it was due to the return of Elvis Presley from his period of Army service – and I suppose there might be something in that.

'But you know, I have never really placed myself in the cate-

*Ricky Nelson – competition for Presley?*

gory of Elvis – and I can't honestly imagine that I was regarded as his deputy during his absence. I have no doubt, though, that when Elvis came back from Germany, the competition was rather tough for all young male singers.'

## TAYLOR'S CADILLAC WINS PRAISE

Vince Taylor & The Playboys' latest recording 'Brand New Cadillac' is receiving instant praise from critics as being the best British-made rock record since Cliff Richard's 'Move It' and Johnny Kidd's more recent 'Shakin' All Over'.

It was at the birthplace of British Rock – Soho's The 2 I's coffee bar in Old Compton Street – that this handsome 21-year-old Anglo-American first attracted sufficient attention to be signed up to launch Palette Records last August – with his single 'I'll Be Your Hero'/'Jet Black Machine'.

Taylor's much-respected Playboys comprise London's finest: Tony Sheridan (guitar), Brian 'Licorice' Locking (bass) and Brian Bennett (drums).

*Liverpool's Beatles, with (from left) John Lennon, George Harrison & Paul McCartney*

# DARIN: 'ROCK PAVED MY WAY'

Back in the charts with the rocked-up oldie 'You Must Have Been A Beautiful Baby', Bobby Darin gives his personal opinion of the current music scene.

'Nowadays, it's extremely difficult for a fan to stay loyal to any one artist for more than a couple of months. I blame the record companies for much of the trouble. The problem is that they try so hard to interest teenagers in new sounds all the time, that many good artists don't have an opportunity to develop their own style,' he says forcefully.

'Immediately after I had a hit with "Mack The Knife", people started to say that I never liked rock'n'roll at all, and that I only sang it to make money. That's not true. I like any sort of music as long as it's good – rock included.

'Of course I wanted the money – well it isn't only a case of wanting – I *needed* the money. But that isn't the only reason I sang rock.

'Three years ago, I was glad to play club dates for $200 a week, and I could only get work for six or seven weeks a year. That's when I wrote "Splish Splash" – that one song put me on the musical map. And, there was also another rock number, "Queen Of The Hop". A year later, "Dream Lover" became a big hit.

'Without those records to pave the way, I'm certain that "Mack The Knife" would never have been the hit it was,' he adds.

## FAME AT LAST

Impresario Larry Parnes's latest value-for-money package show, 'Star Spangled Nights', commenced 26 twice-nightly British theatre dates at the Essoldo, Cannock on October 17.

The bill featured such crowd-pullers as Billy Fury, Eden Kane, Joe Brown, Tommy Bruce, The Allisons, The Viscounts, The Karl Denver Trio, Peter Jay & The Jaywalkers, and Terry Hale.

The cast also included a most promising newcomer who, in the best Parnes tradition of renaming his discoveries, is transformed from Clive Powell into Georgie Fame!

*Wheeler-dealer Larry Parnes*

## CHARTS

| | | |
|---|---|---|
| US45 | Take Good Care Of My Baby | *Bobby Vee* |
| USLP | At Carnegie Hall | *Judy Garland* |
| UK45 | Johnny Remember Me | *John Leyton* |
| UKLP | The Shadows | *Shadows* |

**— WEEK 2 —**

| | | |
|---|---|---|
| US45 | Take Good Care Of My Baby | *Bobby Vee* |
| USLP | At Carnegie Hall | *Judy Garland* |
| UK45 | Michael | *Highwaymen* |
| UKLP | The Shadows | *Shadows* |

**— WEEK 3 —**

| | | |
|---|---|---|
| US45 | Hit The Road Jack | *Ray Charles* |
| USLP | At Carnegie Hall | *Judy Garland* |
| UK45 | Walkin' Back To Happiness | *Helen Shapiro* |
| UKLP | The Shadows | *Shadows* |

**— WEEK 4 —**

| | | |
|---|---|---|
| US45 | Hit The Road Jack | *Ray Charles* |
| USLP | At Carnegie Hall | *Judy Garland* |
| UK45 | Walkin' Back To Happiness | *Helen Shapiro* |
| UKLP | The Shadows | *Shadows* |

**— WEEK 5 —**

| | | |
|---|---|---|
| US45 | Runaround Sue | *Dion & The Delmonts* |
| USLP | At Carnegie Hall | *Judy Garland* |
| UK45 | Walkin' Back To Happiness | *Helen Shapiro* |
| UKLP | The Shadows | *Shadows* |

## ONE-OFF BEAT-MAKERS

Top Liverpool groups The Beatles and Gerry & The Pacemakers merged to become 'The Beat-Makers' for a one-off performance at the Litherland Town Hall on 19 October. The line-up comprised:

Gerry Marsden (vocal/lead guitar), George Harrison (lead guitar), Paul McCartney (rhythm guitar), John Lennon (vocal/piano), Les Chadwick (bass guitar), Les Maguire (saxophone), Pete Best and Freddy Marsden (drums) plus vocalist Karl Terry from The Cruisers.

*Dick James (centre) has a tea-time chat with producer George Martin (left)*

## THE GRAPEVINE

■ Booker Little Jr, one of the most promising trumpet stars on the US scene has died, of uraemia, aged 22.

■ Big Joe Williams and new prodigy Bob Dylan have appeared as guests on legendary blues artist Victoria Spivey's new album.

■ Former UK dance band vocalist Dick James has launched his self-named music publishing house.

■ John Barry has visited Hollywood to discuss possibilities of composing for movies.

*Country singer Jimmie Rodgers*

*Tex – no hick from the sticks*

# MOTOWN MOVES ON

*Tamla's first chart toppers, The Marvelettes*

Tamla Records' boss, Berry Gordy Jr, recently inaugurated a second label which he has called Motown (an abbreviation of Detroit's popular nickname 'The Motor City') with a single by male vocal harmony foursome The Satintones, called 'My Beloved'.

This record was a rush-replacement for The Satintones scheduled disc debut 'Tomorrow And Always' – an 'answer' record to The Shirelles' 'Will You Still Love Me Tomorrow'. At the very last minute, 'Tomorrow And Always' was hastily withdrawn from distribution when Gordy was threatened with a hefty lawsuit which claimed copyright infringement of The Shirelles' original international hit.

Undaunted however, Gordy didn't allow this minor set-back to interfere at all with celebrations surrounding Tamla Records' first national No. 1 single, 'Please, Mr Postman' by a local all-girl group, The Marvelettes. This more than compensated for the minor hit status afforded the debut single of another local girl group, first known as The Primettes when recording for Lu-Pine, but renamed The Supremes for their Tamla release 'I Want A Guy'.

With albums from The Miracles ('Hi! We're The Miracles') and Marvin Gaye ('The Soulful Moods Of . . .') accounting for healthy sales figures, Berry Gordy is optimistic of his two labels success in 1962 and is openly enthusing about a new artist soon to debut – Steveland Judkins, the 11-year-old blind son of one of Tamla's regular cleaning ladies.

Gordy has renamed the gifted singer and instrumentalist Little Stevie . . . Little Stevie Wonder.

## TEX X 100

Tex Ritter, country music legend and hit recorder of 'High Noon', has set something of a precedent in terms of promotion.

He recently recorded more than *100* different versions of 'Hillbilly Heaven', – his new single for Capitol Records – with each including the names of different peak-listening disc jockeys in the lyric. The records were then mailed out with a personal letter from ol' Tex to the various radio stations concerned!

And Webb Pierce has purchased a $20,000 car which has pistol butts for door handles and gear lever, rifles mounted on the tail-lights and *1000* silver dollar pieces as interior decor.

As the saying goes: if you've got it, flaunt it!

*Going solo II – Floyd Cramer*

# TWISTMANIA HITS US, UK AND FRANCE

*Joey Dee and the Starlighters – house-band at the New York temple of twist, the Peppermint Lounge*

Over the last few months, The Twist has exploded world-wide as the single biggest popular music phenomenon since 'Rock Around The Clock' and, as a dance craze, even more popular than the cha-cha.

The man who made it all happen, Philadelphia's 20-year-old Chubby Checker, is currently second only to Elvis as the world's best-known singer! As the tubby twister's cover of the Nov '58 Hank Ballard original has now chalked up 23 consecutive weeks on the US charts (making it the longest unbroken chart run to date), Checker – also the star of quickie-producer Sam Katzman's Bill Haley movie re-make *Twist Around The Clock* and *Don't Knock The Twist* – has given his account of how he devised the Twist dance:

'One day, my lower half twisted one way and my upper half twisted the other . . . right to the rhythm of the song.' With regard to the dance steps, Checker revealed: 'I pretended I was putting out a cigarette with both feet!'

New York's Peppermint Lounge on West 45th Street has now become the official temple of Twist. The dynamic house-band – Joey Dee & The Starlighters – have released their 'live' at the Lounge LP and have been signed up to star in the movie *Hey, Let's Twist* together with Teddy Randazzo and Jo-Ann Campbell.

More movies are on their way, including *Teenage Millionaire* which features Jimmy Clanton, Jackie Wilson, Dion, The Bill Black Combo and Chubby Checker performing 'Let's Twist Again'.

Outside the US, France has been the first country to capitulate to Twistmania, with two French-language 'Let's Twist Again' covers sharing No. 1. Meanwhile, in London, a double bill of *Twist Around The Clock* and *Gidget Goes Hawaiian* opened on New Year's Eve at the New Victoria where The Lionel Blair Dancers were booked to demonstrate The Twist 'live' on stage, daily at 5.30 and 9.10 pm.

## CHARTS

| | | |
|---|---|---|
| US45 | Big Bad John | *Jimmy Dean* |
| USLP | At Carnegie Hall | *Judy Garland* |
| UK45 | Take Good Care Of My Baby | *Bobby Vee* |
| UKLP | Another Black And White Minstrel Show | *TV Cast* |

### WEEK 2

| | | |
|---|---|---|
| US45 | Big Bad John | *Jimmy Dean* |
| USLP | At Carnegie hall | *Judy Garland* |
| UK45 | Tower Of Strength | *Frankie Vaughan* |
| UKLP | Another Black And White Minstrel Show | *TV Cast* |

### WEEK 3

| | | |
|---|---|---|
| US45 | Please Mr. Postman | *Marvelettes* |
| USLP | Blue Hawaii | *Elvis Presley* |
| UK45 | Tower Of Strength | *Frankie Vaughan* |
| UKLP | Another Black And White Minstrel Show | *TV Cast* |

### WEEK 4

| | | |
|---|---|---|
| US45 | The Lion Sleeps Tonight | *Tokens* |
| USLP | Blue Hawaii | *Elvis Presley* |
| UK45 | Tower Of Strength | *Frankie Vaughan* |
| UKLP | Blue Hawaii | *Elvis Presley* |

### WEEK 5

| | | |
|---|---|---|
| US45 | The Lion Sleeps Tonight | *Tokens* |
| US LP | Blue Hawaii | *Elvis Presley* |
| UK45 | Moon River | *Danny Williams* |
| UKLP | Blue Hawaii | *Elvis Presley* |

## DECEMBER 1961

## STAR QUOTE
### FRANK SINATRA

'I want to avoid having bad rock'n'roll records associated with my new Reprise label and the policy will be, in the main, to concentrate on quality performers. That's why I've signed personalities like Sammy Davis Jr.'

## THE GRAPEVINE

■ Johnny Halliday has topped almost every European chart with his French-language version of 'Let's Twist Again'.

■ Cliff Richard & The Shadows' latest movie has been premiered in London to rave reviews.

■ Sandy Nelson's 'Let There Be Drums' has gone Top 10 in both the US and UK.

■ Chubby Checker and Chris Barber's Jazz Band have teamed up to tape a UK-TV Special *Trad With A Twist.*

*Johnny Halliday with Sylvie Vartan*

## A & R ROLE FOR MEEHAN

Having maintained a low-profile since he suddenly quit The Shadows on September 30, Decca Records have maximized public interest by announcing that the group's former drum star, Tony Meehan, has joined the company in a two-fold capacity.

Apart from pursuing a solo career as a recording artist, Meehan is also a new addition to Decca's A&R department, where his duties will be both to discover and develop potential hit-making artists for the label.

# JANUARY 1962

## THE COLONEL RAISES THE STAKES

Now that it has been revealed that Frank Sinatra's $250,000 private jet is fitted with a small stage, an electric piano and a fully stocked cocktail bar, Colonel Tom Parker – with an eye for similar basic creature comforts – has informed the world that Elvis' fee for a one-hour TV special has increased to a mere $400,000.

## BEATLES FAIL AUDITION, DECCA SIGN POOLE

Liverpudlian group The Beatles undertook an unsuccessful studio audition under the supervision of Decca Records' A&R man Mike Smith, at the company's West Hampstead Studios in London.

Among the 15 songs taped, there were three compositions by the group's John Lennon and Paul McCartney – 'Like Dreamers Do', 'Hello Little Girl' and 'Love Of The Loved'.

The remainder were all cover versions – 'To Know Him Is To Love Him', 'Three Cool Cats', 'Memphis Tennessee', 'The Sheik of Araby', 'Money (That's What I Want)', 'Oh Carol', 'Till There Was You', 'Red Sails In The Sunset', 'Please, Mr. Postman', 'What'd I Say', 'Lend Me Your Comb' and 'I Forgot To Remember To Forget'.

Also auditioned and signed to the label, were a five-piece from Dagenham, England, Brian Poole & The Tremeloes.

*Brian Poole & The Tremeloes – preferred by Decca to the Beatles*

# TWISTING ROUND TRAD JAZZ

The Twist looks like it has sidelined trad jazz as Britain's latest teenage trend, as Chubby Checker dances into the charts with two singles featuring his biggest Stateside hits, 'Let's Twist Again' and 'The Twist'. Joey Dee & The Starlighters have also clicked with 'The Peppermint Twist'.

While the British public are eager to buy any single with 'Twist' in the title, opinions within the British music business have been mixed. Trad jazz star Mr Acker Bilk has been quoted as saying: 'I don't think the public is going to swallow this one whole! In America, they needed a new craze – something to revive interest in rock'n'roll. The Twist filled the bill, but over here you should remember we've already got one new fad – It's Trad, Dad!'

Cliff Richard is among the more vocal Twist supporters: 'Sure, I dig The Twist. It knocks me out!'

Party-goer Helen Shapiro finds The Twist 'tremendous', adding: 'It's bound to catch on with the girls . . . after all, let's face the facts, the hip swinging movement is almost a natural for us!'

Frankie Vaughan, who has entered the race with 'Don't Stop, Twist', is ecstatic: 'I think that The Twist is the greatest musical thing to hit England since rock'n'roll.'

*Ernest Evans, a.k.a. Chubby Checker*

## THE GRAPEVINE

■ Thailand has banned all Elvis movies following riots prior, during and following the screening of *Blue Hawaii*.

■ Cliff Richard's 'The Young Ones' 45 has been released with 500,000 advance U.K. sales.

■ The Marketts' 'Surfer Stomp' making much chart noise Stateside.

■ Billy Fury has been filming *Play It Cool*.

■ Folk favourites, Peter, Paul & Mary have been signed to Warner Bros Records.

## BEACH BOYS BREAK THROUGH

The Beach Boys' debut single, 'Surfin'', has entered Billboard Magazine's chart at No. 118.

Formerly known as The Pendletons (named after a fashionable wide-stripe shirt), The Beach Boys comprise the three Wilson brothers – Brian (who writes the songs), Carl and Dennis, their cousin Mike Love and a friend, David Marks.

To date, their only appearance was when they received $300 to play a Ritchie Valens New Year's Eve memorial dance at Long Beach Municipal Auditorium.

## STAR QUOTE

### DENNIS WILSON

on the first time The Beach Boys heard 'Surfin' on the radio

*'We got so excited hearing our record on the radio that Carl threw up, and I ran down the street screaming!'*

# BRUBECK: CLOSET HOLLY FAN

*Brubeck – Sunday Night with Buddy*

*The Crickets: Jerry Allison (top), Buddy Holly, Joe B. Mauldin*

Innovative West-Coast 'Cool School' modern jazz pianist/composer Dave Brubeck, who has repeated his 'Take Five' hit status of last year with the equally catchy 'It's A Raggy Waltz', has revealed that one of his closest, yet most unlikely, musical buddies was called Holly – Buddy Holly!

'One of the least-reported of all friendships was mine with the late, great Buddy Holly,' confessed the coolest of cats. 'I had known Buddy for some time before he died, and I always regretted that I did not see him as often as I would have liked.

'Almost the last occasion we met was when he was in London for concerts, and he appeared on *Sunday Night at the London Palladium*. That evening, I called on him in his dressing room, and we chatted about music – Buddy had a great knowledge of this subject. He knew as much about the modern jazz scene as he did about what was happening in rock and blues and country.

'I saw him only twice more for fleeting moments before I was shattered by the news of his death. It's just a pity that we never did get to record something together.'

## CHARTS

| | | |
|---|---|---|
| US45 | Peppermint Twist | Joey Dee & The Starliters |
| USLP | Blue Hawaii | Elvis Presley |
| UK45 | The Young Ones | Cliff Richard |
| UKLP | The Young Ones | Cliff Richard |

**WEEK 2**

| | | |
|---|---|---|
| US45 | Peppermint Twist | Joey Dee & The Starliters |
| USLP | Blue Hawaii | Elvis Presley |
| UK45 | The Young Ones | Cliff Richard |
| UK.P | The Young Ones | Cliff Richard |

**WEEK 3**

| | | |
|---|---|---|
| US45 | Duke Of Earl | Gene Chandler |
| USLP | Blue Hawaii | Elvis Presley |
| UK45 | The Young Ones | Cliff Richard |
| UKLP | The Young Ones | Cliff Richard |

**WEEK 4**

| | | |
|---|---|---|
| US45 | Duke Of Earl | Gene Chandler |
| USLP | Blue Hawaii | Elvis Presley |
| UK45 | Let's Twist Again | Chubby Checker |
| UKLP | Blue Hawaii | Elvis Presley |

## BROKEN LEG LED DENVER TO HIT

One-time merchant seaman Karl Denver was pretty much a rough diamond before becoming a professional singer.

The tattoo on the back of the left hand of this 26-year-old Glaswegian is a reminder of 30 days spent in an Egyptian jail for hitting an Arab policeman ('I had the tattoo done to pass the time away'), while a broken leg was indirectly responsible for his second U.K. hit, 'Wimoweh'.

Karl confesses: 'About ten years ago, when I'd just turned sixteen, the ship I was serving on docked at a South African port. That evening, I went on one big binge with some pals.

'On the way back to my cabin, I fell down a gangway and broke my leg. I found I had plenty of spare time for convalescence, so I toured the local beauty spots, and came across an African tribe in the middle of a ceremonial dance. They were singing "Wimoweh" in Swahili, and I kept the song in my head ever since.'

# 1962

## CHUBBY CHECKS INTO UK CHARTS

On the other side of the Atlantic, Chubby Checker is thrilled-to-bustin' with three singles in the UK Top 30: 'Let's Twist Again' (7), 'Slow Twistin'' (20) and a duet with Bobby Rydell, 'Teach Me To Twist' (26).

Despite his worldwide success, Chubby is being cautious with his cash. Seemingly, his one luxury is a Thunderbird Convertible.

Says Chubby, who won't be 21 until October: 'My parents are investing my money in real estate just in case, but I'm allowed *thirty-five dollars* a week spending money!'

*Bobby Rydell rides the Twist craze*

## ELVIS'S DREAM

United Artists' Studios have released *Follow That Dream* with Elvis Presley (Toby Kwimper) at the centre of a strictly-for-laughs conflict between shiftless Florida poor folks and corrupt local authorities.

*Elvis as Toby Kwimper*

# TWIST DISCS DOMINATE US CHARTS

*Joey Dee & The Starlighters*

No less than *four* Twist singles are featured in the US Top 20 as the craze takes a hold.

Chubby Checker's 'The Twist' is at No. 5, while Joey Dee & The Starlighters' 'The Peppermint Twist' holds down the No. 9 slot, Gary US Bonds' 'Dear Lady Twist' is at No. 11 and Billy Joe & The Checkmates' 'Perculator Twist' is at No. 27.

Meanwhile, a spot-check of New York's Temple of Twist – The Peppermint Lounge on West 45th Street – reveals that the Big Apple's most popular Twist albums are:
(1) Chubby Checker: 'For Twisters Only', (2) Chubby Checker: 'Let's Twist Again', (3) Chubby Checker: 'Your Twist Party', (4) Ray Charles: 'Do The Twist', (5) Joey Dee: 'Doin' The Twist Live At The Peppermint Lounge' and (6) Louis Prima: 'Doin' The Twist'.

## THE GRAPEVINE

■ The Beatles have made their radio debut on the BBC's *Teenager's Turn – Here We Go*.

■ Helen Shapiro has become the first British artist to top the Japanese charts with 'You Don't Know Me'.

■ The Shadows have become the first British group to headline the prestigious L'Olympia Theatre, Paris.

■ Chicago blues legend Howlin' Wolf (Chester Burnett) has been touring the UK with Chris Barber's Jazz Band.

## CHARTS

| | |
|---|---|
| US45 | Duke Of Earl *Gene Chandler* |
| USLP | Blue Hawaii *Elvis Presley* |
| UK45 | Let's Twist Again *Chubby Checker* |
| UKLP | Blue Hawaii *Elvis Presley* |

— WEEK 2 —

| | |
|---|---|
| US45 | Hey ! Baby ! *Bruce Channel* |
| USLP | Blue Hawaii *Elvis Presley* |
| UK45 | March Of The Siamese Children *Kenny Ball* |
| UKLP | Blue Hawaii *Elvis Presley* |

— WEEK 3 —

| | |
|---|---|
| US45 | Hey ! Baby ! *Bruce Channel* |
| USLP | Blue Hawaii *Elvis Presley* |
| UK45 | Wonderful Land *Shadows* |
| UKLP | Blue Hawaii *Elvis Presley* |

— WEEK 4 —

| | |
|---|---|
| US45 | Hey ! Baby ! *Bruce Channel* |
| USLP | Blue Hawaii *Elvis Presley* |
| UK45 | Wonderful Land *Shadows* |
| UKLP | Blue Hawaii *Elvis Presley* |

— WEEK 5 —

| | |
|---|---|
| US45 | Don't Break The Heart That Loves You *Connie Francis* |
| USLP | Blue Hawaii *Elvis Presley* |
| UK45 | Wonderful Land *Shadows* |
| UKLP | Blue Hawaii *Elvis Presley* |

## DYLAN DEBUT RELEASED

CBS Records have released a self-titled debut album by Bob Dylan. Of the 22 folk and blues tracks he recorded with just his own guitar accompaniment between November 20 and 22 1961, a total of 13 songs are premiered.

Most of young Dylan's influences are in evidence: 'You're No Good' (Jesse Fuller), 'Talkin' New York' (Dylan), 'In My Time Of Dyin' (Jesus Gonna Make Up My Dyin' Bed)' (Blind Willie Johnson), 'Man Of Constant Sorrow' (trad., arr. Dylan), 'Fixin To Die' (Bukka White), 'Pretty Peggy-O' (trad., arr. Dylan), 'Highway 51' (Curtis Jones), 'Gospel Plow' (trad., arr. Dylan), 'Baby, Let Me Follow You Down' (Eric Von Schmidt), 'House Of The Risin' Sun' (trad.), 'Freight Train Blues' (trad.), 'Song To Woody' (Dylan), 'See That My Grave Is Kept Clean' (Blind Lemon Jefferson).

# IT'S ALL GO FOR ACKER!

Trumpeter Kenny Ball woos the Kremlin

A Band of Thieves led by Acker Bilk (left)

Mr Acker Bilk & His Paramount Jazz Band have topped off the most hectic period in their career by commencing the first day's filming on their first full-length movie, *Bank of Thieves*, at Pinewood Studios.

Earlier that week, the popular bowler-hatted jazz clarinettist was an unsuspecting victim of the *This Is Your Life* (BBC-TV) team, and was also awarded a gold disc for a million-plus sales of 'Stranger On The Shore'.

The single, with 21 consecutive weeks on the UK charts, is only five weeks short of Shirley Bassey's all-time best of 26 weeks with 'As Long As He Needs Me'.

In the interim, 'Stranger On The Shore' has repeated the recent Stateside success of fellow-Brit Kenny Ball's 'Midnight In Moscow' million-seller by moving up to No. 4 on *Billboard* magazine's Hot 100.

## THE GRAPEVINE

- Chubby Checker's *Don't Knock The Twist* movie has been premiered in New York.

- With 'Apache', The Shadows are the first British instrumental group to sell over a million singles domestically.

- Steve Allen Lewis – three year old son of Jerry Lee and Myra – has drowned in the family swimming pool.

## NME NO. 1 – OFFICIAL!

In the *New Musical Express'*, Tin Pan Alley offices in Soho's Denmark Street, London, the staff haven't only been celebrating the paper's 10th anniversary, but the good news that, for the first time ever, the paper's circulation now exceeds 200,000 copies weekly.

The certified circulation figure is not only the biggest in the world for any kind of musical paper, but it is greater than the combined weekly sales of all other British music papers.

## EX-BEATLE SUTCLIFFE DIES

Following a brain haemorrhage the previous day, former Beatles bassist Stuart Sutcliffe died, aged 21, in the arms of his German fiancée, photographer Astrid Kirchherr, in the back of an ambulance carrying him to a Hamburg hospital.

Since leaving The Beatles last year, Sutcliffe had been studying art in his adopted city.

Sutcliffe's untimely death may have been brought about as a result of being savagely kicked in the head outside a Liverpool dance hall, two years earlier.

Brenda Lee, unbilled but still dynamite!

The Brooks Brothers

## CHARTS

| | | |
|---|---|---|
| US45 | Johnny Angel | *Shelley Fabares* |
| USLP | Blue Hawaii | *Elvis Presley* |
| UK45 | Wonderful Land | *Shadows* |
| UKLP | Blue Hawaii | *Elvis Presley* |
| | WEEK 2 | |
| US45 | Johnny Angel | *Shelley Fabares* |
| USLP | Blue Hawaii | *Elvis Presley* |
| UK45 | Wonderful Land | *Shadows* |
| UKLP | Blue Hawaii | *Elvis Presley* |
| | WEEK 3 | |
| US45 | Good Luck Charm | *Elvis Presley* |
| USLP | Blue Hawaii | *Elvis Presley* |
| UK45 | Wonderful Land | *Shadows* |
| UKLP | Blue Hawaii | *Elvis Presley* |
| | WEEK 4 | |
| US45 | Good Luck Charm | *Elvis Presley* |
| USLP | Blue Hawaii | *Elvis Presley* |
| UK45 | Wonderful Land | *Shadows* |
| UKLP | Blue Hawaii | *Elvis Presley* |

## POLL-WINNERS SHOW

The NME annual Readers' Poll-Winners Concert was again staged at London's Wembley Pool on April 15.

Those who performed included: Cliff Richard & The Shadows, Billy Fury, Adam Faith, American rocker Johnny Burnette, Eden Kane, Joe Brown, Shane Fenton, Mr Acker Bilk, The Karl Denver Trio, Jet Harris, The Brooks Brothers, John Leyton, Bert Weedon, Helen Shapiro, Danny Williams, The Springfields, Red Price, Ted Heath & His Music and Bob Miller & The Millermen.

Also appearing, as unbilled guest star, was America's 'Miss Dynamite', Brenda Lee.

## CHARTS

| | | |
|---|---|---|
| US45 | Soldier Boy | *Shirelles* |
| USLP | West Side Story | *Soundtrack* |
| UK45 | Wonderful Land | *Shadows* |
| UKLP | Blue Hawaii | *Elvis Presley* |

— W E E K 2 —

| | | |
|---|---|---|
| US45 | Soldier Boy | *Shirelles* |
| USLP | West Side Story | *Soundtrack* |
| UK45 | Nut Rocker | *B. Bumble & The Stingers* |
| UKLP | Blue Hawaii | *Elvis Presley* |

— W E E K 3 —

| | | |
|---|---|---|
| US45 | Soldier Boy | *Shirelles* |
| USLP | West Side Story | *Soundtrack* |
| UK45 | Good Luck Charm | *Elvis Presley* |
| UKLP | Blue Hawaii | *Elvis Presley* |

— W E E K 4 —

| | | |
|---|---|---|
| US45 | Stranger On The Shore | *Acker Bilk* |
| USLP | West Side Story | *Soundtrack* |
| UK45 | Good Luck Charm | *Elvis Presley* |
| UKLP | Blue Hawaii | *Elvis Presley* |

# A STING IN THE TALE

British fans have much cause for complaint over the lack of attention given to B. Bumble & The Stingers' 'Nut Rocker' by BBC Radio djs.

Though 'Nut Rocker' (or as one observer commented: 'a diabolical liberty taken with Mr Tchaikovsky's "Nutcracker Suite"') has been featured 'live' by a number of BBC studio performers, the original Kim Fowley-produced Stateside recording has made the UK Top 10 without any BBC airplay!

It wasn't that the record was banned, it was just ignored. Only when 'Nut Rocker' reached the upper reaches of the charts under its own steam did it receive a solitary spin on Alan Freeman's *Top Ten Show* as a matter of course.

The only way British fans could hear the record was by tuning into European based Radio Luxembourg, where it was on the playlist of all the station's EMI Records sponsored shows. It was due entirely to this that The Stingers buzzed into the British bestsellers lists.

Ironically, 'Nut Rocker' has proved to be one of Top Rank Records' biggest-ever selling hits at a time when the label is about to be discontinued, and the cata-logue absorbed into other EMI divisions. To complete the bizarre circumstances that have surrounded 'Nut Rocker's' success, heavyweight piano-poundin' B. Bumble is persistently miffed that nobody believes that he's recorded under his *real* name: B (Bill) Bumble!

*Kim Fowley tries to retrieve his nutcrackers from a hungry pillar box*

# IS THERE A DOCTOR IN THE CHARTS?

*Chamberlain, the singing doctor*

The trend for actor-singer continues: Richard Chamberlain – the handsome 26-year-old actor who stars in the title role of hit US-TV hospital drama, *Dr Kildare* – has released his vocal version of the programme's popular theme tune under the title 'Three Stars Shine Tonight'.

Chamberlain, whose daily fan mail is reported to exceed 3,500 letters is, so MGM Studios inform the press, a quiet, studious chap who doesn't drink, rarely goes to nightclubs and doesn't have a steady girlfriend.

However, he takes his new-found fame as a singer as seriously as his acting, and has already named Elvis's 'Love Me Tender' as a likely follow-up.

# OL' BLUE EYES TWISTS

Frank Sinatra, who was once quoted as saying he didn't want 'bad rock and roll records' on his Reprise record label, has sent his most devoted finger-poppin' fans into shock by jumping aboard Chubby Checker's commercial bandwagon and releasing a single, 'Ev'rybody's Twistin'', an update of an old jazz standard, 'Ev'rybody's Truckin''.

## THE GRAPEVINE

■ Don and Phil Everly have been discharged from the US Marines.

■ Cliff Richard & The Shadows have been filming *Summer Holiday* in Greece.

■ The two most-played jukebox hits in the US in 1961 were Jimmy Dean's 'Big Bad John' and Chubby Checker's 'The Twist'.

■ Blues legend John Lee Hooker has made the UK charts for the first time with 'Boom Boom'.

# SINATRA HONOURS UK WRITERS

The main event in London this month has been Frank Sinatra's three days of recording – before invited audiences of fans and friends – at Pye's Marble Arch studios. With Robert Farnon conducting a 40-piece orchestra (and visitor Nelson Riddle occasionally advising from the sidelines), Sinatra recorded a selection of 11 ballads, all from the pens of British composers, to be released on Reprise as 'Great Songs From Great Britain'.

Among those recorded were 'The Very Thought Of You' and 'We'll Meet Again'.

Midway through the first session, Sinatra indicated that he would be returning next year to complete a companion L.P.

## CHARTS

**WEEK 1**
- US45 I Can't Stop Loving You / *Ray Charles*
- USLP West Side Story / *Soundtrack*
- UK45 Good Luck Charm / *Elvis Presley*
- UKLP Blue Hawaii / *Elvis Presley*

— WEEK 2 —
- US45 I Can't Stop Loving You / *Ray Charles*
- USLP West Side Story / *Soundtrack*
- UK45 Good Luck Charm / *Elvis Presley*
- UKLP Blue Hawaii / *Elvis Presley*

— WEEK 3 —
- US45 I Can't Stop Loving You / *Ray Charles*
- USLP West Side Story / *Soundtrack*
- UK45 Good Luck Charm / *Elvis Presley*
- UKLP Blue Hawaii / *Elvis Presley*

— WEEK 4 —
- US45 I Can't Stop Loving You / *Ray Charles*
- USLP Modern Sounds In Country & Western Music / *Ray Charles*
- UK45 Come Outside / *Mike Sarne*
- UKLP West Side Story / *Soundtrack*

— WEEK 5 —
- US45 I Can't Stop Loving You / *Ray Charles*
- USLP Modern Sounds In Country & Western Music / *Ray Charles*
- UK45 Come Outside / *Mike Sarne*
- UKLP West Side Story / *Soundtrack*

## CAROLE'S BABY-SITTING BLUES

*Summer rain doesn't worry Carole King*

*No babysitting blues for Little Eva*

Deciding that the end product is so good, songwriter Carole King (of Goffin & King fame) has been persuaded to release her studio demo of 'It Might As Well Rain Until September' on the Dimension label.

Keeping it in the family, Carole King's babysitter, Eva Narcissus Boyd has recorded and released 'The Loco-Motion' under the name of Little Eva to become a summertime chart-topper. The single was written by her erstwhile employers, who were impressed by the ex-babysitter's singing around the house.

Now the only question is: where on earth are they going to find another babysitter?

## THE GRAPEVINE

- The Beatles have been signed to UK Parlophone Records.
- Owen Gray's 'Twist Baby' is the first release on Chris Blackwell's recently formed Island label.
- Bruce Channel, Delbert McClinton, Frank Ifield and Johnny Kidd & The Pirates have been touring the UK together.
- Swedish guitar combo The Spotnicks have twanged their way into the UK charts with 'Orange Blossom Special' update.

## DAVE CLARK BOWS IN

Fronted by their 19-year-old drum-thumping leader, The Dave Clark Five – from the North London area of Tottenham – have made their disc debut with 'That's What I Said'.

The group, apart from Clark, comprises: Mike Smith (vocals and organ), Denny Payton (tenor sax), Lenny Davidson (guitar) and Rick Huxley (bass).

Formed two years ago during the skiffle music craze, they have built up a local following playing at Tottenham's South Grove Youth Club.

## CORDET HIT FOR EX-SHADOW MEEHAN

Louise Cordet, daughter of TV-presenter Helen Cordet, has become the newest object of affection for Britain's male youth following the release of her coquettish 'I'm Just A Baby'.

The single was produced by Tony Meehan shortly before he left his A&R post with Decca Records, to rejoin his former colleagues, Cliff Richard & The Shadows (from whom he split last year), as A&R chief of their newly formed Shad-Rich record production company. However, he will not be involved with either Cliff or The Shadows in a performing capacity.

Though no longer on Decca's team of salaried globe-trotting talent scouts, Meehan (19) will continue to record for the label in a solo capacity.

*Meehan – a star looking for new talent*

# 1962

## STAR QUOTE

### JOE BROWN

*'I have the world's most shocking memory . . . I only manage to remember the words of my songs because they're in rhyme!'*

*Mr Memory – Joe Brown*

## STONES ROLL IN

With a line-up comprised of Mick Jagger (vocals), Keith Richards and Elmo Lewis (Brian Jones) on guitars, Ian 'Stu' Stewart (piano), Dick Taylor (bass) and Mick Avery (drums), The Rolling Stones make their London Marquee Club debut deputizing for the club's regular Thursday Night R&B attraction – Alexis Korner's Blues Incorporated who are broadcasting 'live' on the BBC's weekly *Jazz Club* radio programme.

# ANKA'S AWAY !

Paul Anka, now 21, has the legal freedom to spend the hundreds of thousands of dollars he has been earning for years as a minor!

Some measure of how much that may be can be gauged from the fact that not only has Anka been awarded 20 gold discs (each in recognition for over one million records sold), but that many of them, like 'Lonely Boy' and 'Puppy Love', were self-penned.

Biggest of all has been 'Diana'. This song is said to have been covered 320 times in 22 countries in the past six years, total sales of such recordings being close to ten million records, while Paul's own sales worldwide stand at more than 30 million. Additionally, his current deal with RCA is said to be worth a minimum of one million dollars over the next five years.

Coupled to this, twangy guitar man Duane Eddy has recently signed to Anka's production company Camay, which is distributed by RCA-Victor. His first disc for Anka/Camay is 'Deep In The Heart Of Texas', and shows a return to his familiar hit formula.

Meanwhile, Anka – whose upcoming single is 'Eso Beso' –

has had one of his paintings accepted by the United Nations Art Club. It is to be hung in the General Assembly building in New York prior to being auctioned off by UNICEF.

## CHARTS

| | | |
|---|---|---|
| US45 | The Stripper | *David Rose & His Orchestra* |
| USLP | Modern Sounds In Country & Western Music | *Ray Charles* |
| UK45 | A Picture Of You | *Joe Brown* |
| UKLP | Pot Luck | *Elvis Presley* |

**————— WEEK 2 —————**

| | | |
|---|---|---|
| US45 | Roses Are Red | *Bobby Vinton* |
| USLP | Modern Sounds In Country & Western Music | *Ray Charles* |
| UK45 | I Can't Stop Loving You | *Ray Charles* |
| UKLP | Pot Luck | *Elvis Presley* |

**————— WEEK 3 —————**

| | | |
|---|---|---|
| US45 | Roses Are Red | *Bobby Vinton* |
| USLP | Modern Sounds In Country & Western Music | *Ray Charles* |
| UK45 | I Remember You | *Frank Ifield* |
| UKLP | Pot Luck | *Elvis Presley* |

**————— WEEK 4 —————**

| | | |
|---|---|---|
| US45 | Roses Are Red | *Bobby Vinton* |
| USLP | Modern Sounds In Country & Western Music | *Ray Charles* |
| UK45 | I Remember You | *Frank Ifield* |
| UKLP | Pot Luck | *Elvis Presley* |

## TWIST AND TRAD GAIN GROUND

With both the Twist and trad jazz taking sales away from the previously rock'n'roll dominated singles market, NME's analysis of the paper's weekly charts for the period January 1 – June 30 makes compulsive reading.

Looking at the Top 10 positions, Elvis again is secure at No. 1 followed by Cliff Richard, but with Chubby Checker fast gaining ground at No. 3. There are no other US artists in this top half of the results.

Trad jazz is represented by Mr Acker Bilk at No. 4 and Kenny Ball at No. 7. The remaining best-sellers are: Karl Denver (No. 5), Billy Fury (No. 7), The Shadows (No. 8), Eden Kane (No. 9) and Helen Shapiro who, at No. 10 is a full eleven places ahead of her closest female rival, Brenda Lee!

## THE GRAPEVINE

■ Connie Francis has slipped behind the Iron Curtain to represent the USA at the Polish Music Festival.

■ Following their release from the US Marines, The Everly Brothers have engaged in a six-week 'comeback' tour of the States.

■ British disc jockey Jimmy Savile has made his disc debut with 'Ahab The Arab'.

■ Buddy Holly clone, Tommy Roe is in the US charts with 'Sheila'.

*Connie – polishing up her act*

*Tommy Roe – charting with 'Sheila'*

# CHECKER CHAT

It's not so much a case of biting the beat that feeds him, but for all the hysteria that has surrounded The Twist phenomenon, 20-year-old Chubby Checker has still been able to take a realistic and unbiased view of the circumstances that have placed his records on all the world's major charts, and elevated him to the position of being the first major star of the Sixties.

As far as Chubby is concerned, his seemingly overnight success was as much a case of inspired opportunism than any other fancy theory that has been put forward.

'There is absolutely nothing new about The Twist,' Checker admits. 'People have been doing the same sort of thing for centuries – wiggling their hips and their shoulders in time to music, especially people who can't dance properly.

'Now, I've just been smart enough to exploit something which the public failed to recognize was no more than swaying naturally to musical rhythms.

'And, I'm not worried if it doesn't last. Right now, I'm looking for something else that's been done for years, so that I can exploit that in a way the public won't recognize!'

## THE GRAPEVINE

■ Previously The Four Lovers, Vee-Jay Records' The Four Seasons have hit paydirt first time out with 'Sherry'.

■ Memphis-based Booker T & The MGS are charting everywhere with 'Green Onions'.

■ Robert Allen Zimmerman has legally changed his name to Bob Dylan.

■ Motown vocal group, The Contours, are enjoying heavy action with 'Do You Love Me'.

## BEST OUT, STARR JOINS BEATLES

Officially a Beatle, drummer Ringo Starr has made his controversial Cavern Club debut on August 14, during which scuffles broke out inside the venue, guitarist George Harrison received a black eye and manager Brian Epstein's car was vandalized in the street outside the club.

The series of events began five days earlier when Epstein contacted Ringo Starr, then resident at Butlin's Holiday Camp, Skegness, with Rory Storme & The Hurricanes to offer him the soon-to-be-vacant drum stool with The Beatles.

It was too good an offer for Mr Starr to refuse!

The fact that Pete Best was easily the most popular member of the group was – in the opinion of John, Paul and George – quite incidental. The fact remained that EMI's George Martin had expressed concern about Best's potential as a recording drummer. On hearing these remarks, Epstein and The Beatles instantly rectified the problem, which could easily have jeopardized their upcoming recording plans.

On August 16, Epstein – at the behest of John, Paul and George – informed Pete Best that he was no longer The Beatles' drummer. Two days later, Ringo Starr made his public debut with the group at the Hulme Hall, Port Sunlight. Liverpool fans were not happy – hence the Cavern kerfuffle.

### CHARTS

| | |
|---|---|
| US45 | Roses Are Red *Bobby Vinton* |
| USLP | Modern Sounds In Country & Western Music *Ray Charles* |
| UK45 | I Remember You *Frank Ifield* |
| UKLP | West Side Story *Soundtrack* |

— WEEK 2 —

| | |
|---|---|
| US45 | Breaking Up Is Hard To Do *Neil Sedaka* |
| USLP | Modern Sounds In Country & Western Music *Ray Charles* |
| UK45 | I Remember You *Frank Ifield* |
| UKLP | Pot Luck *Elvis Presley* |

— WEEK 3 —

| | |
|---|---|
| US45 | Breaking Up Is Hard To Do *Neil Sedaka* |
| USLP | Modern Sounds In Country & Western Music *Ray Charles* |
| UK45 | I Remember You *Frank Ifield* |
| UKLP | Pot Luck *Elvis Presley* |

— WEEK 4 —

| | |
|---|---|
| US45 | The Locomotion *Little Eva* |
| USLP | Modern Sounds In Country & Western Music *Ray Charles* |
| UK45 | I Remember You *Frank Ifield* |
| UKLP | West Side Story *Soundtrack* |

*Pete Best (far right) has been elbowed out of The Beatles' line up and is replaced by Hurricanes' drummer Ringo Starr*

# 1962

## THE GRAPEVINE

■ Connie Francis' first book, 'For Every Young Heart' has been published.

■ The Spotnicks back in the UK charts with 'Rocket Man'.

■ Buddy Holly has scored a posthumous hit with 'Reminiscin'.

■ This year's novelty disc is US rock-horror recording 'The Monster Mash' by Bobby 'Boris' Pickett & The Crypt-Kickers.

## CHARTS

| | |
|---|---|
| US45 | Sheila<br>*Tommy Roe* |
| USLP | Modern Sounds In Country & Western Music<br>*Ray Charles* |
| UK45 | I Remember You<br>*Frank Ifield* |
| UKLP | West Side Story<br>*Soundtrack* |

—— WEEK 2 ——

| | |
|---|---|
| US45 | Sheila<br>*Tommy Roe* |
| USLP | Modern Sounds In Country & Western Music<br>*Ray Charles* |
| UK45 | I Remember You<br>*Frank Ifield* |
| UKLP | West Side Story<br>*Soundtrack* |

—— WEEK 3 ——

| | |
|---|---|
| US45 | Sherry<br>*Four Seasons* |
| USLP | Modern Sounds In Country & Western Music<br>*Ray Charles* |
| UK45 | She's Not You<br>*Elvis Presley* |
| UKLP | West Side Story<br>*Soundtrack* |

—— WEEK 4 ——

| | |
|---|---|
| US45 | Sherry<br>*Four Seasons* |
| USLP | Modern Sounds In Country & Western Music<br>*Ray Charles* |
| UK45 | She's Not You<br>*Elvis Presley* |
| UK.P | West Side Story<br>*Soundtrack* |

—— WEEK 5 ——

| | |
|---|---|
| US45 | Sherry<br>*Four Seasons* |
| USLP | West Side Story<br>*Soundtrack* |
| UK45 | She's Not You<br>*Elvis Presley* |
| UKLP | West Side Story<br>*Soundtrack* |

# HATS OFF TO DEL!

Such was the speed with which former US Army serviceman Del Shannon topped the charts on both sides of the Atlantic last Spring with 'Runaway', it was assumed the 22-year old from Grand Rapids, Michigan was just another in the line of one-hit-wonders.

Shannon quickly silenced those sceptics with a quick-fire succession of self-penned hits which included 'Hats Off To Larry', 'So Long Baby', 'Hey Little Girl', 'Cry Myself To Sleep', 'Swiss Maid' and currently 'Little Town Flirt'.

As to the circumstances surrounding his initial Big Break, Shannon (real name Charles Westover) has revealed that, back in Michigan, it was local entrepreneur Ollie McLaughlin who motivated him to go for the big one.

'He heard me performing in a club and told me to look him up when I had written a song I thought stood some chance of being a hit!' he says. 'Immediately after the gig, I sat up all night trying to think up new words to songs, and, eventually, I had 'Runaway' — something easy to remember, but still sufficiently out of the ordinary.'

## ELVIS GETTING BIGGER

Elvis's dresser, Sy Devore has to kit out the singer with a new $9,300 wardrobe for an upcoming movie. Seeing how Elvis earns $10,000-plus a day singing and dancing before the cameras, Devore has to hire a stand-in with identical measurements to Elvis.

There is one problem — sources close to the star have intimated that Elvis is having weight problems!

*Big 'Bossa Nova' Charlie Byrd finds Brazilian rhythm his route into the US charts*

## BYRD'S NEW BEAT

Among the more unusual souvenirs guitarist Charlie Byrd brought back home to Washington DC from his US State Department Tour of South America, was a bag full of Brazilian rhythms.

One in particular — the *bossa nova* (the new beat) — intrigued both him and tenor saxist Stan Getz, with the result that a single plucked from their best-selling 'jazz samba' album, 'Desafinado (Slightly Out Of Tune)', has charted and, in doing so, prompted dozens of artists to ride the bossa nova bandwagon.

*Tenor saxist Stan Getz — Charlie Byrd's partner and certainly not 'desafinado' with the US record-buying public*

# JB – OUTTA SIGHT

## CHARTS

| | | |
|---|---|---|
| US45 | Sherry | Four Seasons |
| USLP | West Side Story | Soundtrack |
| UK45 | Telstar | Tornados |
| UKLP | West Side Story | Soundtrack |
| | WEEK 2 | |
| US45 | Sherry | Four Seasons |
| USLP | West Side Story | Soundtrack |
| UK45 | Telstar | Tornados |
| UKLP | West Side Story | Soundtrack |
| | WEEK 3 | |
| US45 | Monster Mash | Bobby 'Boris' Pickett |
| USLP | Peter, Paul & Mary | Peter, Paul & Mary |
| UK45 | Telstar | Tornados |
| UKLP | West Side Story | Soundtrack |
| | WEEK 4 | |
| US45 | Monster Mash | Bobby 'Boris' Pickett |
| USLP | Peter, Paul & Mary | Peter, Paul & Mary |
| UK45 | Telstar | Tornados |
| UKLP | Out Of The Shadows | Shadows |

It's reported that prior to The James Brown Revue commencing yet another headlining season at New York's world-famous Apollo Theater, Harlem, Syd Nathan (the head of King Records) argued vigorously against Brown's wish to record his complete act.

'You mean,' said Nathan, 'you want to record your stage show *live*! – you can't keep on recording the same songs over and over . . . nobody's going to buy that!'

When Brown explained that his hits sounded infinitely better when performed against a gale-force blast of his screamin' fans, Nathan thought the idea quite crazy and made no commercial sense. Nathan's final word on the subject was that, if Brown was so obsessed with the project, he should fund it entirely from out of his own pocket.

King Records, insisted Nathan, won't contribute a cent! The bottom line for recording is $5,700, so JB laid his money down and recorded all four of the shows he gave on Wednesday, October 24.

It's a time of historical importance for 'the hardest working man in show business'. Unsatisfied with the Apollo's financial arrangements, JB has set a precedent by insisting that he will cancel his shows unless he's allowed to rent the venue for the duration of his season.

In this way, once all the overhead costs have been covered, JB will earn something nearer his true box-office worth.

## PHIL EVERLY ALONE

Don Everly flew out of London en route for the States on October 15, leaving younger brother Phil with the daunting task of completing a bill-topping Everly Brothers UK tour, solo!

The circumstances behind this bizarre situation took place two days earlier, on Sunday, October 13. During a rehearsal at London's Prince of Wales Theatre, brother Don broke down completely during 'Crying In The Rain' and was immediately rushed to the nearby Charing Cross Hospital before being taken on to the Middlesex Hospital for treatment not unconnected with medicine he has been taking.

## IF YOU HAVE TO ASK . . .

Asked Elvis Presley's going rate for inaugurating the lavish New York Americana Hotel, Colonel Tom Parker replied: 'The first ten floors!'

## THE GRAPEVINE

■ Parlophone are said to have selected two Lennon & McCartney originals, 'Love Me Do' and 'P.S. I Love You' as the debut single from The Beatles.

■ Bobby 'Boris' Pickett's 'Monster Mash' has been banned by BBC radio and TV for being 'offensive'.

■ Cliff Richard, The Shadows and Frank Ifield were the token pop acts on Royal Command Variety Performance.

*Elvis (left) – a fair day's work for a fair day's pay?*

*Hank Marvin (right) – he and the Shadows are considered suitable viewing for the Royal Family*

## NOVEMBER 1962

## HOT NEWS FROM NJF

The British National Jazz Federation/Marquee Club 'house' publication *Jazz News* has printed its first weekly 'Rhythm & Blues Column' noting:

'Alexis Korner and Blues Incorporated have been Thursday residents at famous Marquee Club in Oxford Street for some months now . . . audiences now reach almost 700 nearly every session . . . an exciting line-up including Dick Heckstall-Smith, Graham Bond, Peter 'Ginger' Baker, Jack Bruce, and Johnny Parker guarantees the jazz content . . . jiving, twisting, raving, just listening, that's the Marquee on Thursdays.

'Mick Jagger and The Rolling Stones are touring the local clubs to appreciative audiences, with a history of appearances at the first R&B club in London, the Ealing Saturday Club, where Korner used to play.'

*Alexis Korner and Blues Incorporated – Marquee residents*

*The Rolling Stones – one time regulars at the Ealing Club*

# LITTLE RICHARD ROCKS BACK

When Little Richard agreed to headline a UK tour supported by Sam Cooke and Jet Harris, it was in the belief that it was in his three-year old adopted role of gospel music performer.

On the opening night (8 October) at the Gaumont Theatre, Doncaster, Richard took the stage for the first of two evening shows dressed in the long robes favoured by gospel preachers and, with teenage Billy Preston at the Hammond organ, began to sing such familiar old-time quasi-religious standards as 'Peace In The Valley' and 'I Believe'.

The house-full audience, who had anticipated a full-throttle rock'n'roll assault from the Georgia Peach, went into shock and the promoter into a panic.

At the second show, Sam Cooke, delayed from making the earlier performance, whipped the audience into a frenzy prior to intermission time and left them howling for more. Sensing a serious challenge to his reputation, Richard abandoned his gospel set to rock out in a rough impromptu manner and secure his bill-topping status. And that's how it con-tinued for the remainder of the tour, which culminated in Brian Epstein booking Richard to headline an all-Merseyside 5½-hour/12 group marathon at the Tower Ballroom, New Brighton and, two weeks later, to headline at the Empire Theatre, Liverpool. On both occasions, The Beatles also appeared.

Though he was now singing rock'n'roll, Richard was determined to quash rumours that he was in fact godless and deceitful.

*Richard sidekick – Billy Preston*

## CHARTS

| | | |
|---|---|---|
| US45 | He's A Rebel | *Crystals* |
| USLP | Peter, Paul & Mary | *Peter, Paul & Mary* |
| UK45 | Telstar | *Tornados* |
| UKLP | West Side Story | *Soundtrack* |

#### — WEEK 2 —

| | | |
|---|---|---|
| US45 | He's A Rebel | *Crystals* |
| USLP | Peter, Paul & Mary | *Peter, Paul & Mary* |
| UK45 | Lovesick Blues | *Frank Ifield* |
| UKLP | West Side Story | *Soundtrack* |

#### — WEEK 3 —

| | | |
|---|---|---|
| US45 | Big Girls Don't Cry | *Four Seasons* |
| USLP | Peter, Paul & Mary | *Peter, Paul & Mary* |
| UK45 | Lovesick Blues | *Frank Ifield* |
| UKLP | West Side Story | *Soundtrack* |

#### — WEEK 4 —

| | | |
|---|---|---|
| US45 | Big Girls Don't Cry | *Four Seasons* |
| USLP | Peter, Paul & Mary | *Peter, Paul & Mary* |
| UK45 | Lovesick Blues | *Frank Ifield* |
| UKLP | On Stage With | *George Mitchell Minstrels* |

## THE GRAPEVINE

■ A new disc has just been released this month by The Miracles – 'You Really Got A Hold On Me'.

■ EMI Parlophone producer George Martin has announced that he's to record The Beatles 'live' at The Cavern Club.

■ A new release from The Four Seasons: 'Big Girls Don't Cry'.

## HARRIS, MEEHAN JOIN FORCES

The Shadows' former bass player and drummer – Jet Harris and Tony Meehan – have announced that they've chosen to join forces as an instrumental team and promise a spectacular debut early in the New Year.

# CHRIS MONTEZ STEPS OUT

Chris Montez — inspired by Presley and Haley and stepping into Valens' shoes

The logical successor to the late lamented Ritchie Valens, is how 17-year old Chicano, Chris Montez is being hailed. 'Let's Dance' with its piping-hot organ, thunderbolt drums and Montez's nasal invitation to hit the floor in style, carries on where Valens' 'C'mon, Let's Go' left off.

Actually, it was only a chance encounter with some old Presley and Haley discs that got this young Los Angelino rockin' 'n' rollin'. 'That stuff really set me off – I was hooked. After that, I used to spend all my pocket money buying second-hand discs in junk shops, trying to build a collection,' Montez admits.

He also reveals how 'Let's Dance' almost didn't get released! 'That's not for me, I told my manager, when I first heard it,' he says. The fact that it was his manager Jim Lee who had

penned the tune didn't colour his initial judgement. However, Jim was convinced that Chris should at least record the song and then decide upon its fate.

'I agreed to do so only after realising that Jim had a great deal of faith in his composition,' Chris says. 'It wasn't conceit, it was conviction, and by the time he'd hired musicians and had worked out a good backing, I decided the song was for me after all.

'We tried to achieve a new sound on 'Let's Dance'. I think this had a lot to do with it becoming a success, because frankly I don't have big ideas about my ability as a singer. I should think that most kids bought it just to dance to. After all, that's what it's about – not to listen to me!'

Dusty R&B fan

## PRESLEY: LUCKY 13 HITS

'Return To Sender' has given Elvis Presley his 50th entry in the NME singles chart – an unprecedented achievement which is unlikely to be equalled in the forseeable future.

On the subject of Elvis chart statistics: since his first UK No. 1 'All Shook Up', Elvis has occupied the coveted top slot for a total of 52-weeks – in other words, he's been No. 1 on the UK charts for a total of one year, with the longest run of nine consecutive weeks being with 'It's Now Or Never'.

The grand total of 52-weeks at No. 1 was accumulated by 13 separate singles.

## CHARTS

| | |
|---|---|
| US45 | Big Girls Don't Cry *Four Seasons* |
| USLP | My Son The Folk Singer *Allan Sherman* |
| UK45 | Lovesick Blues *Frank Ifield* |
| UKLP | On Stage With *George Mitchell Minstrels* |

**WEEK 2**

| | |
|---|---|
| US45 | Big Girls Don't Cry *Four Seasons* |
| USLP | My Son The Folk Singer *Allan Sherman* |
| UK45 | Lovesick Blues *Frank Ifield* |
| UKLP | On Stage With *George Mitchell Minstrels* |

**WEEK 3**

| | |
|---|---|
| US45 | Big Girls Don't Cry *Four Seasons* |
| USLP | The First Family *Vaughan Meader* |
| UK45 | Return To Sender *Elvis Presley* |
| UKLP | On Stage With *George Mitchell Minstrels* |

**WEEK 4**

| | |
|---|---|
| US45 | Telstar *Tornados* |
| US LP | The First Family *Vaughan Meader* |
| UK45 | Return To Sender *Elvis Presley* |
| UKLP | On Stage With *George Mitchell Minstrels* |

**WEEK 5**

| | |
|---|---|
| US45 | Telstar *Tornados* |
| USLP | The First Family *Vaughan Meader* |
| UK45 | The Next Time *Cliff Richard* |
| UKLP | On Stage With *George Mitchell Minstrels* |

Elvis the record breaker

# RULE BRITANNIA – BRITISH BEAT INVADES AMERICA

It's interesting to note that each time popular music has gone off the boil in the 35 years covered by this book, history reveals that a return to the roots will usually provide rehabilitation. The first time it occurred was the most significant, back in 1964, when an event known in the US as "The British Invasion" took place.

Rock'n'roll music was hardly ten years old, but already its youthful audience had demonstrated one of its most noticeable characteristics, one which still continues today – a short attention span coupled with an insatiable appetite for something new. Early rock'n'roll's first hero, Bill Haley,

seemed too old, Elvis Presley's stint as a GI seemed to have made his music soft, Jerry Lee Lewis was in disgrace for marrying his 13 year old cousin, Little Richard had got religion, Chuck Berry was in prison, Buddy Holly was dead, and the new stars who had risen seemed less exciting and flamboyant.

Very few British records had penetrated the US chart before 1964 – you could almost count them on the fingers of one hand: Laurie London, Lonnie Donegan, The Tornados, maybe one or two more. However, in the wake of Donegan, innumerable semi-professional British groups had sprung up all over Great

Britain, most of them playing songs they'd heard on records by Americans, in particular songs with a strong rhythm & blues bias à la Berry or Holly.

Liverpool (the port where many ships from America docked) was one port where American sailors sold their records, London was obviously another, and it was these international cities which became the headquarters of the British beat group phenomenon. In fact, many of the best Liverpool bands had already ventured to Hamburg (the Liverpool of West Germany), where they not only played music in the style of the great rock'n'roll

*Overnight success – The Stones*

*Herman's Hermits*

*The Dave Clark Five*

*DJ John Peel made it first in US*

*The Kinks regularly toured the States*

pioneers, but also began writing original (if primitive) material. The Beatles, Gerry & The Pacemakers, The Searchers and others were rocking in Hamburg while the US and UK were pretending that the twist, ersatz rockers like Frankie Avalon and Bobby Rydell, and in Britain, Cliff Richard & The Shadows, were filling the gap caused by the demise of original rock'n'roll.

It initially happened in Britain. The charts for the first three months of 1963 were dominated by Cliff & Co., then Liverpool acts shut out virtually all the competition for the top slot in the UK singles chart. Initially, the United States was unenthusiastic, despite the fact that the rest of the English-speaking world had capitulated, but the appearance of The Beatles on the influential 'Ed Sullivan Show' opened the floodgates for literally dozens of British groups to achieve commercial success in the New World. Some acts, such as Dave Clark, Herman and The Zombies (from St. Albans), found greater success in North America than they would ever achieve in their own country. Ultimately, virtually every British group of any note from the mid-1960s made it in the States, including The Who, The Rolling Stones, The Hollies, The Yardbirds, The Moody Blues, Cream, Traffic, Pink Floyd and The Troggs (although in some cases, success did not occur overnight as it had for The Beatles and The Stones).

For the first time since rock'n'roll was born, America wasn't totally predominant, and American acts like The Walker Brothers and later Jimi Hendrix successfully launched themselves in Britain before returning to reap the bigger rewards provided in their homeland.

America's return to control came via '60s soul music and then psychedelia – both these styles had much in common with R&B and country music, the joint sources of rock'n'roll, and their victory over the marauding Brits came much more gradually than the tidal wave bearing British beat music. What was different – and remains one of the British Invasion's most impressive achievements – was that Britain would henceforth be taken seriously as an inventive and trend-setting source of popular music.

*Manfred Mann*

*Original UK export Lonnie Donegan*

*Bigger in the US – Peter and Gordon*

*The Beatles – opened the floodgates*

## BLIND BOY GRUNT

In London, Bob Dylan adopted the unlikely pseudonym 'Blind Boy Grunt' when he dropped by Doug Dobell's Jazz Record Shop at 77, Charing Cross Road to blow harmonica on a Dick Farina and Eric Von Schmidt recording session taking place on the premises.

The reason for Dylan's visit to London was to perform 'Blowin' In The Wind' and 'Swan On The River' in his role as a hobo in BBC-TV's drama 'Mad House On Castle Street'.

## ELVIS ACAPULCO-BOUND

With Swedish femme fatale Ursula Andress cast as his leading lady, Elvis Presley has been a little more eager than usual to begin work on a new movie.

This time around, the sun'n' sand scenario has been entitled 'Fun In Acapulco'. In sticking close to a Mexican theme, the soundtrack material will include 'Bossa Nova Baby' and '(There's) No Room To Rhumba In A Sports Car'.

# 1, 2, 3 FOR EX-SHADS, SHADS AND BOSS

An amazing set of circumstances has resulted in a most unique chart hat-trick: Jet Harris and Tony Meehan — once The Shadows' rhythm section — have leap-frogged to No. 1 on the UK charts with their duo debut, 'Diamonds'.

In the process of establishing themselves as a new instrumental chart force to be reckoned with, Jet and Tony pushed their former colleagues' 'Dance On' from the top slot down to No. 2, while front man Cliff Richard's 'Bachelor Boy' has moved up to No. 3 and his 'The Next Time' rests at No. 7.

Other artists with two singles each in this week's UK Top 30: The Tornados ('Globetrotter' at No. 4 and 'Telstar' at No. 22) and Frank Ifield ('The Wayward Wind' at No. 17 while 'Lovesick Blues' is at No. 19).

*Tony (left) and Jet — 'Diamonds' takes ex-Shads to the top*

## THE GRAPEVINE

■ Hollywood's latest rock spot, The Whiskey-A-Go-Go discotheque has opened on Sunset Boulevard.

■ A second UK single from The Beatles: 'Please Please Me' backed with 'Ask Me Why'.

■ Phil Everly has married Jackie Ertel.

■ 'Rhythm Of The Rain' by The Cascades promises to be one of the month's more endurable hits.

■ The Beatles have signed to Chicago's Vee-Jay label for the States.

*Beatles records to be released Stateside*

## TORNADOS DOUBLE GOLD

Joe Meek-produced instrumental five-piece and singer Billy Fury's backing group The Tornados, have received a second Gold Disc in recognition of their hit 'Telstar' having sold in excess of two million copies world-wide.

The Tornados are the third British-based act to gain this coveted double-gold award inside twelve months.

Mr Acker Bilk with his lyrically haunting 'Stranger On The Shore' was the first. Similarly, Aussie singer Frank Ifield struck double-gold with his reworked oldie, 'I Remember You'.

## CHARTS

| | |
|---|---|
| US45 | Telstar *Tornadoes* |
| USLP | The First Family *Vaughn Meader* |
| UK45 | Dance On *Shadows* |
| UKLP | On Stage With *George Mitchell Minstrels* |
| | WEEK 2 |
| US45 | Go Away Little Girl *Steve Lawrence* |
| USLP | The First Family *Vaughn Meader* |
| UK45 | Dance On *Shadows* |
| UKLP | West Side Story *Soundtrack* |
| | WEEK 3 |
| US45 | Go Away Little Girl *Steve Lawrence* |
| USLP | The First Family *Vaughn Meader* |
| UK45 | Dance On *Shadows* |
| UKLP | West Side Story *Soundtrack* |
| | WEEK 4 |
| US45 | Walk Right In *Rooftop Singers* |
| USLP | The First Family *Vaughn Meader* |
| UK45 | Diamonds *Jet Harris & Tony Meehan* |
| UKLP | West Side Story *Soundtrack* |

## TRAD AT PALACE

It's still Trad, Dad! — the single biggest trad jazz event to be staged in Britain, has taken place in the Great Hall of North London's Alexandra Palace.

Held from 10 pm on Friday until 7 am the following morning, hosts George Melly and Diz Disley introduced the New Orleans-style jazz of such popular British bandleaders as Mr Acker Bilk, Chris Barber, Kenny Ball, Alex Welsh, Ken Colyer, Monty Sunshine, Bob Wallis, Bruce Turner, Mick Mulligan and at least half-a-dozen others.

# AUSSIE FRANK CLEANS UP

*Ifield's yodelling hat trick*

## ELVIS – NEW RCA DEAL

In the space of just 12 months, clean-cut blond Australian singer Frank Ifield has emerged from obscurity to slip in comfortably behind both Elvis Presley and Cliff Richard as the third most popular best-selling recording artist in the UK during 1962.

This has been achieved on the strength of three consecutive country-pop oldies which have all grabbed the No. 1 position: 'I Remember You', 'Lovesick Blues' and 'Wayward Wind' – the first two being million-plus gold record winners in double-quick time.

Ifield (25), a successful recording artist back in Australia, arrived in Britain an unknown and that's how things remained for three years until, after a few false starts, he clicked in a big way – both here and in the US – with 'I Remember You'.

This hitmaker, whose vocal trade mark is a small yodel, confessed: 'When I arrived in Britain, I thought to myself, "Well, one thing that's out of the act now is yodelling!" After I got here, I gave myself five years to get to the top, but I did it in three.'

His worldwide success has made Ifield a much in-demand performer and his 1963 diary is almost filled. A debut album is to be released next month, and it has been announced that he's to be the main attraction during the London Palladium's prestigious 1963 resident Summer Revue. Meanwhile, he's considering offers to star in a full-length semi-autobiographical movie.

Elvis Presley, who has sold the equivalent of 100 million singles in eight years, has renewed his contract with RCA-Victor. This new deal, which lasts for ten years, guarantees Elvis a minimum of around two million dollars with scope to earn much more.

From his records and movies alone, Presley's personal income is now reported to be in excess of one-and-a-half million dollars a year. The lucrative long-term contract is viewed within the record industry as RCA's faith in Presley's world-wide staying power as a major recording star.

Aside from movies and records – the former bringing him approximately $10,000-a-day on the set, Elvis is said to receive 2.5% of all souvenir products retailed in the US in his name. These include soft toys, record players, stationery, jewellery and clothes, and sales of these are estimated to reach two million dollars.

*Clint Eastwood – Rowdy record*

## CHARTS

| | | |
|---|---|---|
| US45 | Walk Right In | *Rooftop Singers* |
| USLP | The First Family | *Vaughn Meader* |
| UK45 | Diamonds | *Jet Harris & Tony Meehan* |
| UKLP | Summer Holiday | *Cliff Richard* |

——— W E E K  2 ———

| | | |
|---|---|---|
| US45 | Hey Paula | *Paul & Paula* |
| USLP | The First Family | *Vaughn Meader* |
| UK45 | Diamonds | *Jet Harris & Tony Meehan* |
| UKLP | Summer Holiday | *Cliff Richard* |

——— W E E K  3 ———

| | | |
|---|---|---|
| US45 | Hey Paula | *Paul & Paula* |
| USLP | The First Family | *Vaughn Meader* |
| UK45 | Diamonds | *Jet Harris & Tony Meehan* |
| UKLP | Summer Holiday | *Cliff Richard* |

——— W E E K  4 ———

| | | |
|---|---|---|
| US45 | Hey Paula | *Paul & Paula* |
| USLP | The First Family | *Vaughn Meader* |
| UK45 | The Wayward Wind | *Frank Ifield* |
| UKLP | Summer Holiday | *Cliff Richard* |

## THE GRAPEVINE

■ Helen Shapiro plus The Beatles have embarked on a twice-nightly 15-city UK tour.

■ Paul Anka has married Anne De Zogheb – daughter of Comte and Comtess Charles Zogheb – in Paris.

■ Actor Clint Eastwood has attempted to capitalize on his popular *Rawhide* TV role as cowpoke Rowdy Yates, with a single 'Rowdy'.

■ Publisher Dick James has started Northern Songs to handle the songs of Lennon and McCartney.

# PATSY CLINE KILLED IN PLANE CRASH

Country music stars Patsy Cline (30), Lloyd 'Cowboy' Copas (50) and Harold 'Hawkshaw' Hawkins (41) all perished when the light aircraft carrying them home after a benefit concert in Kansas City crashed at Camden, Tennessee, on March 5.

Patsy Cline was best known for a string of hits that included 'Walking After Midnight' and 'I Fall To Pieces'. Cowboy Copas had recently enjoyed a chart comeback with 'Alabam', while Hawkshaw Hawkins had 'Sunny Side Of The Mountain' and 'Lonesome 7-7203' to his credit.

Only two years ago, Patsy Cline narrowly escaped death in a road crash. She was a passenger in her brother's car when it was involved in a collision in which a man in another vehicle was killed. She overcame her serious injuries and fought her way back to the top again, winning Billboard magazine's dj poll last autumn as best female country vocalist.

Early reports suggest that the plane carrying Cline and friends may have been flying upside down when it crashed — it was in the middle of a severe windstorm at the time, which could account for it being flipped over.

*Chart newcomer Otis Redding*

*Marriott borrows from Buddy?*

## THE GRAPEVINE

■ Otis Redding has made his first chart appearance with 'These Arms Of Mine'.

■ Tommy Roe and Chris Montez upstaged by both The Beatles and their fans on their 21-day UK trek.

■ Cockney child actor Steve Marriott has made his disc debut with Buddy Holly-inspired 'Give Her My Regards'.

■ Merseysiders Gerry & The Pacemakers also on disc for the first time with 'How Do You Do It?'.

## TORME: I'M NO ROCKER!'

Mel Torme, currently enjoying crossover chart success with 'Comin' Home Baby', is attempting to distance himself from the rest of the hit parade pack.

'Please, please, don't call it rock and roll,' he says of his single. 'I do not like rock and roll and I do not sing rock and roll.

'Now that I have a hit record — which is a great feeling for both ego and wallet — I still won't sing rock and roll. 'Comin' Home Baby' is a jazz song. To be more specific, it's rhythm'n'blues that started life as a jass instrumental on an album by jazz flute player, Herbie Mann and written by bassist Ben Tucker.

'And, I hope it is sung by jazz singer — Melvin Howard Torme. That's me! The teenage market may be where the big money is today, and they may well be the ones who are buying it. But it's not rock and roll!' he added.

## BERRY SUES BRIAN

Brian Wilson was audacious enough to have fitted a brand new set of self-penned lyrics to Chuck Berry's 'Sweet Little Sixteen', retitled it 'Surfin' U.S.A.', and put it out as The Beach Boys' latest single for Capitol.

Natch, Chuck and his music publisher have sued, but a co-composer name-check and a sackful of greenbacks have helped make the injured parties feel less hurt!

*Chuck makes up with The Beach Boys*

*Gerry & The Pacemakers rehearse their action-packed show. How do they do it?*

# EPSTEIN LAUNCHES BILLY J

On what appears to be an un-stoppable winning streak, Brian Epstein has launched his very latest Liverpudlian protegées, Billy J. Kramer & The Dakotas, and ensured them instant success with their first Parlophone single by pairing two valuable Lennon & McCartney compositions 'Do You Want To Know A Secret' and 'I'll Be On My Way'.

As with other NEMS managed acts such as The Beatles, Gerry & The Pacemakers, The Fourmost and Cilla Black, ballad-singing Billy J. Kramer's records have been produced by George Martin.

So as not to feel outdone, Manchester's answer to NEMS – Kennedy Street Enterprises' local comic-rockers, Freddie & The Dreamers – have also debuted with a cover of James Ray's R&B waltz-time classic, 'If You Gotta Make A Fool Of Somebody'.

*Billy J. cuts Beatlesongs*

## PYE RELEASE CHESS IN UK

Having acquired the UK rights to the Chicago-based Chess label catalogue, Pye Records have proudly launched their red and yellow label 'Chicago R&B series with albums from Chuck Berry and Bo Diddley, plus inaugural singles from Sonny Boy Williamson, Howlin' Wolf, Bo Diddley and local Marquee Club favourites, harmonica man Cyril Davies & His All Stars.

*Cavern cloakroom attendant Priscilla White, one of the NEMS stars*

## OLDHAM, EASTON SIGN STONES

Flamboyant pop publicist, Andrew 'Loog' Oldham and his boss, theatrical manager Eric Easton, have signed London R&B group The Rolling Stones to an exclusive management contract.

At the recommendation of George Harrison, both Oldham and Easton drove out to The Crawdaddy Club, Richmond on April 28, to catch The Rolling Stones in action.

Easton was impressed by the group's energy, but had certain reservations about just how commercial they were. There were no such doubts for Oldham, who admitted gazing at the prancing Mick Jagger the way Sylvester looks at Tweetie Pie.

'I knew what I was looking at,' confessed the pole-axed publicist as The Stones worked the audience up into a frenzy. 'It was SEX. And, I was 48 hours ahead of the pack.'

## ROE SOUNDS OFF

In a candid interview, America's Tommy Roe expressed his views on the current crop of UK groups:

'Somebody asked me if I liked British pop music, and I'm afraid I had to tell them the truth: I don't. Not most of it anyway,' he said.

'I don't mean they are of poor quality – I was constantly impressed by the high standard of singing and production. It's just that there is something about the 'feel' of them, the atmosphere, that I feel unable to appreciate.

'Perhaps that's why British vocal discs haven't done so well in the States . . . all the big British hits have been instrumentals like 'Stranger On The Shore', 'Telstar' and 'Midnight In Mosow'.

'There's only one British group I rave over – it's The Beatles. They have a truly fantastic *American* sound. If they went to the States, they couldn't go wrong!'

### CHARTS

| | |
|---|---|
| US45 | He's So Fine<br>*Chiffons* |
| USLP | Songs I Sing On The Jackie Gleason Show<br>*Frank Fontaine* |
| UK45 | How Do You Do It<br>*Gerry & The Pacemakers* |
| UKLP | Summer Holiday<br>*Cliff Richard* |
| **WEEK 2** | |
| US45 | He's So Fine<br>*Chiffons* |
| USLP | Songs I Sing On The Jackie Gleason Show<br>*Frank Fontaine* |
| UK45 | How Do You Do It<br>*Gerry & The Pacemakers* |
| UKLP | Summer Holiday<br>*Cliff Richard* |
| **WEEK 3** | |
| US45 | He's So Fine<br>*Chiffons* |
| USLP | West Side Story<br>*Soundtrack* |
| UK45 | How Do You Do It<br>*Gerry & The Pacemakers* |
| LKLP | Summer Holiday<br>*Cliff Richard* |
| **WEEK 4** | |
| US45 | I Will Follow Him<br>*Little Peggy March* |
| USLP | West Side Story<br>*Soundtrack* |
| UK45 | From Me To You<br>*Beatles* |
| UKLP | Summer Holiday<br>*Cliff Richard* |

*Bo Diddley for Pye*

### THE GRAPEVINE

■ Bob Dylan has given his first major solo concert, to ecstatic reviews, at New York's Town Hall.

■ A third Parlophone single has been produced by The Beatles: 'From Me To You'.

■ Having scored sales of 60-million records, Fats Domino has quit Imperial Records to sign with ABC-Paramount.

■ This month's dance floor-filler: Ray Barretto's 'El Watusi'.

# MAY 1963

# DYLAN'S DREAM: NO HASSLES

The fact that Bob Dylan's album debut has only sold 5,000 copies has prompted many CBS Records' executives to be less than enthusiastic over the young protest singer's immediate future on the label.

Only producer John Hammond's valuable patronage and the unshakeable support of Johnny Cash, have led to the release of a second LP, 'The Freewheelin' Bob Dylan'.

However, before the record reached the public, a number of behind-the-scenes dramas were enacted. Firstly, Dylan's New York Town Hall Concert of April 12 was taped for release and then promptly shelved.

On May 12, Dylan failed to make his national TV debut on 'The Ed Sullivan Show', when CBS top brass vetoed Dylan's plan to perform his controversial 'Talking John Birch Society Blues' on the programme. The decision prompted him to turn on his boot-heels and walk.

The knock-on effect was that CBS Records scrapped 'Freewheelin's' original track listing and replaced four songs – 'Rocks And Gravel', 'Alabama Woman Blues', 'Let Me Die In My Footsteps', 'Ramblin', Gamblin Willie' and the ultra-sensitive 'Talking John Birch Paranoid Blues' – with four Dylan had recorded on April 24: 'Girl From The North Country', 'Masters Of War', 'Bob Dylan's Dream' and 'Talking World War III Blues'.

*Fury: last of a line?*

## THE GRAPEVINE

■ Bob Dylan, Joan Baez, Pete Seeger, Peter, Paul & Mary, The Weavers and Mance Lipscomb headlined the first Monterey Folk Festival in California.

■ Innovative Mississippi-bluesman Elmore James has died, aged 45.

■ Billy Fury has released his first album of all-new material in three years.

■ The once outlawed Jerry Lee Lewis has returned for a UK tour with Gene Vincent.

*Not-quite-folk, not-quite-pop, but a success formula for chart-toppers The Springfields*

## SPRINGFIELDS MAKE HITS FROM FOLK

Though voted No. 1 British vocal group in NME's 1961 and 1963 readers' poll, things have moved slowly chartwise in the UK for folk-pop trio The Springfields – currently in the top five with 'Say I Won't Be There'.

However, it has been the success of their uptempo rewrite of the traditional French song 'au Clair de Lune', and their previous single 'Island Of Dreams' which has transformed them into one of Britain's major musical exports.

Londoners all, The Springfields comprise brother and sister Tom and Dusty Springfield (Dion and Mary O'Brien), and Mike Hurst (Michael Longhurst-Pickworth).

'Say I Won't Be There' has followed The Springfields' pattern of re-interpreting traditional folk material.

Their disc debut, 'Dear John' was the American Civil War song 'Marching Thro' Georgia' with new lyrics and 'Silver Threads And Golden Needles' yet another country folk standard.

Recalling the group's early days, Tom Springfield revealed: 'Once, when we auditioned for a BBC producer, he told us we had to make a decision. We either had to be a folk group or a pop group if we were going to have any success at all. But, of course, we fell between the two!'

## CHARTS

| | |
|---|---|
| US45 | I Will Follow Him *Little Peggy March* |
| USLP | Days Of Wine And Roses *Andy Williams* |
| UK45 | From Me To You *Beatles* |
| UKLP | Summer Holiday *Cliff Richard* |
| **WEEK 2** | |
| US45 | I Will Follow Him *Little Peggy March* |
| USLP | Days Of Wine And Roses *Andy Williams* |
| UK45 | From Me To You *Beatles* |
| UKLP | Please Please Me *Beatles* |
| **WEEK 3** | |
| US45 | If You Wanna Be Happy *Jimmy Soul* |
| USLP | Days Of Wine And Roses *Andy Williams* |
| UK45 | From Me To You *Beatles* |
| UKLP | Please Please Me *Beatles* |
| **WEEK 4** | |
| US45 | If You Wanna Be Happy *Jimmy Soul* |
| USLP | Days Of Wine And Roses *Andy Williams* |
| UK45 | From Me To You *Beatles* |
| UKLP | Please Please Me *Beatles* |

# LENNON LASHES OUT

Though there was much amusement when Paul McCartney was dragged out of Abbey Road Studios two days earlier by John, George and Ringo and publicly bumped to celebrate his 21st birthday, the atmosphere at a party held in Liverpool on June 20 turned violent.

Bob Wooler, the Cavern Club d.j, loudly insinuated to anyone who'd listen, that Brian Epstein and John Lennon were lovers, and was promptly gifted with a black-eye from the latter for his troubles.

Although news of the fracas made an item in the first edition of the next morning's Liverpool Echo, the NEMS PR machine went into overdrive to stop the news spreading further afield. Within days, the fight was no more than an unsubstantiated rumour, with everyone at the party maintaining a wall of secrecy.

Cover up – The Beatles

## CHARTS

| | | |
|---|---|---|
| US45 | It's My Party | Lesley Gore |
| USLP | Days Of Wine And Roses | Andy Williams |
| UK45 | Do You Want To Know A Secret | Billy J Kramer |
| UKLP | Please Please Me | Beatles |
| | WEEK 2 | |
| US45 | It's My Party | Lesley Gore |
| USLP | Days Of Wine And Roses | Andy Williams |
| UK45 | Do You Want To Know A Secret | Billy J Kramer |
| UKLP | Please Please Me | Beatles |
| | WEEK 3 | |
| US45 | Sukiyaki | Kyu Sakamoto |
| USLP | Days Of Wine And Roses | Andy Williams |
| UK45 | I Like It | Gerry & The Pacemakers |
| UKLP | Please Please Me | Beatles |
| | WEEK 4 | |
| US45 | Sukiyaki | Kyu Sakamoto |
| USLP | Days Of Wine And Roses | Andy Williams |
| UK45 | I Like It | Gerry & The Pacemakers |
| UKLP | Please Please Me | Beatles |
| | WEEK 5 | |
| US45 | Sukiyaki | Kyu Sakamoto |
| USLP | Days Of Wine And Roses | Andy Williams |
| UK45 | I Like It | Gerry & The Pacemakers |
| UKLP | Please Please Me | Beatles |

## THE GRAPEVINE

■ The BBC have launched a new Radio series: 'Pop Go The Beatles'.

■ The late Buddy Holly is back in the UK charts for the second time this year with 'Bo Diddley'.

■ The Rolling Stones have released their reworking of Chuck Berry's 'Come On'.

■ 'Fingertips Part 2' by 12-year old blind singer-instrumentalist Little Stevie Wonder turning into a hot summer hit.

## LOW-KEY STONES DEBUT, SWEETER FOR SEARCHERS

The Rolling Stones' debut single – a cover of Chuck Berry's seldom-heard 'Come On' – has been given a somewhat low-key launch by Decca Records.

Over the last few weeks there has been much more media interest in the first singles from three Manchester groups: The Hollies '(Ain't That) Just Like Me', Wayne Fontana & The Mindbenders 'Roadrunner' and comic rockers Freddie & The Dreamers 'If You Gotta Make A Fool Of Somebody'.

Popular London band Manfred Mann have made it on to vinyl with 'Why Should We Not', while on Merseyside, it's been The Swinging Blue Jeans with 'It's Too Late' and Freddie Starr & The Midnighters who tried their luck with 'Who Told You'.

But the biggest interest has been centred on The Searchers, whose combination of high-pitched nasal vocals and jingly-jangly guitars has made them one of the 'Pool's most popular local groups. They have only just released their first single on Pye, a

## MARTIN: 'NO LIVERPOOL SOUND'

'There is no such thing as a Liverpool Sound,' George Martin, Britain's leading record producer insists. 'I prefer to talk of the Beatles sound – after all, they started it!'

Martin, who has masterminded massive hits for such acts as The Beatles, Gerry & The Pacemakers and Billy J. Kramer & The Dakotas, explains his theory:

'I'm not suggesting that other groups copy The Beatles. Quite the contrary, for their styles are wholly different. That's why you can't lump them together under the heading of a Liverpool Sound.'

Jerry Lee – Bible part?

## STAR QUOTE

### JERRY LEE LEWIS

'Though it's a little hard to imagine, I wanna get a part in a Bible movie . . . 'bout the only thing I could do is be a slave or somethin' . . . that would really be a good lick!'

highly-personalized treatment of The old Drifters' song 'Sweets For My Sweet'.

The Searchers, who all sing, comprise Mike Pender (lead guitar), John McNally (rhythm guitar), Tony Jackson (bass) and Chris Curtis (drums).

Sweets sound of Searchers

# CHARLES: 'NO ROOM FOR COMPLACENCY'

Ray Charles's influence on a broad spectrum of contemporary American popular music is immeasurable.

From fashioning soul music through to incorporating elements of blues, jazz, gospel, R&B, pop and country & western into his work, he has scored countless worldwide crossover hits such as 'What'd I Say', 'Georgia On My Mind', 'I Got A Woman', 'Busted', 'Hit The Road Jack', 'One Mint Julep', 'I Can't Stop Loving You' plus such best-selling LPs as 'The Genius Of Ray Charles', 'Genius + Soul = Jazz' and 'Modern Sounds In Country & Western'.

Not for nothing is Ray Charles referred to as 'The Genius Of Soul'. The man and his music are inseparable.

'I try to put on a show . . . a band show that is, not just a band of musicians playing a set pattern of numbers and nothing else. That's why I branched out into what people call pop material, although I reckon some of my early blues singing and playing was popular enough,' he explains.

'But I don't want to get known as a labelled man. I want to work any kind of concert, to fit in anywhere. I used to sing a lot more of the down home blues, but since songs like 'I Can't Stop Loving You', I have really broadened out.

'About the only concrete thing you can say about my singing, as far as I'm concerned, is that I try to instil a little bit of soul into everything. It comes from suffering some sort of depression, some kind of hard times.

'Right now, there's no question of hard times, but these things have a habit of lingering,' he adds. 'You remember them – those early years of struggle. And, you also remember that nobody has it made. I can't afford to slip into a rut, into complacency.'

## VEE-JAY IN UK

Launched in Britain to meet and fuel the growing demand among young clubgoers for authentic American R&B singles without having to pay inflated import prices, EMI's Stateside label has got it right first time with a trio of singles leased from Chicago's Vee-Jay operation: John Lee Hooker's insistent and commercial 'Boom Boom', Jimmy Reed's 'Shame, Shame, Shame' and Roscoe Gordon's 'Just A Little Bit'.

*Miracles, with leader Smokey Robinson*

## THE GRAPEVINE

■ 'Mickey's Monkey' is the latest release from The Miracles.

■ Del Shannon has become the first US artist to make Billboard's charts with a Beatles' cover – 'From Me To You'.

■ Former Tornadoes' bassist Heinz has released his Joe Meek-produced Cochran tribute, 'Just Like Eddie'.

■ Billy J. Kramer is backing another winner with two more unheard Lennon & McCartney songs: 'Bad To Me' and 'I Call Your Name'.

## MORE MERSEY BEAT

Liverpool hasn't been completely plundered of talent.

All those Merseyside groups that were not immediately signed up by London recording managers looking for another Beatles have been assembled by producer John Schroeder on to two Oriole LPs entitled 'This Is Mersey Beat'.

Among those featured are such local heroes as Faron's Flamingoes, The Mojos and Rory Storme & The Hurricanes.

*More Merseybeat from the Mojos*

*Blues hero John Lee Hooker*

# JAN AND DEAN SURF TO THE TOP

*Beat from the beach with surf songsters Jan and Dean*

Britain might not have the climate in which to emulate Southern California's highly-desirable sun-soaked surfin' lifestyle, but it has a keen ear for the accompanying soundtrack, as supplied by such recent UK chart entries as The Chantays ('Pipeline'), The Surfaris ('Wipeout'), The Beach Boys ('Surfin' USA') and Jan & Dean ('Surf City').

The latter are Los Angelinos Jan Berry (21) and Dean Torrance (22), boyhood friends who were scoring close-harmony hits when still at university.

Following the initial success of local label hits, a switch to Liberty and a nation-wide best-seller – 'Linda' – made the duo turn their attention more towards music-making.

Soon after, a link-up with Brian Wilson (and his songwriting partner Roger Christian) quickly made Jan & Dean an even bigger attraction than The Beach Boys, by virtue of 'Surf City'. A furious Capitol Records threatened to sue The Beach Boys because of Brian Wilson's audible contributions to the record's success.

Jan & Dean's sun-bleached athletic good-looks have come to epitomise the surfin' image ('Surfin'' all day – sturdy surf bunnies by night!') especially since it became known that for all The Beach Boys' endeavours to promote this new beach culture, only drummer Dennis Wilson actually surfs!

## CHARTS

| | | |
|---|---|---|
| US45 | So Much In Love | *Tymes* |
| USLP | Days Of Wine And Roses | *Andy Williams* |
| UK45 | Sweets For My Sweet | *Searchers* |
| UKLP | Please Please Me | *Beatles* |

### WEEK 2

| | | |
|---|---|---|
| US45 | Fingertips Part II | *Stevie Wonder* |
| USLP | Days Of Wine And Roses | *Andy Williams* |
| UK45 | Sweets For My Sweet | *Searchers* |
| UKLP | Please lease Me | *Beatles* |

### WEEK 3

| | | |
|---|---|---|
| US45 | Fingertips Part II | *Stevie Wonder* |
| USLP | Days Of Wine And Roses | *Andy Williams* |
| UK45 | Sweets For My Sweet | *Searchers* |
| UKLP | Please Please Me | *Beatles* |

### WEEK 4

| | | |
|---|---|---|
| US45 | Fingertips Part II | *Stevie Wonder* |
| USLP | Little Stevie Wonder | *Stevie Wonder* |
| UK45 | Bad To Me | *Billy J Kramer & The Dakotas* |
| UKLP | Please Please Me | *Beatles* |

### WEEK 5

| | | |
|---|---|---|
| US45 | My Boyfriend's Back | *The Angels* |
| USLP | My Son, The Nut | *Allan Sherman* |
| UK45 | Bad To Me | *Billy J Kramer & The Dakotas* |
| UKLP | Please Please Me | *Beatles* |

## DYLAN: VOICE OF PROTEST

With 'The Freewheelin' Bob Dylan' having sold in excess of 250,000 copies, Dylan has become acknowledged as America's foremost folk singer.

Peter, Paul & Mary have transformed two 'Freewheelin'' tracks – 'Blowin' In The Wind' and 'Don't Think Twice, It's All Right' – into Top 40 hits and protest movement anthems, Joan Baez features many of Dylan's songs in her concert repertoire and is frequently joined onstage by the singer-composer.

As the protest movement gathers momentum across the United States, Bob Dylan makes his position clear, in words and music.

## SUTCH FOR PARLIAMENT?

Screamin' Lord Sutch has announced that he will stand as an independent candidate in the forthcoming Stratford-On-Avon by-election.

Should he win, the optimistic Lord David Sutch – a rock horror performer noted for such endearing ballads as 'Jack The Ripper' – insists that he will give up the pop business altogether to concentrate on his political career as a responsible Member of the British parliament. His loyal backing group, The Savages, will carry on their flamboyant act alone.

However, just in case the prized Stratford-On-Avon seat is, by a strange twist of fate, won by a member of one of the established political parties, His Lordship's manager has taken the precaution of booking an October UK tour for Sutch, to be followed by a Paris engagement.

## THE GRAPEVINE

■ The Beatles collected £300 ($900) for their last-ever Cavern Club date, and the first edition of 'The Beatles Monthly' has gone on sale.

■ Jerry Lee Lewis has announced that he's not resigning from Sun Records: Liberty have guaranteed him $10,000 a year until 1968.

■ A new movie trend is catching on Stateside with 'Beach Party' starring Frankie Avalon, Annette Funicello and Dick Dale & The Del-Tones.

## STAR QUOTE

GERRY MARSDEN

*'The Beatles and ourselves (The Pacemakers) – we let go when we get on-stage. I'm not being detrimental, but in the south, I think the groups have let themselves get a bit too formal. On Merseyside, it's beat, beat, beat all the way. We go on and really have a ball.'*

*More beach fun: Frankie Avalon*

# PACEMAKERS – HOW DO THEY DO IT?

In the space of just eight brief months, chirpy Liverpudlians Gerry & The Pacemakers have earned themselves the un-precedented distinction of becoming the first act ever to reach the UK chart top slot with their first three consecutive single releases.

First, there was the breezy 'How Do You Do It?' – the Mitch Murray composition The Beatles had earlier vetoed – followed by an equally carefree Murray ditty 'I Like It'. And, now they have made it a hat-trick with a com-plete change of mood and an anthemic big beat ballad treat-ment of Rodgers & Hammer-stein's 'You'll Never Walk Alone' from the hit US musical, 'Carousel'.

At the time of preparing both this crucial third single, plus a bunch of their stage show covers for their upcoming LP debut, 'How Do You Like It?' Gerry openly confessed his anxieties as well as his immediate plans.

'I can't begin to tell you how we're worried about our next single: getting the number just right and so on,' he said. 'I don't even know what it's going to be,

though the chances are on a cer-tain little ditty I've written myself!'

He wasn't disclosing too much about the mainly R&B material he and The Pacemakers have been recording over the previous weeks, except to enthuse over 'You'll Never Walk Alone', which has long been a popular cornerstone of The Pacemakers' 'live' performances.

'I'm really made up by the way that turned out. Because we play it every night in our set, there wasn't any difficulty recording it,' he confided.

## RICHARD ROCKS TO THE RESCUE!

Little Richard, who'd previously vowed he'd never do another rock tour, is being airlifted into Britain by local promoter Don Arden to take over as headline attraction on The Everly Brothers flagging 30-date UK tour.

Richard, who is regarded by British and European rock fans as the nearest thing to perfect, is to join up with the tour on October 5 hopefully to boost hitherto bad box-office business.

Surprisingly, the support bill of US R&B cult star Bo Diddley and The Rolling Stones, plus

Julie Grant and Mickie Most, hasn't been sufficient to create more than half-full halls.

However, before leaving for the UK, Little Richard has the task of informing his family and friends that after years of reli-gious studies – and despite the fact that he's soon to qualify as a

Billy Graham-style evangalist preacher – the emergence of the British beat boom, the threat of The Beatles ('I taught them how to rock!') and the continued suc-cess of his friend Sam Cooke, has convinced him to leave the Church for what he truly does best – rockin' and rollin' . . .

## THE GRAPEVINE

- Buddy Holly has notched up his third posthumous UK hit this year with 'Wishin''.

- 'We Want Billy' – a live LP from Billy Fury & The Tornados has been this month's hot UK long-player.

- Jet Harris and his singer girlfriend Billie Davis have been badly hurt in auto accident.

- Despite insisting that he's to join Elvis at RCA, Jerry Lee Lewis has signed to Smash.

'What's the most distinctive sound of our group? We often wondered what it is ourselves. Really, it is the sound we had when we recorded 'Apache' – that kind of Hawaiian sounding lead guitar . . . plus the beat.'

*Out of the Shadows, with Hank B. Marvin (left) on lead guitar*

*Richard to the rescue of the Everly Brothers tour*

# COLONEL PARKER DISMISSES PRESLEY MOVIE CRITICS

As Elvis Presley records the truly dreadful soundtrack for his equally-dreadful MGM Li'l Abner-style *Kissin' Cousins* movie, Colonel Tom Parker chooses to ignore grumblings from fans concerning the quality and quantity of Elvis's conveyor-belt movie vehicles.

When pressed on why he didn't demand approval, the Colonel insisted: 'We have approval, but only on money. Anyway, what does Elvis need? A couple of songs, a little story and some nice people to go with him!'

According to the Colonel, he actually returned the script of *Kissin' Cousins* to the studio, unread. Attached to it was a personal memo: 'If you want an opinion or evaluation of this script, it will cost you an additional $25,000.'

To the movie's hapless director, Gene Nelson, the Colonel remarked: 'We don't know how to make movies. We have you for that. All we want are songs for an album.'

## THE GRAPEVINE

■ France's most popular singer, Edith Piaf, has died in Paris, aged 48.

■ Voluptuous ex-Mouseketeer and Beach movie star, Annette (Funicello) celebrated her 21st birthday.

■ There were incredible airport scenes this month as thousands of fans greeted The Beatles return home from a tour of Sweden.

■ A second Searchers' single, 'Sugar and Spice', has been released.

Funicello gets the vote and chooses Fabian

## STAR QUOTE

### FREDDIE
of The Dreamers

'The Dreamers and I have always been daft. You couldn't call me a sex-idol, could you? Collectively, we're no glamour boys!'

Freddie the Dreamer proves he's daft!

## CHARTS

| | | |
|---|---|---|
| US45 | Blue Velvet | *Bobby Vinton* |
| USLP | My Son, The Nut | *Allan Sherman* |
| UK45 | Do You Love Me | *Brian Poole & The Tremeloes* |
| UKLP | Please Please Me | *Beatles* |

WEEK 2

| | | |
|---|---|---|
| US45 | Sugar Shack | *Jimmy Gilmer & The Fireballs* |
| USLP | My Son, The Nut | *Allan Sherman* |
| UK45 | Do You Love Me | *Brian Poole & The Tremeloes* |
| UKLP | Please, Please Me | *Beatles* |

WEEK 3

| | | |
|---|---|---|
| US45 | Sugar Shack | *Jimmy Gilmer & The Fireballs* |
| USLP | My Son, The Nut | *Allan Sherman* |
| UK45 | Do You Love Me | *Brian Poole & The Tremeloes* |
| UKLP | Please Please Me | *Beatles* |

WEEK 4

| | | |
|---|---|---|
| US45 | Sugar Shack | *Jimmy Gilmer & The Fireballs* |
| USLP | Peter, Paul & Mary | *Peter, Paul & Mary* |
| UK45 | You'll Never Walk Alone | *Gerry & The Pacemakers* |
| UKLP | Please Please Me | *Beatles* |

## LOCKING QUITS SHADOWS, WELCH STAYS

Brian 'Licorice' Locking has announced that he's to leave The Shadows, while Bruce Welch has reversed his earlier decision and will stay with the group.

Locking, who replaced bass guitarist Jet Harris 17 months ago, has secretly been thinking of vacating his position for several months. A Jehovah's Witness, Locking believes that he would better further his religious beliefs working in one place, as opposed to constantly touring with The Shadows.

In the case of rhythm guitarist Bruce Welch – who previously had insisted his final appearance with The Shadows would be a bill-topping spot on the September 22 edition of the top-rated *Sunday Night At The London Palladium* TV show he is now determined to overcome the nervous ailment that he claimed was responsible for him giving notice to quit.

Said Welch: 'I feel much

better. After my three week holiday in Barbados with my wife, and filming in The Canary Islands, I should be fine by March, when we are due to tour again.'

On the same day, Dusty Springfield – who announced she was going solo following The Springfields' final performance together on October 6 – revealed that her solo debut, 'I Only Want To Be With You', will be released November 8, to coincide with the start of a UK tour she is making with The Searchers, Brian Poole & The Tremeloes and Freddie & The Dreamers as opening acts.

Dusty – no more Springfields

# NOVEMBER 1963

## LENNON'S ROYAL QUIP

The Beatles performed before the Queen Mother, Princess Margaret and Lord Snowdon at this year's Royal Variety Command Performance held at London's Prince Of Wales Theatre.

Midway through the group's performance, Lennon rose to the occasion by requesting: 'On the next number, would those in the cheap seats clap their hands? The rest of you rattle your jewellery!'

The House Of Windsor did the latter.

### CHARTS

| | | |
|---|---|---|
| US45 | Sugar Shack | Jimmy Gilmer & The Fireballs |
| USLP | In The Wind | Peter, Paul & Mary |
| UK45 | You'll Never Walk Alone | Gerry & The Pacemakers |
| UKLP | Please Please Me | Beatles |

— WEEK 2 —

| | | |
|---|---|---|
| US45 | Sugar Shack | Jimmy Gilmer & The Fireballs |
| USLP | In The Wind | Peter, Paul & Mary |
| UK45 | You'll Never Walk Alone | Gerry & The Pacemakers |
| UKLP | Please Please Me | Beatles |

— WEEK 3 —

| | | |
|---|---|---|
| US45 | Deep Purple | Nino Tempo & April Stevens |
| USLP | In The Wind | Peter, Paul & Mary |
| UK45 | You'll Never Walk Alone | Gerry & The Pacemakers |
| UKLP | Please Please Me | Beatles |

— WEEK 4 —

| | | |
|---|---|---|
| US45 | I'm Leaving It Up To You | Dale & Grace |
| USLP | In The Wind | Peter, Paul & Mary |
| UK45 | She Loves You | Beatles |
| UKLP | Please Please Me | Beatles |

— WEEK 5 —

| | | |
|---|---|---|
| US45 | Sugar Shack | Jimmy Gilmer & The Fireballs |
| USLP | In The Wind | Peter, Paul & Mary |
| UK45 | She Loves You | Beatles |
| UKLP | With The Beatles | Beatles |

# JFK DEAD – SPECTOR CANCELS CHRISTMAS

As a nation mourned the assassination of President John Kennedy in Dallas on November 22, distraught whizkid record producer Phil Spector immediately withdrew his all-star Philles label seasonal meisterwerk, 'A Christmas Gift To You', from the stores out of personal respect.

'Nobody's going to want happy Christmas songs this year,' Spector was quoted as saying.

During the summer, Spector had devoted considerable time to what he envisaged as a no-expense-spared celebration of his distinctive Wall Of Sound approach to creating, what he fondly termed, 'Little symphonies for the kiddies!'

With arrangements by Jack Nitzsche and performances from Philles' stars The Crystals, The Ronettes, Darlene Love and Bob B. Soxx & The Blue Jeans, here was a collection of familiar Yuletide pop standards as you'd never heard them before. It was a concept album of varied moods, which reached its peak on The Crystals' snowcap-melting romp through 'Santa Claus Is Comin' To Town'.

Finally, Spector's closing salutations over 'Silent Night', in the current circumstances, evoked an atmosphere of eerie sentimentality.

*Dylan – Commie claim claptrap!*

## RED FOLKIE SCARE

With Peter, Paul & Mary's interpretations of two Bob Dylan songs 'Blowin' In The Wind' and 'Don't Think Twice, It's All Right' chartbound on both sides of the Atlantic, it has been left to UK music writer Derek Johnson to go boldly into print and publicly dismiss as rubbish scarestories in Britain's more lurid Sunday tabloids which claim the current worldwide folk music trend masks subversive tactics by the Kremlin to 'poison young minds'!

These fantasy stories have implied that folk music is having a 'conditioning, brain-washing effect upon its followers', that the songs have an 'insidious, detrimental effect' upon the younger generation because the majority of folk singers such as Bob Dylan, Peter, Paul & Mary and their ilk are 'communists'.

Johnson jokingly asks whether the sudden leap into the UK charts by this winsome trio's 'Blowin' In The Wind' is all down to the fact that, unbeknown to the public, Russian leader Mr Kruschev has taken a hand in the hit parade!

*We'll love The Shirelles tomorrow*

*Duane – touring with Richard*

## THE GRAPEVINE

■ The Rolling Stones are the latest group to try their chart luck with a Lennon & McCartney song – 'I Wanna Be Your Man'.

■ Meanwhile, Billy J. Kramer continues his John & Paul association with 'I'll Keep You Satisfied'.

■ Little Richard, Duane Eddy and The Shirelles are touring the UK together.

# QUEEN DINAH FOUND DEAD

It'll be a blue Christmas without her! The 'Queen Of The Blues', Dinah Washington, was found dead from an overdose of sleeping pills in her Detroit home on December 14. She was 39.

Born Ruth Jones, in Tuscaloosa, Alabama, August 29, 1924, this one-time singer with the Lionel Hampton Orchestra scored 36 chart entries between 1949 and 1963. Of these, the most popular were her Mercury label recordings 'What A Difference A Day Makes' and 'September In The Rain'.

Dinah Washington also enjoyed world-wide chart success with her 1960 hit duets with Brook Benton, 'Baby (You've Got What It Takes)' and 'A Rockin' Good Way'.

Her private life was text-case turmoil – just five months prior to her tragic death, Dinah Washington married her *seventh* husband, Detroit Lions' football star, Dick 'Night Train' Lane.

## SONNY BOY VS YARDBIRDS

*Yardbirds – slagged off by Sonny Boy Williamson*

Almost semi-resident in the UK, harmonica bluesman Sonny Boy Williamson's appearance with The Yardbirds at London's R&B Crawdaddy Club has been recorded for a proposed 'Live In London' Fontana Records release.

Sometimes over-critical of even the most enthusiastic wide-eyed locals, the Chess Records' star's own opinion of The Yardbirds is less than flattering: 'They want to play the blues so badly, and that's how they play it, badly!' he's reported as saying.

# BEATLES XMAS CRACKER

Following one-nighters in Bradford (December 21) and Liverpool (December 22), Brian Epstein's production 'The Beatles' Christmas Show' – a combination of music, laughter and traditional pantomime – began a season at The Finsbury Park Astoria, London on December 24 until January 11.

Apart from the bill-topping Beatles (who also acted in comedy sketches) the show featured Billy J. Kramer & The Dakotas, Cilla Black, The Fourmost and Tommy Quickly, plus light entertainment from Australian Rolf Harris and comedy group The Barron-Knights featuring Duke D'Mond.

With a top ticket price of 75p ($2), all available 100,000 tickets were sold by November 16.

*New from NEMS – Tommy Quickly*

*Crazy! Joe Brown, Sid James & Co.*

## CHARTS

| | | |
|---|---|---|
| US45 | Dominique | *The Singing Nun* |
| USLP | The Singing Nun | *The Singing Nun* |
| UK45 | I Want To Hold Your Hand | *Beatles* |
| UKLP | With The Beatles | *Beatles* |
| **WEEK 2** | | |
| US45 | Dominique | *The Singing Nun* |
| USLP | The Singing Nun | *The Singing Nun* |
| UK45 | I Want To Hold Your Hand | *Beatles* |
| UKLP | With The Beatles | *Beatles* |
| **WEEK 3** | | |
| US45 | Dominique | *The Singing Nun* |
| USLP | The Singing Nun | *The Singing Nun* |
| UK45 | I Want To Hold Your Hand | *Beatles* |
| UKLP | With The Beatles | *Beatles* |
| **WEEK 4** | | |
| US45 | Dominique | *The Singing Nun* |
| USLP | The Singing Nun | *The Singing Nun* |
| UK45 | I Want To Hold Your Hand | *Beatles* |
| UKLP | With The Beatles | *Beatles* |

## JFK – A MEMORIAL

As a shocked America mourns, Premium Records have released 'John Fitzgerald Kennedy – A Memorial Album (The Last Hours)' for just 99 cents.

It sold four million copies in six days, thereby qualifying it as the fastest-ever selling record in history, and assuring it a place in the famous Guinness Book of World Records.

Compiled by producer Eli Oberstein and son Maurice from broadcasts on the day of the assassination, 'The Last Hours' marks a coup for the former RCA A&R man, previously best known for his productions of black and country artists, including Duke Ellington.

*The Teddy Bears, Spector on left*

*The Righteous Brothers*

*Ike and Tina Turner*

*Archetypal girl group The Crystals*

*Spector rehearses for that Wall of Sound*

*Bruce Lee – Spector's fabled bodyguard*

*The Ronettes*

*Spector with session singer Ronee Blakeley*

# THE TYCOON OF TEEN

One of the several books written about Phil Spector is sub-titled 'The Truth About Rock & Roll's Legendary Madman', and it's certainly true that there are almost as many possibly apocryphal anecdotes about Spector as there are utterly amazing and timeless records which he produced.

Spector's first success came in 1958, when 'To Know Him Is To Love Him', a song written by him topped the 'Billboard' singles chart and sold a million copies, but it wasn't until the end of 1960 that Spector was again responsible for a Top 10 hit ('Corinna Corinna' by Ray Peterson, which he produced). The end of 1961 saw the first release on Spector's own label, Philles Records. That was 'There's No Other (Like My Baby)' by The Crystals, and it reached the US Top 20, as did a follow up, 'Uptown', in spring 1962. In the autumn of that year, a third Crystals single, 'He's A Rebel', topped the US chart. This was swiftly followed by another US Top 10 hit, 'Zip-A-Dee-Doo-Dah', performed by Bob B. Soxx & The Blue Jeans. In 1963, Spector began producing hits for Darlene Love while The Crystals remained successful with Top 10 hits like 'Da Doo Ron Ron' and 'Then He Kissed Me.

Part of the appeal of these records was Spector's so called 'Wall Of Sound' – where other records were produced by overdubbing a single guitarist as many times as required, Spector preferred to have several guitarists playing in unison together, and the same for each instrument involved in a track. The result was certainly unique, although other producers have called this method, which calls for numerous musicians, expensive and self-indulgent.

By this point, Spector had discovered another female vocal trio who were based in New York, The Ronettes, and was captivated by the voice and the exotic beauty of lead singer Veronica 'Ronnie' Bennett, with whom he instantly fell in love. The first and biggest Ronettes hit was 'Be My Baby', and soon after it peaked in the US chart, Spector's problems can be seen to have begun. The Crystals, Bob B. Soxx and Darlene Love were all effectively forgotten as Spector concentrated his energy and ingenuity on recording masterpieces with The Ronettes, although the other three acts were also represented on what is often critically regarded as Spector's finest work, an album of seasonal songs titled variously 'A Christmas Gift For You' or

'Phil Spector's Christmas Album'. The album was first released only days before the assassination of President John F. Kennedy, and immediately after Kennedy's death, America in general was too stunned to think of buying records of any sort. By the middle of January, 1964, America had discovered The Beatles, and Spector's Christmas Album was forgotten.

But things began to improve at the end of that year, when he started producing Bill Medley and Bobby Hatfield, a white juo known as The Righteous Brothers, whose approach to singing was known as "blue eyed soul". The first hit Spector produced for them was the unforgettable 'You've Lost That Lovin' Feelin'', which topped charts around the world. The Righteous Brothers had several more Spector-produced hits like 'Unchained Melody' and 'Ebb Tide', before they fell out with their Svengali-like producer, who only worked with one other act during 1965, The Ronettes.

In mid-1966, after admiring Tina Turner's vocal ability when they worked together on a TV show, he proposed to her then husband, Ike, that he produce records for Tina. The single which first resulted from these sessions, 'River Deep - Mountain High', was another masterpiece, which reached the Top 3 in Britain, but was an utter failure in the US.

Phil Spector had always been admired by the aristocrats of British pop music, The Beatles and The Rolling Stones. The first album by The Stones included a song titled 'Now I've Got A Witness (Like Uncle Phil & Uncle Gene)', referring to Messrs. Spector and Pitney, who were present at the recording sessions for the album. The Beatles were not quite so close to Spector, but when Allen Klein suggested Spector to remix the recordings made for the group's 'Let It Be' album, the idea was favourably received.

This led to Spector producing George Harrison's classic triple album, 'All Things Must Pass' (which included 'My Sweet Lord') and several albums for John Lennon, among them 'John Lennon/Plastic Ono Band' and 'Imagine' and several hit singles, such as 'Instant Karma' and 'Happy Xmas (War Is Over)', as well as the 'Concert For Bangla Desh' triple album and part of what was eventually released as 'Rock'n'Roll' by John Lennon, an album which Spector had previously licensed without Lennon's approval.

That was in 1975, since when Spector has only occasionally emerged from his Hollywood mansion for shortlived one-off projects like albums with Dion, Leonard Cohen and The Ramones. There are many who think its time he ended this self-imposed exile . . . .

*The recluse of rock*

# 1964

## TOTP LAUNCHED

'It's No. 1, it's *Top Of The Pops!*'

In Britain, BBC-Television has inaugurated its weekly look at the British record charts.

## THE GRAPEVINE

■ The Beach Boys have adopted the pseudonym The Survivors for a Brian Wilson-produced one-off single, 'Pamela Jean'.

■ Elvis has paid $55,000 for Franklin D. Roosevelt's former presidential yacht, 'Potomac'.

■ The Beatles were the UK's top record selling act last year with 18 weeks at No. 1.

■ Pye Records have signed North London R&B foursome, The Kinks.

## CHARTS

| | |
|---|---|
| US45 | There! I've Said It Again *Bobby Vinton* |
| USLP | The Singing Nun *The Singing Nun* |
| UK45 | I Want To Hold Your Hand *Beatles* |
| UKLP | With The Beatles *Beatles* |

—— WEEK 2 ——

| | |
|---|---|
| US45 | There ! I've Said It Again *Bobby Vinton* |
| USLP | The Singing Nun *The Singing Nun* |
| UK45 | I Want To Hold Your Hand *Beatles* |
| UKLP | With The Beatles *Beatles* |

—— WEEK 3 ——

| | |
|---|---|
| US45 | There ! I've Said it Again *Bobby Vinton* |
| USLP | The Singing Nun *The Singing Nun* |
| UK45 | Glad All Over *Dave Clark Five* |
| UKLP | With The Beatles *Beatles* |

—— WEEK 4 ——

| | |
|---|---|
| US45 | There ! I've Said It Again *Bobby Vinton* |
| USLP | The Singing Nun *The Singing Nun* |
| UK45 | Glad All Over *Dave Clark Five* |
| UKLP | With The Beatles *Beatles* |

# DYLAN: NEW ALBUM, NEW PRODUCER

Although Bob Dylan's SRO New York Carnegie Hall concert of October 26 1963 was recorded for release (and given the catalogue number 77110) it has remained unheard. In the interim Dylan's new manager, Albert Grossman, has unsuccessfully attempted to renegotiate his client's original royalty deal with CBS.

In the course of much unpleasantness, Grossman secured Tom Wilson instead of John Hammond (who discovered and signed Dylan to CBS) to produce Dylan's third studio album, 'The Times They Are A-Changin''.

Recorded in August and October 1963, it comprises ten Dylan originals.

## PARIS: NO BEATLEMANIA

The Beatles picked The Cyrano Theatre, Versailles, Paris to warm-up prior to their season at the world-famous L'Olympia Theatre with Trini 'If I Had A Hammer' Lopez and France's most popular 'pop' femme, Sylvie Vartan.

The following evening (16th), Beatlemania was not visible in Paris when Les Fabs attempted to impress unimpressionable L'Olympia patrons on the first night of a three week variety season.

# STONES ON THE ROAD

*Stones Watts, Jagger and Richards*

The Rolling Stones and The Ronettes opened their UK tour at The Granada, Harrow, supported by The Swinging Blue Jeans, Marty Wilde & The Wildcats, Dave Berry & The Cruisers, The Cheynes (with Peter Green and Mick Fleetwood) and Johnny Kidd & The Pirates.

Recordwise, The Stones' first EP has entered the singles chart and the group have acted as un-billed back-up band for their friend Cleo (Sylvester) who debuted with a cover of 'To Know Him Is To Love Him'.

# CYRIL DAVIES DIES

*British blues father-figure Cyril Davies, with the All Stars, including Long John Baldry (second from right)*

January 7 was a black day for British R&B – Cyril 'Squirrel' Davie, pioneering British R&B harmonica star, died of leukemia, aged 32.

Along with Alexis Korner, Davies co-formed Blues Incorporated which, at one time or another, featured Mick Jagger, Eric Burdon, Charlie Watts, Jack Bruce, Ginger Baker, Graham Bond and Paul Jones as singers and musicians.

Equal in musical status to most of the US blues stars he sought to emulate, Davies quit Blues Inc. in November 1962, to form his own All-Stars (featuring Long John Baldry) and to record his remarkable 'Country Line Special' (Pye).

# KINSLEY QUITS MERSEYBEATS

Billy Kinsley, bass-guitarist and vocalist with The Merseybeats, has quit the group – in the UK charts at the moment with 'I Think Of You' – to marry hairdresser Pat Allman.

While most groups who lose a key member gloss over such predicaments, Merseybeats founder Tony Crane admitted: 'We're in trouble. Things are really starting to happen now we're in the charts, but now Billy has walked out on us, we've had to stop everything and return to Liverpool to find a replacement as quickly as possible.

'It's not easy, because Billy has been with me since we were a double act called The Mavericks.'

With drummer John Banks and Aaron Williams on guitar, they became known as The Merseybeats.

Tony continued: 'Don't ask my why Billy should leave just as we're on the verge of getting somewhere. I mean, he played on both 'I Think Of You' and our previous hit 'It's Love That Really Counts' – then out of the blue he told me he doesn't like the life, and that's that!'

For the moment, The Mersey-beats are honouring bookings as a trio. 'Surprisingly, we sounded quite reasonable. This could be because we feature quite a few slow numbers. We didn't deliberately start out to be a quiet group – it just happened that way,' said Tony.

'We got a recording contract some time after a lot of other Liverpool groups and we felt we'd just be lost in the crowd if we did wild numbers like the rest.'

It's likely that ex-Big Three bass player and frontman Johnny Gustavson will be Kinsley's replacement.

*Georgie Fame, here seen on guitar rather than his usual Hammond organ*

## FAME AT LAST!

Firmly established on London's flourishing club scene as premier exponents of Hammond 'n' horns urban R&B, scenemakers Georgie Fame & The Blue Flames – who skilfully blend the best elements of Jamaican Blue Beat, James Brown funk, Stax soul, Tamla Motown melodies and hard bop into a danceable crowd-pulling mix – packed mohair mods and US servicemen into the Soho basement of 37 Wardour Street. With the tapes rolling, they recorded their debut album, 'Rhythm And Blues At The Flamingo Club', for release on Columbia.

### STAR QUOTE

JUDITH SIMONS
London *Daily Express*

*'They look like boys whom any self-respecting mum would lock in the bathroom! But The Rolling Stones – five tough young London-based music makers are not worried what mum thinks! . . . The Stones have taken over as the voice of the teens.'*

### THE GRAPEVINE

- The Kinks have made their Pye label debut with a cover of Little Richard's 'Long Tall Sally'.
- The Dave Clark Five less than impressive on ATV's *Sunday Night at the London Palladium*.
- Billy Fury has covered 'Hippy Hippy Shake' and 'Glad All Over' exclusively for Scandinavian single.
- Vee-Jay have released latest Beatlemania cash-in: 'Jolly What! The Beatles and Frank Ifield On Stage'.

## BLUEBEAT'S OWN LABEL

BlueBeat – the latest variant of Jamaican popular dance music – has also loaned its name to a UK-based record label specializing in the popular club phenomenon.

London's two top-selling BlueBeat singles are 'Madness' by Prince Buster and 'Carolina' by The Folks Brothers.

*Brothers Dave and Ray Davies (centre) with bassist Peter Quaife and Mick Avory on drums – The Kinks*

## BEWARE, ANIMALS AT LARGE!

Newcastle R&B group, The Animals, have made their debut with the Mickie Most-produced 'Baby Let Me Take You Home' – a gung-ho rework of an old blues standard the group discovered on Bob Dylan's first album.

Formerly, The Alan Price Combo, they were renamed The Animals by their Tyneside fans because of their wild appearance and stage act!

The Animals comprise: Eric Burdon (vocals), Alan Price (organ), Hilton Valentine (guitar), Chas Chandler (bass) and John Steel (drums).

# BEATLES – THE DOMINATION CONTINUES

The Beatles have pulled off an unprecedented music industry coup, covering all top *five* slots on *Billboard* magazine's singles chart with 'Can't Buy Me Love' at No. 1, 'Twist And Shout' at No. 2, 'She Loves You' at No. 3, 'I Want To Hold Your Hand' at No. 4 and 'Please Please Me' at fifth spot.

Not content with *just* that, Beatles singles also hold down positions 16, 44, 49, 69, 78, 84 and 88 on the same Hot 100.

The group accounted for 60 per cent of *all* records sold in North America during February, according to industry sources.

Meanwhile, John Lennon's first book, *In His Own Write*, has won the presitigious Foyle's Literary Prize in Britain.

As guest speaker at the celebrated literary luncheon held in his honour in London, Lennon's entire acceptance speech was a mumbled: 'Thank you very much. You've got a lucky face!' after which he immediately fled the banquet!

## ELVIS FANS SEE DOUBLE

*Kissin' Cousins* is the latest Elvis epic from the MGM Studios. A Li'l Abner-style hillbilly romp, it has Presley playing both a US Army officer (Josh Morgan) and his hick double (Jodie Tatum) – achieved by the application of a

*Duplicate Elvis with a blond wig – two for the price of one!*

tatty blond wig.

The only selling point of this disaster is that fans get two Elvises for the price of one!

- Filming has begun on Beatles movie, *A Hard Day's Night*.

- Beatles German-language versions of 'I Want To Hold Your Hand (Komm, Gib Mir Deine Hand)' and 'She Loves You (Sie Liebt Dich)' are on sale in the Fatherland.

- Stan Getz has headlined the last show at the Marquee Club's Oxford Street premises in London.

*Getz closes Marquee in Oxford Street*

## SULLIVAN RE-BOOKS DC5

It has been a hectic month for The Dave Clark Five. Hot on the heels of The Beatles, Tottenham's finest made an impressive debut on *The Ed Sullivan Show* on March 8, performing 'Glad All Over'.

Taken with their clean-cut appearance and politeness, Mr Sullivan immediately invited them to return. Having taken the unanimous decision to turn professional on March 14, now that 'Glad All Over' is a chart-topper, The Dave Clark Five cancelled the first night of their week-long season at Liverpool's Empire to make their second appearance on *The Ed Sullivan Show* where they performed 'Do You Love Me', 'Bits And Pieces' and 'Glad All Over'.

# HENTOFF SLAMS BEATLES & CLARK, LIKES SEARCHERS

Noted US critic Nat Hentoff's opinion of The Beatles' recent *Ed Sullivan Show* TV debut was decidely lukewarm: 'Musically, this reviewer cannot understand the fervour of Beatles' admirers, or the scorn of their detractors. Except for their visual uniqueness, The Beatles are a run of the mill rock'n'roll attraction.'

Hentoff's views on The Dave Clark Five's *Sullivan* appearance were equally dismissive: 'Clark leads an ordinary rock'n'roll group with no particular musical direction,' he wrote.

However, Hentoff was more impressed by The Searchers on April 5: 'The Searchers seem to be the most professional British rock group to have appeared in America. To this viewer, the initial impression was more favourable musically than had been the case with The Beatles or The Dave Clark Five.

'They sustained an exuberant mood, punctuated by several unison jumps in the air. They showed a more subtle command of dynamics than the two groups that preceded them.'

## CHARTS

| | | |
|---|---|---|
| US45 | | Can't Buy Me Love *Beatles* |
| USLP | | Meet The Beatles *Beatles* |
| UK45 | | Can't Buy Me Love *Beatles* |
| UKLP | | With The Beatles *Beatles* |

**WEEK 2**

| | | |
|---|---|---|
| US45 | | Can't Buy Me Love *Beatles* |
| USLP | | Meet The Beatles *Beatles* |
| UK45 | | Can't Buy Me Love *Beatles* |
| UKLP | | With The Beatles *Beatles* |

**WEEK 3**

| | | |
|---|---|---|
| US45 | | Can't Buy Me Love *Beatles* |
| USLP | | Meet The Beatles *Beatles* |
| UK45 | | Can't Buy Me Love *Beatles* |
| UKLP | | With The Beatles *Beatles* |

**WEEK 4**

| | | |
|---|---|---|
| US45 | | Can't Buy Me Love *Beatles* |
| USLP | | Meet The Beatles *Beatles* |
| UK45 | | A World Without Love *Peter And Gordon* |
| UKLP | | The Rolling Stones *Rolling Stones* |

## ELVIS: VIVA ROMANCE?

MGM have released *Viva Las Vegas* with Elvis Presley as racing driver Lucky Jordan. Not only has this film been judged as slightly superior in terms of script and soundtrack than critics have come to expect from an Elvis musical, but the dynamic presence of the statuesque Ann-Margret (Rusty Martin) has added to the public's interest.

Gossip columnists have picked up on the fact that the romantic involvement between the two stars wasn't just restricted to the movie set.

Ann-Margret has made no secret about the relationship having passed the 'just good friends' stage. However, Elvis's more loyal fans were most displeased when she said she anticipated announcing wedding plans.

## THE GRAPEVINE

■ The Rolling Stones have broadcast four weekly 15-minute shows for Radio Luxembourg.

■ Roy Orbison, Tony Sheridan, Freddie & The Dreamers, Wayne Fontana & The Mindbenders and Ezz Rico are touring the U.K.

■ The Beatles have completed work on their first feature-length movie, *A Hard Day's Night*.

■ Success by Peter & Gordon with Lennon & McCartney song, 'World Without Love'.

## STAR QUOTE

### BRIAN BENNETT
The Shadows

*'Comparisons between us and The Beatles? No one has said anything to our faces. Occasionally, some of the local press boys ask if we consider ourselves to be slipping, on account of The Beatles' success. Our reply usually varies, depending on our mood!'*

## STONES FOR THE CHOP

Mr Wallace Scowcroft, President of Britain's National Federation of Hairdressers has offered a free haircut to the next No. 1 group or soloist in the pop charts, adding: 'The Rolling Stones are the worst. One of them looks as if he has got a feather duster on his head.'

With The Rolling Stones having defined their rebellious image long before their musical identity, manager Andrew Oldham has taken the unprecedented gamble of exploiting this, by removing all but the Decca logo (including the group's name) from the front of their debut album and selling it on the strength of a highly atmospheric photograph.

The group's rise to the top continues unchecked, with now-obligatory riots accompanying their live appearances.

Security battled with 8,000 Stones fans inside Empire Pool, Wembley during the 'Ready Steady Go Rave Mad Mod Ball'.

Outside, police arrested a battalion of thirty warlike bikers.

*Stones (l to r) Jones, Watts, Jagger, Richard, Wyman keep names off album and annoy hairdressers — business as usual*

*Elvis and Ann-Margret — more than friends?*

# 1964

## THE GRAPEVINE

■ Two pirate radio station ships have begun transmitting off the coast of Britain – Radio Caroline and Radio Atlanta.

■ Wayne Fontana & The Mind-benders have covered 'Duke Of Earl'.

■ An exhibition of ex-Beatle Stuart Sutcliffe's paintings has opened at Liverpool's Walker Gallery.

■ John Mayall's Bluesbreakers have made their debut on disc with 'Crawling Up A Hill'.

# STONES – MORE ROWS, MORE RIOTS

*Mirror mocks Stones*

The London *Daily Mirror* is the latest paper to lambast The Rolling Stones, in an editorial which said: 'Everything seems to be against them on the surface. They are called the ugliest group in Britain. They are not looked on very kindly by most parents, or by adults in general. They are even used to the type of article that asks big brother if he would let his sister go out with one of them.'

Confronted with this and similar criticism, Mick Jagger replies: 'We know a lot of people don't like us 'cause they say we're scruffy and don't wash.

'So what? They don't have to come and look at us, do they? If they don't like me, they can keep away!'

Determined not to keep away, even if they didn't atually have tickets, were Scottish fans at the Stones' May 19 gig at Chantinghall Hotel, Hamilton.

More than 4,000 people tried to gate-crash the gig and found themselves in the middle of a full-scale battle with local police. Unable to control the crush, officers let the fans in.

As final proof of the Stones' popularity, BBC-TV was deluged with over 8,000 postal applications for studio tickets when they announced the group's scheduled appearance on *Juke Box Jury* on June 27.

## THE NIGHT OF THE LIVING LEGENDS

Forget The Beatles and The Stones! London audiences haven't witnessed anything quite as spectacular as when three living legends – Chuck Berry, Gene Vincent and Carl Perkins – headlined a one-nighter at London's Hammersmith Odeon.

In supporting slots: The Animals, The Nashville Teens and Kingsize Taylor & The Dominoes.

*Nashville Teens (right) in Tobacco Road? Possibly not . . .*

*But Gene Vincent (below) probably is*

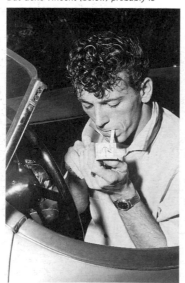

## LENNY'S SIDEKICK SHOOTS HIMSELF

Joe Maini (34), the widely respected madcap sax-playing sidekick of comedian Lenny Bruce, was killed in Los Angeles on May 8 during a bizarre shooting incident at a friend's house.

Maini placed the muzzle of a revolver to his head and, laughing, pulled the trigger, shooting himself fatally.

# GETZ AND THE GIRL FROM RIO

Having instigated the immensely profitable bossa nova phenomenon with his 1962 Grammy Award-Winning Verve Records album, 'Jazz Samba' and the hit single 'Desafinado' (on which he was partnered by guitarist Charlie Byrd), master of the 'cool' jazz tenor Stan Getz is again chartbound with 'The Girl From Ipanema', which has resulted in instant global stardom for singer Astrud Gilberto, who appears on this record by pure accident.

As part of a series of bossa nova albums with various artists, Stan Getz commenced a two-day recording session in New York in March 1963 with top Brazilian singer-composers, Antonio Carlos Jobim and Joao Gilberto.

One of the eight songs they taped was 'The Girl From Ipanema', a gently sensual sun-kissed samba meant to showcase Getz's tenor sax and the voice of guitarist Joao Gilberto. However, it became clear that Gilberto could only sing in Portuguese and could not perform Normal Gimbel's specially commissioned English lyric.

At the session was Gilberto's 24-year-old Bahia-born wife, Astrud. She spoke English and possessed a voice of sorts. Though she had never sung professionally, she was coaxed into softly crooning the wistful lyrics.

At the time of release, Astrud Gilberto's nonchalant vocal contribution was viewed as being so slight she was not name-checked on the album.

Ironically, public demand for a single version of 'The Girl From Ipanema' resulted in the original LP version being drastically cut for commercial appeal. Joao Gilberto's vocal was edited out, leaving just the magical combination of Stan The Man and The Girl From Rio.

In the face of a mounting bossa nova backlash, both the 'Stan Getz/Joao Gilberto Album' and the appearance of 'The Girl From Ipanema' on the charts have proved a point by succeeding in a spectacular manner for entirely artistic reasons.

Below: 'Desafinado' partners Getz (left) and Byrd and (above) Astrud Gilberto

## CHARTS

|  |  |
| --- | --- |
| US45 | Chapel Of Love<br>*Dixie Cups* |
| USLP | Hello Dolly !<br>*Original Cast* |
| UK45 | You're My World<br>*Cilla Black* |
| UKLP | The Rolling Stones<br>*Rolling Stones* |

— WEEK 2 —

|  |  |
| --- | --- |
| US45 | Chapel Of Love<br>*Dixie Cups* |
| USLP | Hello Dolly !<br>*Louis Armstrong* |
| UK45 | You're My World<br>*Cilla Black* |
| UKLP | The Rolling Stones<br>*Rolling Stones* |

— WEEK 3 —

|  |  |
| --- | --- |
| US45 | Chapel Of Love<br>*Dixie Cups* |
| USLP | Hello Dolly !<br>*Louis Armstrong* |
| UK45 | It's Over<br>*Roy Orbison* |
| UKLP | The Rolling Stones<br>*Rolling Stones* |

— WEEK 4 —

|  |  |
| --- | --- |
| US45 | A World Without Love<br>*Peter & Gordon* |
| USLP | Hello Dolly !<br>*Louis Armstrong* |
| UK45 | It's Over<br>*Roy Orbison* |
| UKLP | The Rolling Stones<br>*Rolling Stones* |

## MARTIN MOCKS STONES

For their American debut, The Rolling Stones were set up for ritual slaughter on the network TV show *Hollywood Palace*, where host Dean Martin set them up for a string of cheap laughs.

'Their hair is not long,' quipped Martin. 'It's just smaller foreheads and higher eyebrows.'

Of a trampoline artist also on the show, he said: 'That's the father of The Rolling Stones. He's been trying to kill himself ever since.'

Martin: "Higher eyebrows"

## MEADE LUX DIES

Boogie Woogie piano ace Meade Lux Lewis — best known for his hit 'Honky Tonk Train Blues', plus classic collaborations with fellow Boogie pianomen Albert Ammons and Pete Johnson — has died, aged 58, in a Minneapolis auto accident.

## THE GRAPEVINE

■ Sam Cooke has appeared in cabaret at New York's swish Copacabana Club.

■ Peter & Gordon have charted yet again with a Lennon & McCartney tune, 'Nobody I Know'.

■ The Beatles have kicked off the European leg of their world tour with Jimmy Nicol depping for a sick Ringo.

■ Summer film plans for the proposed Clive Donner-directed Rolling Stones have been shelved.

# JIM REEVES KILLED IN AIR CRASH

Texas-born country music star Jim Reeves became the object of instant cult hysteria when he was killed, aged 40, in an air crash on July 31.

The light aircraft which was carrying Reeves and his manager Dean Manuel, from Arkansas back to Nashville, flew into heavy rain four miles from Beery Field Airport and plunged into thick foliage.

A prolific recording artist, Reeves' innumerable hits included: 'He'll Have To Go', 'I Love You Because', 'Adios Amigo', 'Welcome To My World' and 'You're The Only Good Thing'.

A year before his death, Reeves starred in the title role of a South African-made feature film, *Kimberly Jim*.

## CHARTS

| | |
|---|---|
| US45 | I Get Around *Beach Boys* |
| USLP | Hello Dolly ! *Louis Armstrong* |
| UK45 | House Of The Rising Sun *Animals* |
| UKLP | The Rolling Stones *Rolling Stones* |

WEEK 2

| | |
|---|---|
| US45 | I Get Around *Beach Boys* |
| USLP | Hello Dolly ! *Louis Armstrong* |
| UK45 | House Of The Rising Sun *Animals* |
| UKLP | The Rolling Stones *Rolling Stones* |

WEEK 3

| | |
|---|---|
| US45 | Rag Doll *Four Seasons* |
| USLP | Hello Dolly ! *Original Cast* |
| UK45 | A Hard Day's Night *Beatles* |
| UKLP | A Hard Day's Night *Beatles* |

WEEK 4

| | |
|---|---|
| US45 | Rag Doll *Four Seasons* |
| USLP | A Hard Day's Night *Beatles* |
| UK45 | A Hard Day's Night *Beatles* |
| UKLP | A Hard Day's Night *Beatles* |

## STONES ESCAPE RIOT, EQUIPMENT DOESN'T

Britain's biggest-ever rock'n'roll riot erupted when The Rolling Stones and The Executives played The Empress Ballroom at The Winter Gardens, Blackpool before a crowd of 9,000 fans, which included many drunken holidaying Scots.

Mid-show, Keith Richards lashed out with his boot at troublemakers who spat at Brian Jones. With a blood-hungry gang of drunks on their heels, the Stones fled the building.

The mob then took out their vengeance on the equipment, reducing a grand piano to matchwood. However, they failed to

## THE GRAPEVINE

■ The Beatles' movie *A Hard Day's Night* received a Royal Premiere in London.

■ An impromptu song in Adam Faith's dressing room by 17-year-old fan Sandie Shaw has been rewarded with a Pye Records contract.

■ Big demand in the UK for imported EPs by French 'Yeh! Yeh!' star Francoise Hardy has prompted the WH Smith chain to stock her records nation-wide.

break into the Winter Gardens theatre, where The Dave Clark Five were heading a summer-season variety show.

*Tottenham's finest, the Dave Clark Five, who escaped the rampaging revellers during the Blackpool orgy of destruction*

## HIGH NUMBERS COUNT ON HIT

The High Numbers, who are fast becoming the most popular West London R&B mod group, have made their Fontana label debut with two songs written by their manager, Peter Meadon – 'I'm The Face' (a rewrite of Slim Harpo's 'Got Love If You Want It') and 'Zoot Suit' (based on The Showmen's 'Country Fool').

Both songs, Meaden has insisted, accurately reflect the teenage lifestyle in such mod strongholds as the Goldhawk Club in London's Shepherd's Bush and Soho's Scene Club.

The High Numbers, who are known to smash up pairs of marracas on stage, comprise: Roger Daltrey (vocals), Pete Townshend (guitar), John Entwistle (bass) and newcomer Keith Moon (drums).

The group who, until recently, were known as The Detours, have been booked for some Sunday concerts with The Beatles.

# BEATLES TOUR AMERICA

The Fab Four look set to conquer the U.S. as Beatlemania takes hold

Though The Beatles had previously visited the United States in February for a short promotional expedition, their first full-blown North American concert tour kicked off at San Francisco's Cow Palace before a screaming, jelly-baby-throwing audience of 17,000.

The rest of their previously announced dates are as follows: *August*: (20) The Convention Centre, Las Vegas; (21) The Coliseum, Seattle; (22) Empire Stadium, Vancouver; (23) Hollywood Bowl, Los Angeles; (26) Red Rocks Amphitheatre, Denver; (27) The Gardens, Cincinnati; (28/29) Forest Hills, New York City; (30) The Convention Centre, Atlantic City. *September*: (2) The Convention Hall, Philadelphia; (3) Indiana State Fair Coliseum, Indianapolis; (4) The Arena, Milwaukee; (5) The International Amphitheatre, Chicago; (6) Olympia Stadium, Detroit; (7) Maple Leaf Gardens, Toronto; (8) The Forum, Montreal; (11) The Gator Bowl, Jacksonville; (12) The Garden, Boston; (13) The Civic Centre, Baltimore; (14) The Civic Arena, Pittsburg; (15) The Public Auditorium, Cleveland; (16) City Park Stadium, New Orleans; (17) Municipal Stadium, Kansas City.

## DYLAN IS NOT TAKING SIDES

'Another Side Of Bob Dylan', the eagerly-awaited fourth album from America's most influential contemporary performer, has been released to brisk activity at the nation's check-outs.

Though again accompanied by just his own guitar and occasional piano, the 'Side' of the singer for all to hear isn't quite the Voice of Protest most expected.

Recorded in just one day (June 9), the songs are more of a look inward with eight of the eleven tracks concerned with women. Yet there is still an undercurrent of his often-apocalyptic view of life.

The songs are: 'All I Really Want To Do', 'Black Crow Blues', 'Spanish Harlem Incident', 'Chimes Of Freedom', 'I Shall Be Free No. 10', 'To Ramona', 'Motorpsycho Nitemare', 'My Back Pages', 'I Don't Believe You', 'Ballad In Plain D' and 'It Ain't Me Babe'.

Bob Dylan — an album a day?

## CHARTS

| | | |
|---|---|---|
| US45 | A Hard Day's Night | *Beatles* |
| USLP | A Hard Day's Night | *Beatles* |
| UK45 | A Hard Day's Night | *Beatles* |
| UKLP | A Hard Day's Night | *Beatles* |
| **WEEK 2** | | |
| US45 | A Hard Day's Night | *Beatles* |
| USLP | A Hard Day's Night | *Beatles* |
| UK45 | A Hard Day's Night | *Beatles* |
| UKLP | A Hard Day's Night | *Beatles* |
| **WEEK 3** | | |
| US45 | Everybody Loves Somebody | *Dean Martin* |
| USLP | A Hard Day's Night | *Beatles* |
| UK45 | Do Wah Diddy Diddy | *Manfred Mann* |
| UKLP | A Hard Day's Night | *Beatles* |
| **WEEK 4** | | |
| US45 | Where Did Our Love Go | *Supremes* |
| USLP | A Hard Day's Night | *Beatles* |
| UK45 | Do Wah Diddy Diddy | *Manfred Mann* |
| UKLP | A Hard Day's Night | *Beatles* |
| **WEEK 5** | | |
| US45 | Where Did Our Love Go | *Supremes* |
| USLP | A Hard Day's Night | *Beatles* |
| UK45 | Have I The Right | *Honeycombs* |
| UKLP | A Hard Day's Night | *Beatles* |

## JOHNNY BURNETTE DROWNED

Johnny Burnette has drowned in a fishing accident, aged 30.

Memphis-born Burnette — whose legendary Rock'n'Roll Trio sides for Decca-Coral (1956/57) rank alongside Elvis's Sun sessions as essential seminal rockabilly classics — really only found international recognition once he'd joined Liberty Records, smoothed out both his style and appearance, and charted with such songs as 'Dreamin'', 'You're Sixteen' and 'Little Boy Sad'.

# SEPTEMBER 1964

*More British beat: The Animals headline for ten days at the Brooklyn Paramount*

## CHARTS

| | |
|---|---|
| US45 | House Of The Rising Sun *Animals* |
| USLP | A Hard Day's Night *Beatles* |
| UK45 | Have I The Right *Honeycombs* |
| UKLP | A Hard Day's Night *Beatles* |

**— WEEK 2 —**

| | |
|---|---|
| US45 | House Of The Rising Sun *Animals* |
| USLP | A Hard Day's Night *Beatles* |
| UK45 | You Really Got Me *Kinks* |
| UKLP | A Hard Day's Night *Beatles* |

**— WEEK 3 —**

| | |
|---|---|
| US45 | House Of The Rising Sun *Animals* |
| USLP | A Hard Day's Night *Beatles* |
| UK45 | I'm Into Something Good *Herman's Hermits* |
| UKLP | A Hard Day's Night *Beatles* |

**— WEEK 4 —**

| | |
|---|---|
| US45 | Oh, Pretty Woman *Roy Orbison* |
| USLP | A Hard Day's Night *Beatles* |
| UK45 | I'm Into Something Good *Herman's Hermits* |
| UKLP | A Hard Day's Night *Beatles* |

## MICKIE – MOST SUCCESSFUL!

Mickie Most, who recently returned to the UK after a three year stay in South Africa where he scored 11 consecutive chart-topping singles, has suddenly emerged as Britain's hottest new record producer.

Having already enjoyed phenomenal success world-wide with The Animals ('The House Of The Rising Sun') and The Nashville Teens ('Tobacco Road'), Most is again at No. 1 as a result of having Manchester group Herman's Hermits re-record Earl Jean's jaunty 'I'm Into Something Good'.

# NEW YORK ROCKS

New York City hasn't seen so much super league rock'n'roll action since the late fifties with Brooklyn being the epicentre of this current activity.

On September 4, one of the city's great auditoriums – the Brooklyn Paramount Theatre – re-opened its doors after many years of darkness to welcome 'The House Of The Rising Sun' hit-makers The Animals who, along with Chuck Berry, Jan & Dean, Del Shannon, Bobby Rydell, The Dixie Cups and Dee Dee Sharp, held court for the next ten days.

The smart money says that the show that opened a day earlier (Sept. 3) at the Brooklyn Fox Theatre in competition, amounts to one hot two-dollar fifty ticket.

The Searchers are the token Brit group on a bill which features Marvin Gaye, The Supremes, The Miracles, The Temptations, Martha & The Vandellas and The Contours.

## MARIANNE'S TEARS GO BY

'I need to have a boy friend,' admits 17-year-old former convent girl Marianne Faithfull, whose debut single – Jagger & Richard's 'As Tears Go By' – has jumped ten places to No. 13 on the UK best-sellers. 'Often, I get terribly lonely, and it's so nice if there's always someone there.'

Discussing the music business, Marianne doesn't pull her punches: 'People take it all so seriously, it's stupid. Most people are in it for the money, but they just don't admit it.

## THE GRAPEVINE

■ The Beach Boys have made their *Ed Sullivan* debut.

■ 17-year-old folk-singer Marianne Faithfull has made her professional stage debut.

■ Brian Epstein has vetoed a three-and-one-half million dollar buy-out bid for The Beatles.

■ Rod Stewart has made his recording debut with 'Good Morning, Little Schoolgirl'.

## STAR QUOTE

### JOHNNIE RAY

*I'll tell you one thing: when I had all those teenagers screaming for me, I could control them. If I wanted quiet, I got it. I just told them to be quiet.'*

'I'm not some little girl caught up in the business. I know what I'm doing. I've got two sides. One of them wants money, quick money, and in this business you can make it.

'I thought that I would never be bought. Now I think I have been. Friends of mine say: "Oh Marianne, you're a real mad bird." Yes, that fits me, I'm sure!'

# RONETTES – SEXY AND SUCCESSFUL

Not everyone is buying British to the total exclusion of everything else.

US vocal groups still remain a very hot attraction on both sides of the Atlantic, and none more than The Ronettes, whose teen-angst recordings of 'Be My Baby', 'Baby I Love You' and '(The Best Part Of) Breakin' Up' are not only some of the best-ever recordings made in this genre, but have made the group objects of desire.

The group comprisessisters Veronica and Estelle Bennett and their cousin Nedra Talley. They were originally Twist go-go dance demonstrators at New York's famed Temple Of Twist – The Peppermint Lounge. That was until a chance encounter with whizkid Phil Spector led them to be signed to his Philles label and stardom.

With their long hair piled high upon their heads, heavy eye-makeup, pouting bee-stung lips, tight oriental silk dresses slashed to the thigh and stiletto shoes, they have a sexually-dangerous look that is attractive to both girls – who regard them as role models – and boys, who see them as the answer to their prayers, dreams, fantasies . . .

*Spector Protégées, The Ronettes*

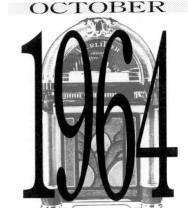

# SULLIVAN SLAMS STONES

Immediately following uncontrollable scenes of mass hysteria in the studio during The Rolling Stones' appearance on prime-time 'The Ed Sullivan Show', an irate Mr. Ed told reporters: 'I promise you they'll never be back on our show. If things can't be handled, we'll stop the whole business. We won't book any more rock'n'roll groups, and we'll ban teenagers from the theatre if we have to.

'Frankly, I didn't see the Rolling Stones until the day before the broadcast. They were recommended by my scouts in England. I was shocked when I saw them.

'Now the Dave Clark Five are nice fellows. They are gentlemen, and they perform well. It took me seventeen years to build this show. I'm not going to have it destroyed in a matter of weeks.'

Sullivan — shocked

# THE GRAPEVINE

■ Mary Wells has been special guest star on The Beatles UK tour.

■ The Rolling Stones have cancelled a South African tour

following talks with the Musicians' Union, which opposes that country's Apartheid policies.

■ CBS have guaranteed Mickie Most £85,000 for the next three years as an independent producer while EMI have signed him to produce new artists for them over the next five years.

J. Frank Wilson: prophetic disc heralds real-life drama as car crash theme comes true

## 'LAST KISS' MAN HURT

An automobile carrying 'Last Kiss' car-crash-death-disc hit-maker J. Frank Wilson was involved in an accident near Memphis. The singer was seriously injured, and his 27-year old record producer, Sonley Rouch, was killed.

## MU BANS SA TOURS

Following the last-minute cancellation of The Rolling Stones' Christmas tour of South Africa, The Swinging Blue Jeans, The Four Pennies, Dave Berry and Freddie & The Dreamers have all called off their scheduled trips. They were told not to go by the British Musicians' Union, which opposes South Africa's apartheid policies. A tour by The Searchers is also threatened. Their agent, Tito Burns, said, 'I haven't cancelled the deal as yet, and I'm hopeful of a M.U. executive meeting next month.'

However, M.U. secretary Harry Francis commented: 'Although South Africa is one of the things our executive committee will discuss, I don't think there's much chance of a change of policy on this issue.'

Mr. Jim Stodel, executive director of African Consolidated Theatres, flew to London from Johannesburg to book artists for South African tours in 1965. But he has already been told by Francis that members of the M.U. will not be permitted to go.

Stodel revealed he would be negotiating with Leslie Grade for Cliff Richard & The Shadows to return to South Africa. Of this, Francis commented: 'We can't speak for Cliff Richard — he is a member of Equity. But as far as we are concerned, The Shadows won't be going.

'The Shadows were not members of the Musicians' Union when they went to South Africa early last year, but they are now. We could never permit our members to work in a country that practises apartheid.'

## TAMI TOPS TV

It's already being said of the Steve Binder-directed spectacular, *The TAMI Show* (The Teenage Command Performance), that in terms of production values it will be the yardstick for all future live-in-concert television and cinema presentations.

Filmed a 'live' in Anaheim, California, the non-stop action was supplied by: The Beach Boys, The Barbarians, Chuck Berry, James Brown & The Famous Flames, Marvin Gaye, Gerry & The Pacemakers, Lesley Gore, Jan & Dean, Billy J. Kramer & The Dakotas, Smokey Robinson & The Miracles, The Rolling Stones and The Supremes.

## CHARTS

| | | |
|---|---|---|
| US45 | Oh, Pretty Woman | *Roy Orbison* |
| USLP | A Hard Day's Night | *Beatles* |
| UK45 | I'm Into Something Good | *Hermin's Hermits* |
| UKLP | A Hard Day's Night | *Beatles* |

### WEEK 2

| | | |
|---|---|---|
| US45 | Oh, Pretty Woman | *Roy Orbison* |
| USLP | A Hard Day's Night | *Beatles* |
| UK45 | Oh, Pretty Woman | *Roy Orbison* |
| UKLP | A Hard Day's Night | *Beatles* |

### WEEK 3

| | | |
|---|---|---|
| US45 | Do Wah Diddy Diddy | *Manfred Mann* |
| USLP | A Hard Day's Night | *Beatles* |
| UK45 | Oh, Pretty Woman | *Roy Orbison* |
| UKLP | A Hard Day's Night | *Beatles* |

### WEEK 4

| | | |
|---|---|---|
| US45 | Do Wah Diddy Diddy | *Manfred Mann* |
| USLP | A Hard Day's Night | *Beatles* |
| UK45 | Oh, Pretty Woman | *Roy Orbison* |
| UKLP | A Hard Day's Night | *Beatles* |

### WEEK 5

| | | |
|---|---|---|
| US45 | Baby Love | *Supremes* |
| USLP | People | *Barbra Streisand* |
| UK45 | Always Something There To Remind Me | *Sandie Shaw* |
| UKLP | A Hard Day's Night | *Beatles* |

The Swingin' Blue Jeans, part of the British Musicians Union ban on groups touring South Africa

# 1964

# NASHVILLE TEENS TO BUY 2ND ALBUM?

British group The Nashville Teens are back in the charts with 'Google Eye' – a song about a fish(!) from the album 'Twelve Sides Of John D. Loudermilk'.

The Teens' first world-wide hit 'Tobacco Road' also came from the same source. It wasn't intended that way, it's just that country music star Loudermilk is a dab hand with a tune and lyrics.

Ramon Phillips, one of The Teens' two lead singers revealed: 'What do you do when someone comes up and says, "You're making another record next week?" Well, we looked at the LP and found 'Google Eye' was the next track.'

Seems the Loudermilk album is the only one the group own: 'So if you want to know what our next ten records are going to be,' joked Phillips, 'Best buy Loudermilk's LP and work your way through it!'

Currently on tour with The Animals, Carl Perkins and Tommy Tucker, The Teens say their upcoming U.S. tour will give them the chance to investigate new material.

They believe it's the overall sound of any record, rather than the lyrical content, that decides whether or not it's a hit.

'You listen to 'Baby Love' by The Supremes,' fellow frontman Art Sharp argued. 'And you won't hear all the words. People go around singing 'Baby love, my baby love,' because that's all they know – only the hook line.'

## ELVIS: THE HONDA THEY FALL

Paramount Pictures have released *Roustabout*. Though Elvis Presley stars and Raquel Welch makes her screen debut, the standard of such formula movies is cause for increasing concern among even die-hard fans.

Elvis' movie double and song choreographer Lance Le Gault offers his thoughts on the subject: 'We shot 'Kissin' Cousins' in seventeen days, and I think that was the turning point. Up until then, certains standards had been maintained. Once they realized they could do a film so quickly, we were on fast pictures.

'The first time I noticed it was in *Roustabout*. Elvis rode a Honda in it. Which is pretty silly, when you think about it, because Elvis rides Harleys. Yet, in the film they put him on a 350 Honda.

'And this is a guy who's playing a drifter whose only mode of transportation is his bike. This is a guy who supposedly goes across country on a machine that's about right for the driveway, a 350 Honda.'

*A still from 'Roustabout', latest Elvis quickie to come out of Hollywood*

## CHARTS

| | | |
|---|---|---|
| US45 | Baby Love | *Supremes* |
| USLP | People | *Barbra Streisand* |
| UK45 | Always Something There To Remind Me | *Sandie Shaw* |
| UKLP | A Hard Day's Night | *Beatles* |

### WEEK 2

| | | |
|---|---|---|
| US45 | Baby Love | *Supremes* |
| USLP | People | *Barbra Streisand* |
| UK45 | Baby Love | *Supremes* |
| UKLP | A Hard Day's Night | *Beatles* |

### WEEK 3

| | | |
|---|---|---|
| US45 | Baby Love | *Supremes* |
| USLP | People | *Barbra Streisand* |
| UK45 | Little Red Rooster | *Rolling Stones* |
| UKLP | A Hard Day's Night | *Beatles* |

### WEEK 4

| | | |
|---|---|---|
| US45 | Leader Of The Pack | *Shangri-Las* |
| USLP | People | *Barbra Streisand* |
| UK45 | Little Red Rooster | *Rolling Stones* |
| UKLP | A Hard Day's Night | *Beatles* |

*Vocalist Judith Durham fronts a new folk-based group from Down Under, The Seekers*

## THE GRAPEVINE

■ Radio Manx – transmitting from a caravan on the Isle of Man – has become Britain's first land-based commercial radio station.

■ The Isley Brothers and Marvin Gaye have appeared on *Ready, Steady, Go!*.

■ Rolling Stones have covered 'Little Red Rooster' as their latest single.

■ The Beach Boys have been in Europe on a radio/TV promo tour.

■ Bluesman Jimmy Reed has been touring UK clubs.

## EMI SIGN AUSSIE GROUP

EMI Records have announced the signing, to their Columbia label, of an Australian group (one girl and three boys) who 'sound like The Springfields' and are called The Seekers.

The comparison is not unsurprising considering that Tom Springfield wrote the 'A' side of their debut single, 'I'll Never Find Another You'. EMI are predicting big things for the group.

Also on the EMI schedule is the 'comeback' disc of The Beatles' music publisher Dick James after a 5-year silence. Best known for his hit recording of the 'Robin Hood' TV theme, James is again aiming high with a sing-a-long medley of Beatles' hits.

# SOUL PIONEER COOKE KILLED

Soul singer Sam Cooke was shot dead by the manageress of a Los Angeles motel on December 10.

Earlier that evening, Cooke picked up a Eurasian girl named Elisa Boyer in a bar and offered to driver her home. Instead, Cooke drove to a motel on South Figueroa, where he signed the register as 'Mr and Mrs Cooke'.

It's alleged that once inside the motel room, Cooke began to rip the woman's clothes off. Then, when he went to the bathroom, Boyer fled from the room with both her clothes and Cooke's, and hid in a nearby telephone booth, from which she called the police.

Emerging from the motel room dressed in nothing but his sports' coat and shoes, Cooke kicked in the door of the manageress Mrs Bertha Lee Franklin. She testified that Cooke punched her twice and that, in self-defence, she fired at him three times with a .22 revolver.

One shot wounded Cooke in the chest. However, this didn't halt his attack, so Franklin bludgeoned him with a stick. Sam Cooke was already dead by the time the police arrived at the scene of the incident.

Unproven rumours within the U.S. music industry suggest that the Mafia had taken out a contract on the singer, who refused to throw in his lot with some of the criminal elements who control part of the record industry.

Born, 22 January 1931 in Chicago, Sam Cooke is revered as a soul music pioneer who, by way of such songs as 'A Change Is Gonna Come', is said to have heralded the Black Power movement.

The vocal purity of his gospel-derived style on hits such as 'You Send Me', 'Cupid', 'Only Sixteen', 'Wonderful World', 'Another Saturday Night', 'Bring It On Home To Me', 'Twistin' The Night Away' and 'Chain Gang' greatly influenced the current generation of soul singers.

## BEATLES XMAS SHOW

*Vocalist Elkie Brooks is the only girl on the Beatles' bill*

A repeat of last year's formula of music, laughter and traditional pantomime is planned for 'Another Beatles Christmas Show'. This year, The Fabs are joined at London's Hammersmith Odeon by a varied bill that includes: The Yardbirds, Freddie & The Dreamers, Elkie Brooks, Jimmy Saville, Michael Haslam, Ray Fell, Sounds Incorporated and The Mike Cotton Sound.

## CHARTS

| | | |
|---|---|---|
| US45 | Ringo | *Lorne Greene* |
| USLP | Beach Boys Concert | *Beach Boys* |
| UK45 | I Feel Fine | *Beatles* |
| UKLP | A Hard Day's Night | *Beatles* |

— WEEK 2 —

| | | |
|---|---|---|
| US45 | Mr. Lonely | *Bobby Vinton* |
| USLP | Beach Boys Concert | *Beach Boys* |
| UK45 | I Feel Fine | *Beatles* |
| UKLP | Beatles For Sale | *Beatles* |

— WEEK 3 —

| | | |
|---|---|---|
| US45 | Come See About Me | *Supremes* |
| USLP | Beach Boys Concert | *Beach Boys* |
| UK45 | I Feel Fine | *Beatles* |
| UKLP | Beatles For Sale | *Beatles* |

— WEEK 4 —

| | | |
|---|---|---|
| US45 | I Feel Fine | *Beatles* |
| USLP | Beach Boys Concert | *Beach Boys* |
| UK45 | I Feel Fine | *Beatles* |
| UKLP | Beatles For Sale | *Beatles* |

*As Brian Wilson (top) quits touring, The Beach Boys go on without him*

## THE GRAPEVINE

■ The Miracles have made their first visit to Britain to appear on ITV's *Ready, Steady, Go!*

■ The Animals have recorded, as their next single, a song normally associated with Nina Simone – 'Don't Let Me Be Misunderstood'.

■ New from Gerry & The Pacemakers: 'Ferry 'Cross The Mersey'.

■ 19-year old Kink Ray Davies has married his 18-year old sweetheart.

## BRIAN WILSON BOWS OUT

The Beach Boys' main-man Brian Wilson suffered a nervous breakdown on a scheduled flight from Los Angeles to Houston.

As a result, he says he's to quit touring with the group to concentrate on song writing and record production.

## CHARTS

| | | |
|---|---|---|
| US45 | I Feel Fine | *Beatles* |
| USLP | Roustabout | *Elvis Presley* |
| UK45 | I Feel Fine | *Beatles* |
| UKLP | Beatles For Sale | *Beatles* |

### WEEK 2

| | | |
|---|---|---|
| US45 | I Feel Fine | *Beatles* |
| USLP | Beatles '65 | *Beatles* |
| UK45 | I Feel Fine | *Beatles* |
| UKLP | Beatles For Sale | *Beatles* |

### WEEK 3

| | | |
|---|---|---|
| US45 | Come See About Me | *Supremes* |
| USLP | Beatles '65 | *Beatles* |
| UK45 | Yeh Yeh | *Georgie Fame* |
| UKLP | Beatles For Sale | *Beatles* |

### WEEK 4

| | | |
|---|---|---|
| US45 | Downtown | *Petula Clark* |
| USLP | Beatles '65 | *Beatles* |
| UK45 | Go Now | *Moody Blues* |
| UKLP | The Rolling Stones No.2 | *Rolling Stones* |

### WEEK 5

| | | |
|---|---|---|
| US45 | Downtown | *Petula Clark* |
| USLP | Beatles '65 | *Beatles* |
| UK45 | Go Now | *Moody Blues* |
| UKLP | The Rolling Stones No.2 | *Rolling Stones* |

# AMERICA SHUTS OUT BRITISH GROUPS

*Nashville Teens, victims of visa embargo Stateside*

Official action by the US Government seems destined to put an end to the tours by British rock groups which proved so popular and lucrative during 1964. The Labor Department in Washington, without stating any clear reasons for the decision, has declared that no UK rock groups will in future be granted H-1 visas – the type necessary for a US tour.

This has already washed out New Year tours by The Zombies, The Nashville Teens and The Hullaballoos, all of whom were working in New York over Christmas on lesser H-2 visas. Existing bookings have already been cancelled.

US journalist Nat Hentoff notes: 'Individual promoters of each concert could apply for a group to work in their town, but setting up a tour this way would be time-consuming and impractical. It is likely, therefore, that British groups will only come to America for TV, radio, or New York stage engagements in future.'

## ANIMALS QUARANTINED IN HARLEM

Two live shows by The Animals at the Apollo Theatre in Harlem on January 21 and 22 – which were to be recorded live by MGM Records for a spring album – were cancelled by the US immigration department.

Only a last-minute decision by the department allowed the group to fulfil their TV booking on *The Ed Sullivan Show*, on which they performed their new single 'Don't Let Me Be Mis-

understood'.

Producer Mickie Most said: 'The Apollo shows were specially set up so I could record a live LP, but as they were preparing to go on stage on Thursday, an official stopped the show.

'Apparently, our American agents had only got permission for the Sullivan show. As a result of our breaking a rule by appearing at the Apollo, The Animals almost lost the TV show too.'

## SPECTOR'S LOVIN' TRIUMPH

Concerned that The Righteous Brothers' 'You've Lost That Lovin' Feeling' hit might be eclipsed in the UK by Cilla Black's George Martin cover version, Rolling Stones' producer Andrew Loog Oldham took the following quarter-page ad in the NME on his own initiative:

'This advertisement is not for commercial gain. It is taken as something must be said about the great new Phil Spector record - The Righteous Brothers singing "You've Lost That Lovin' Feelin'", already in the American Top 10.

'This is Spector's greatest production, the last word in tomorrow's sound today, exposing the overall mediocrity of the music industry, and typifying his greatness.'

*Spector's latest, the Righteous Brothers*

## WESTERN MOVIE FOR THE BEATLES

The Beatles are expected to film a famous western story next year. It will be based on Richard Condon's novel *A Talent For Loving*, which centres on a 1,400-mile horse race which took place in 1871 between the Rio Grande and Mexico City.

Condon, who also wrote *The Manchurian Candidate*, which was filmed by Frank Sinatra, is currently working on the screenplay at his Geneva home.

The movie is to be made by Pickfair Films, a production company formed by Brian Epstein with former United Artists executive Bud Ornstein, and will be shot on location in England and Spain.

However, this is not expected to be the third Beatles film which they will make in the autumn — that is almost certain to be the last of a three-picture deal with United Artists, which began with *A Hard Day's Night*.

Meanwhile, the group fly to the Bahamas on February 22 to begin work on their second film, which will be premiered August and released simultaneously in Britain and the US.

# ONLY EIGHT US GOLD SINGLES IN 1964?

The Record Industry Association Of America has announced that eight singles were given gold discs last year for RIAA-certified US sales of over one million.

They were 'Rag Doll' by The Four Seasons, 'I Get Around' by The Beach Boys, Dean Martin's 'Everybody Loves Somebody', Roy Orbison's 'Oh, Pretty Woman', and four by The Beatles: 'I Want To Hold Your Hand' (the year's biggest seller), 'Can't Buy Me Love', 'A Hard Day's Night' and 'I Feel Fine'.

It is believed that several more singles also reached gold status in the US in 1964, but were not applied for by RIAA companies. These include Louis Armstrong's 'Hello Dolly' (on Kapp), The Animals' 'House Of The Rising Sun' (on MGM), Manfred Mann's 'Do Wah Diddy Diddy' (Ascot), and three further Beatles singles: 'She Loves You' (a two million seller for Swan), 'Twist And Shout' and 'Love Me Do' (both on Tollie).

The Tamla-Motown group, America's most successful independent record company, is not an RIAA member, but had a clutch of 1964 million-sellers with Mary Wells' 'My Guy', Martha & The Vandellas' 'Dancing In The Street', and three singles by The Supremes: 'Where Did Our Love Go', 'Baby Love' and 'Come See About Me'.

## THE GRAPEVINE

■ Gene Pitney has recorded an album of duets in Nashville with country star George Jones. Pitney commented: 'George is a real deep-down, bass-y singer, and next to him I sounded like a shrieking witch. But I was really singing country, and I found George was going pop on me, bending words and so on . . . a fantastic experience.'

*Manfred 'Diddy' Mann*

*The Four Seasons (left) and Beach Boys (above) among last year's US million-sellers*

## CRICKETS – NO MORE CHIRPIN'

The Crickets, the group originally fronted by Buddy Holly, and which in the years since Holly's death has scored particularly strongly in Britain with hits like 'Don't Ever Change', 'My Little Girl' and 'They Call Her La Bamba', have disbanded.

Although leader and drummer Jerry Allison retains ownership of The Crickets' name, and may re-form the group at some future date for recording purposes, the hit-making line-up will not be reunited. The recent single 'Now Hear This' was the band's final disc.

Vocalist Jerry Naylor has been ill and is convalescing, while Sonny Curtis is to concentrate on his music publishing business in Los Angeles. As a songwriter Curtis has hits like The Everlys' 'Walk Right Back' under his belt.

Pianist Glenn Hardin has also turned to songwriting, as well as appearing as a session player every week on Jack Good's *Shindig* TV show.

# UK TOUR SELL-OUT FOR FOLK FAVOURITE DYLAN

Announcements of a British tour in May by Bob Dylan, acknowledged as the world's leading folk singer, have resulted in a rapid sell-out and the addition of extra dates to the original itinerary – including a second night in London at The Royal Albert Hall. The Beatles are expected to be in the audience for this show, and many other celebrities – including the UK's own new folk star Donovan – have also sought tickets.

Promoter Tito Burns announced: 'Without a single poster having been printed, every ticket was sold for Dylan's concerts in Manchester on May 7 and at The Albert Hall three nights later. His other appearances, at Liverpool, Sheffield, Leicester, Birmingham and Newcastle are also almost sold out already.

'I have to cable this week to tell him that if he wanted to avoid riots in London – and my blood being shed – he must do an extra date at The Albert Hall, which he agreed to.'

While in the UK, Dylan will film his own TV special, and Burns is currently deciding between offers from two of the four major ITV companies for its screening.

CBS Records, meanwhile, has released the title track of Dylan's LP 'The Times They Are A-Changin'' as his first British single, and plans to follow up with his new US 45 'Subterranean Homesick Blues' on the eve of the tour.

## THE GRAPEVINE

■ Andrew Oldham recorded Rolling Stones concerts at Liverpool and Manchester on March 6 and 7, in order to extract live tracks for a Stones EP to be titled 'Got Live If You Want It' for Decca release in April.

■ Decca is also seeking to record Tom Jones' first major concert date, for an eventual similar live EP.

■ Jeff Beck, formerly with the Tridents, has replaced Eric Clapton as lead guitarist with The Yardbirds.

*Rolling Stones, live on the road if you want it*

*Jones' concert debut*

# HELP! COMES TO THE BEATLES

The title of The Beatles' forthcoming film has now been switched to *Help!* after a new song written by John Lennon and Paul McCartney, which the group recorded in a night-time studio session on Tuesday, 13 April.

This will also be their next single, timed for release about a fortnight before the movie is premiered. The previous working title, *Eight Arms To Hold You*, was scrapped before Lennon and McCartney attempted the daunting task of writing a title song around it!

British comedian Frankie Howerd is now slated for a guest role in the film, in the role of an elecution teacher to The Beatles.

## HERMAN'S HERMITS HITS

*Mrs. Brown and daughter herald huge hit for Herman*

Herman's Hermits' single 'Mrs Brown You've Got A Lovely Daughter' after massive US airplay as a track on their debut album, has been issued as a single by public demand, despite the group's 'Can't You Hear My Heartbeat' still being in the US Top Five, and the recently released 'Silhouettes' already soaring Top 10-wards.

The day before release, advance orders for the single totalled over 600,000, and it leapt on to the *Billboard* singles chart as No. 12, the highest first-week entry since Sheb Wooley's 'Purple People Eater' debuted in the Top 10 in 1958.

## ROULETTE SPONSORS PIRATE RADIO AIRTIME

For the first time, a record company-sponsored show is being broadcast by one of the UK's offshore pirate radio stations, Radio Caroline – despite the British record industry's call to the government to ban the stations.

The sponsor is US label Roulette Records, which is presenting an hour-long show five evenings a week, recorded in the US with DJ Jack Spector. Tapes for the first shows arrived in London on April 10, and were immediately rushed to Caroline's North and South stations, off the Isle of Man and the Essex coast respectively, for first transmission two days later.

A Caroline spokesman said: 'Our contract with Roulette is for

### CHARTS

| | | |
|---|---|---|
| US45 | Stop ! In The Name Of Love | *Supremes* |
| USLP | Goldfinger | *Soundtrack* |
| UK45 | The Last Time | *Rolling Stones* |
| UKLP | The Rolling Stones No.2 | *Rolling Stones* |

— WEEK 2 —

| | | |
|---|---|---|
| US45 | I'm Telling You Now | *Freddie & The Dreamers* |
| USLP | Goldfinger | *Soundtrack* |
| UK45 | The Minute You're Gone | *Cliff Richard* |
| UKLP | The Rolling Stones No.2 | *Rolling Stones* |

— WEEK 3 —

| | | |
|---|---|---|
| US45 | I'm Telling You Now | *Freddie & The Dreamers* |
| USLP | Goldfinger | *Soundtrack* |
| UK45 | Ticket To Ride | *Beatles* |
| UKLP | The Rolling Stones No.2 | *Rolling Stones* |

— WEEK 4 —

| | | |
|---|---|---|
| US45 | Game Of Love | *Wayne Fontana & The Mindbenders* |
| USLP | Goldfinger | *Soundtrack* |
| UK45 | Ticket To Ride | *Beatles* |
| UKLP | Beatles For Sale | *Beatles* |

*Freddie: dreams come true*

## THE GRAPEVINE

■ Over a four-day period, Mercury Records received orders for 142,000 copies of its first US album by Freddie & The Dreamers, topping the singles chart with their two-year-old UK hit 'I'm Telling You Now'. The advance sale of this LP so far breaks the all-time advance order record for any LP in the label's 18-year history.

two years, and is worth a lot of money to us – it runs into five figures. In addition to the show, Roulette is to take advertising spots.'

The label's UK licensee is EMI, one of the industry's anti-pirate leaders, and none too pleased by the development. An EMI spokesman stated: 'We have written to Roulette Records giving them full details of the attitude of the British record industry - and of the British government – to the pirate stations in general.'

# 1965

# PRICE LEAVES ANIMALS

Alan Price, The Animals' organist, who originally formed the group in Newcastle as The Alan Price Combo, has quit. His replacement is Dave Rowberry, previously with The Mike Cotton Sound.

Price's decision was forced upon him by an increasing fear of flying, which came to a head just as the group were due to depart for live dates in Sweden.

He announced: 'My nerve broke just a few hours before we were due to fly to Scandinavia,' and added that he was now resting in Newcastle on doctor's orders, with no immediate plans for the future.

Animals' guitarist Hilton Valentine confirms that Price 'said he was sorry, but he just couldn't force himself on to the plane'.

At short notice, the group recruited 19-year-old Mickey Gallagher, of South Shields group

Flying fear grounds Price

Chosen Few, as temporary organist for the nine-day Swedish trek. Rowberry was then recruited as full-time replacement on their return.

Comments vocalist Eric Burdon: 'Alan was a good blues organist, but I think Dave Rowberry's a better musician. We've been working out some arrangements with him on numbers like the Everlys' 'Bye Bye Love'. We believe the group will be even better.'

## FREDDIE, BY GUM

A major US manufacturer of bubble gum is introducing a new series of Freddie & The Dreamers cards to be given free with packs of gum.

There will be a set of 66 cards in all, which, when they are all placed together, will make a 3ft square picture of the British group.

### CHARTS

| | |
|---|---|
| US45 | Mrs. Brown, You've Got A Lovely Daughter *Herman's Hermits* |
| USLP | Goldfinger *Soundtrack* |
| UK45 | Ticket To Ride *Beatles* |
| UKLP | Beatles For Sale *Beatles* |

— WEEK 2 —

| | |
|---|---|
| US45 | Mrs. Brown, You've Got A Lovely Daughter *Herman's Hermits* |
| USLP | Goldfinger *Soundtrack* |
| UK45 | Ticket To Ride *Beatles* |
| UKLP | Beatles For Sale *Beatles* |

— WEEK 3 —

| | |
|---|---|
| US45 | Mrs. Brown, You've Got A Lovely Daughter *Herman's Hermits* |
| USLP | Goldfinger *Soundtrack* |
| UK45 | Ticket To Ride *Beatles* |
| UKLP | The Freewheelin' Bob Dylan *Bob Dylan* |

— WEEK 4 —

| | |
|---|---|
| US45 | Ticket To Ride *Beatles* |
| USLP | Goldfinger *Soundtrack* |
| UK45 | Where Are You Now *Jackie Trent* |
| UKLP | Bringing It All Back Home *Bob Dylan* |

— WEEK 5 —

| | |
|---|---|
| US45 | Help Me Rhonda *Beach Boys* |
| USLP | Goldfinger *Soundtrack* |
| UK45 | Long Live Love *Sandie Shaw* |
| UKLP | Bringing It All Back Home *Bob Dylan* |

Author Lennon with wife Cynthia

# THE GRAPEVINE

■ John Lennon's second book, *A Spaniard In The Works*, is to be published in the UK on June 24 by Jonathan Cape, although Lennon will be out of the country at the time, playing with The Beatles in their debut live appearance in Milan, Italy.

■ Simon & Schuster are to publish the book in the US, where Lennon's previous volume, *In His Own Write*, sold 175,000 copies.

# POLITICIANS ENTER US VISA ROW

On May 13, as 30 leading American theatrical agents met in New York to formulate a policy in the face of US Government policy apparently aimed at preventing British rock groups from being able to work in America, their cause was joined by a number of US Senators opposed to the current situation.

Meanwhile, on the other side of the Atlantic, Kenneth Lomas, Member of Parliament for Huddersfield West, sought action from the British government.

Having been told that the British government 'cannot accept responsibility for the laws of another country', Lomas told the NME: 'The only other way I could draw attention to this problem was by asking the Minister of Labour to restrict permits to Americans who wish to work in Britain, as a reciprocal measure.'

The Minister, in a written reply, refused to introduce reciprocal action.

# WHO'S DALTREY: HE'D RATHER DIE THAN GROW OLD

The Who's vocalist Roger Daltrey, in his first NME interview, somewhat unnerved writer Alan Smith – as did the rest of the group.

Assesses Smith: 'There's a sort of vicious strangeness about these four beatsters from Shepherds Bush – and they admit it. They talk quite happily about the way guitarist Pete Townshend smashes his guitar against an amplifier when the mood takes him. Pete says it produces an unusual sound, and I can well believe him.'

Daltrey, after startling his interviewer with the opening observation: 'I never want to grow old – I want to stay young forever,' asserts that The Who were not particularly pleased with their debut hit 'I Can't Explain': 'We just did it to get known. As time goes by, we'll do the kind of thing we really like, really way out.'

'Arguments? Sure, we have 'em all the time. That's why we get on so well; it kind of sharpens us up. We've all got kind of - well, explosive temperaments — and it's like waitin' for a bomb to

go off. If it wasn't like this, we'd be nothin'. I mean it: if we were always friendly and matey . . . well, we'd all be a bit soft. We're not mates at all. When we've finished a show and we've got time off, that's it, we go our own ways.'

Daltrey feels that James Brown is going to be the next craze. The Who have been playing his material for some time,

*The Who: explosive*

and think that it will catch on quicker than people suspect.

Pete Townshend is described by Daltrey as 'very political, a right Bob Dylan', while of himself, he says, with all seriousness: 'If I wasn't with a group, I don't know what I'd do. It means everything to me. I think I'd do myself in.'

## THE GRAPEVINE

■ In an apparent reciprocation against the continued refusal of work visas to UK acts in the US, American singer Bobby Vinton was refused a work permit when he arrived in Britain for two weeks of radio and TV dates. A planned appearance on *Top of the Pops* was an early casualty. Ironically, the single Vinton hopes to plug in Britain is 'Don't Go Away Mad'.

*Visa veto vexes Vinton*

## JONES BECOMES A HOME-OWNER

Tom Jones has paid £8,000 to buy himself and his family their first home of their own.

His 25th birthday present to himself is a newly built open-plan house of ultra-modern design, in Shepperton, Middlesex, in the comfortable outer London suburbs. He expects to move wife Linda and eight-year-old son Mark in as soon as he returns from a US trip towards the end of June.

Comments Jones: 'This is the first real home of our own we've had since we were married. We used to live with our in-laws in Pontypridd. I can't wait to move in!'

# KINKS KAUGHT IN A SONG TUG-OF-WAR

Release of the new Kinks' single has been held up because of a dispute between Larry Page, one of their managers, and Shel Talmy, the producer contracted to record them for Pye. Both men had recorded the group on new Ray Davies compositions, and each barred the other from allowing Pye to release either track.

Talmy, who produced 'See My Friend' with the group before their recent US trip, said: 'I served legal notice on the group while they were in America, restraining them from recording without me.'

Page, who produced a session with The Kinks in Hollywood at the end of the US tour, said: 'I want what is best for the boys — and 'Ring The Bells' is the best record. As publisher of Ray's compositions, I have the final say on any recordings.'

Page also claimed that as publisher/manager he was legally entitled to record the group in Hollywood on one of its own compositions.

A few days after the deadlock was joined, and following The Kinks' return to London from the US, Page resolved the row by agreeing to the release of the Talmy-produced 'See My Friend'.

*Kontract krisis for Kinks*

## ORBISON SIGNS DUAL RECORD DEAL

Roy Orbison's long-term recording contract with Monument Records, which has brought him almost five years of hits, has expired and not been renewed.

The singer made his last recordings with Monument's owner/producer Fred Foster last month, some of which may yet emerge as singles.

For the future, however, Orbison has taken the unprecedented step of signing parallel deals, each understood to be for 20 years, with different record companies in the US and UK. At home, he will be released on MGM, a company which is also committed to building — via its parent film division — his career in movies.

In Britain, the singer has signed directly to Decca Records for release on its London-American label — the same outlet which previously handled his Monument repertoire in the UK. Orbison is reported to have been so happy with Decca's work (in 1964, he sold more records in the UK than any other US act), that he was keen to see the relationship continue.

The basis of both deals is that Orbison will supervise his own recording sessions at a studio near his Nashville home. From these, master tapes will be delivered to both MGM and Decca for release.

## THE GRAPEVINE

■ It has been agreed in the London High Court that The Honeycombs' hit 'Have I The Right' was the work of the group's managers, Ken Howard and Alan Blaikeley.

Composer Geoff Goddard agreed to drop allegations that he, not they, had written the song.

■ Dusty Springfield has recorded an EP titled 'Mademoiselle Dusty', with versions of 'Will You Love Me Tomorrow', 'Summer Is Over', 'Losing You' and 'Stay Awhile' all sung in French.

*Honeycombs men have right to song*

# BEATLES: MASSIVE SHEA CONCERT AND TV SHOW PLANS

The Beatles played to a massive audience of 56,000 fans at New York's Shea Stadium on August 15, in a concert which was filmed for TV by Ed Sullivan Productions in conjunction with Brian Epstein, who is 'confident that it will be suitable for presentation on British television at Christmas'.

The concert's promoter, Sidney Bernstein, has offered the group a record $350,000 to return to the venue next July or August. Their share from the recent Shea concert was $160,000.

Meanwhile, John Lennon and Paul McCartney will host a 50-minute Granada TV spectacular devoted to their songwriting, to be recorded in the autumn for screening before Christmas. They are unlikely to sing in the show, which is to be produced by John Hamp, but will introduce guests such as Cilla Black, Billy J. Kramer, Peter & Gordon, The Silkie, and other acts singing their hit versions of the duo's songs.

American artists are likely to be featured in film clips, including Ella Fitzgerald, who had a hit with 'Can't Buy Me Love'.

Hamp produced a similar Granada spectacular built around Burt Bacharach, and had discussions with Lennon, McCartney and Brian Epstein concerning the content of the forthcoming show, prior to The Beatles' departure for their US tour.

## TOP PRODUCERS FORM NEW INDEPENDENT COMPANY

Four of Britain's top record producers – George Martin, Ron Richards and John Burgess from EMI, and Peter Sullivan from Decca - have formed their own production company, to be known as Associated Independent Records (London) Limited, or AIR for short.

Each of the four will continue to work with the acts he has handled on behalf of his previous employer – which amounts to many of EMI's and Decca's top acts, including The Beatles, Tom Jones, Cilla Black, The Hollies, Lulu and P.J. Proby.

George Martin told the NME: 'This will not affect my position as The Beatles' recording manager. Both the group and Brian Epstein stressed that they would like me to continue, and I am happy to do so.'

AIR intends to sign further artists of its own, and there is a possibility that some of those already produced could sign directly with the company after present contracts expire. For the moment, EMI will have first option on AIR's productions, except where the act concerned is currently signed to Decca.

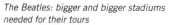
The Beatles: bigger and bigger stadiums needed for their tours

(Below) Five get mobbed in Chicago

## THE GRAPEVINE

■ Dave Clark Five vocalist Mike Smith had two ribs broken when the group was mobbed in Chicago on the first date of its current US tour, while Clark and sax player Dennis Payton lost their jackets and had their shirts torn. After hospital treatment, Smith was allowed to rejoin the group, his chest strapped and in plaster.

# 1965

# STAR MEETING IN HAWAII – HERMAN QUESTIONS, ELVIS DODGES

Herman's Hermits fulfilled a long-held ambition when they met Elvis Presley on the set of his film, *Paradise Hawaiian Style*, while the group were appearing in Honolulu.

Said Herman's singer Peter Noone: 'I told Sam Katzman, who was producing the film we were in, that I would love to meet El. He was also producing Elvis' picture, and arranged for us to get together when we flew to Hawaii.

'I expected him to be a bit moody, but he was a really nice guy. He told me how much he liked our recordings of 'Mrs Brown' and 'Henry VIII', and Colonel Tom Parker chipped in and said that his wife was always singing 'Henry VIII'!

'Elvis looks *exactly* like he appears on film, and was perfectly natural. He's got a very broad Tennessee accent, and his favourite expressions are "why, sure" and "yessir".

'When I asked him about long hair, and why he didn't grow his, he reminded me that ten years ago, he had long sideburns. It was difficult for me to realize that he was that old!

'We talked for about an hour . . . Elvis said how much he liked British groups, especially The Beatles and The Stones, and said that he was sorry he couldn't meet The Beatles. Every time I mentioned his records to him, though, he seemed to dodge the question.

'I also asked him a few questions about his films, but again he discreetly avoided answering. Colonel Parker protects him all the time. He listens to everything Elvis says, and he won't let him be photographed except by his own photographers.'

**THE GRAPEVINE**

■ Decca has guaranteed The Animals £100,000 to issue their records outside North America, once the group's contract with producer Mickie Most expires in

February 1966. MGM Records, is paying $250,000 for the group's contract for the US and Canada.

■ Husband and wife act Sonny and Cher are reported to be considering the film script of *The Marriage Game*, submitted to them in New York by producer Charles Casher.

## CHARTS

| | | |
|---|---|---|
| US45 | Help! | *Beatles* |
| USLP | Out Of Our Heads | *Rolling Stones* |
| UK45 | (I Can't Get No) Satisfaction | *Rolling Stones* |
| UKLP | Help! | *Beatles* |

WEEK 2

| | | |
|---|---|---|
| US45 | Help! | *Beatles* |
| USLP | Help! | *Beatles* |
| UK45 | (I Can't Get No) Satisfaction | *Rolling Stones* |
| UKLP | Help! | *Beatles* |

WEEK 3

| | | |
|---|---|---|
| US45 | Help! | *Beatles* |
| USLP | Help! | *Beatles* |
| UK45 | (I Can't Get No) Satisfaction | *Rolling Stones* |
| UKLP | Help! | *Beatles* |

WEEK 4

| | | |
|---|---|---|
| US45 | Eve Of Destruction | *Barry McGuire* |
| USLP | Help! | *Beatles* |
| UK45 | Tears | *Ken Dodd* |
| UKLP | Help! | *Beatles* |

*Herman and the group (top) meet long-time hero Elvis, chaperoned as usual by the Colonel*

## RADIO LONDON IN THRILLER MOVIE

The MV Galaxy, offshore home of UK pirate radio station Radio London, will be one of the locations for the movie *Deadline For Diamonds*, a thriller now going into production at Pinewood Studios, London.

The film will also feature performance cameos by several acts including The Small Faces and Kiki Dee, and some Radio London DJs may also appear.

## GERRY TO MARRY

Gerry Marsden of Gerry & The Pacemakers has announced that he will marry his former fan club secretary Pauline Behan in Liverpool on October 11. The couple will then honeymoon for two weeks before Gerry and the group resume UK cabaret dates.

The three Pacemakers – all already married – will be among the guests at the ceremony.

# FAITH AND ROULETTES SPLIT

Adam Faith has parted company with his backing group, The Roulettes, after a three-year partnership, and told reporters: 'It's a friendly parting: they've gone to concentrate on their own career.'

Both singer and group will continue to record individually for EMI's Parlophone label, but The Roulettes have also left the Starcast organisation of Evelyn Taylor (who manages Faith), to Unit 4+2's managers John Barker and Anne Niven.

Faith is currently auditioning other groups who could work with him on his few personal appearances, and in their own right at other times.

During the association, The Roulettes backed Faith on several chart singles, beginning with the 1963 UK Top five hit 'The First Time', and including his biggest US success 'It's Alright'. They also released six singles and one album of their own.

## CHARTS

| | |
|---|---|
| US45 | Hang On Sloopy / *McCoys* |
| USLP | Help! / *Beatles* |
| UK45 | Tears / *Ken Dodd* |
| UKLP | Help! / *Beatles* |
| **WEEK 2** | |
| US45 | Yesterday / *Beatles* |
| USLP | Help! / *Beatles* |
| UK45 | Tears / *Ken Dodd* |
| UKLP | Help! / *Beatles* |
| **WEEK 3** | |
| US45 | Yesterday / *Beatles* |
| USLP | Help! / *Beatles* |
| UK45 | Tears / *Ken Dodd* |
| UKLP | Help! / *Beatles* |
| **WEEK 4** | |
| US45 | Yesterday / *Beatles* |
| USLP | Help! / *Beatles* |
| UK45 | Tears / *Ken Dodd* |
| UKLP | Help! / *Beatles* |
| **WEEK 5** | |
| US45 | Yesterday / *Beatles* |
| USLP | Help! / *Beatles* |
| UK45 | Tears / *Ken Dodd* |
| UKLP | The Sound Of Music / *Soundtrack* |

## ELVIS BASSIST DIES

Bill Black the bass player who appeared on all Elvis Presley's pre-army recordings and live dates, as well as in the films *Loving You* and *Jailhouse Rock*, died on October 21 in Memphis, aged 39. He had been ill for some time, and had undergone surgery at the Baptist Hospital on a brain tumour, from which he did not recover.

After parting from Presley, Black formed his own instrumental outfit, The Bill Black Combo, which scored eight US Top 30 hits between 1959 and 1962, including an instrumental reworking of Elvis' 'Don't Be Cruel'.

*Cliff turns to Stones*

## THE GRAPEVINE

■ UK comedian Lance Percival is to dub the voices of Paul McCartney and Ringo Starr for US TV's Beatles cartoon series.

■ Cliff Richard plans to record a Mick Jagger/Keith Richards song, 'Blue Turns to Grey'.

■ Them's lead singer Van Morrison has cut a session at London's Decca Studios which may yield a debut solo single for late October release.

*Van takes a vocal vocation from Them*

## LUXEMBOURG BOOSTS ITS AIR POWER

The switching on of Radio Luxembourg's new medium wave transmitter means widespread improved reception of the station's 208 metre English language pop music service, which is beamed at the British Isles but listened to across Europe.

A recent survey in the UK by Gallup indicates that the British weekly audience for Luxembourg is nearly three times as great as that for offshore pirate stations Radios London and Caroline combined.

The poll states that Luxembourg's audience in the UK and Ireland exceeds 37 million – compared to 13 million claimed by London and Caroline after their own survey.

Also, several of 208's top-rated shows have more than two million listeners apiece, compared with 500,000 late-night listeners claimed by BBC radio. The station's leading show, *Top 20*, based on the NME singles chart, claims more than three million listeners between 11pm and midnight each Sunday.

## MARIANNE IS A MUM

Marianne Faithfull and husband John Dunbar found themselves the parents of a son on November 10, somewhat earlier than anticipated.

Marianne fell on the steps of her Chelsea home that morning, went into labour, and gave birth – almost two months prematurely - during the afternoon at a London nursing home. The boy is to be named Nicholas.

## BAROQUE BEATLES

Elektra Records, best known as a folk music label, is to release an album of Beatles compositions arranged in baroque style and performed by a small chamber orchestra.

The group reportedly gave their permission for the project, though otherwise have no involvement in it. Title of the LP will be 'Eine Kleine Beatle Musik'.

## THE GRAPEVINE

■ The Small Faces, hitmakers in the UK with their debut single 'Whatcha Gonna Do About It', have had a personnel switch. Organist Jimmy Winston has left to form his own group, and has been replaced by 18-year-old Ian McLagan, formerly with The Boz People. McLagan played his debut with the group on a ballroom date at London's Lyceum on November 2.

*McLagan (left), the newest Small Face*

# P.J. PROBY: DOWN AND NEARLY OUT?

The turbulent career of P.J. Proby has lurched from crisis to crisis even more than usual in recent weeks.

Firstly, he parted company with his manager John Heyman after a 12-month association – 'by mutual consent and on friendly terms', according to both parties. On November 10, a new management pact was signed with the partnership of London club owner Bernie Green and former Bachelors publicist Mel Collins.

However, within days this agreement too was terminated, again 'by mutual agreement', though with no further explanation by either side.

New management offers were being discussed at the end of the month: the next to take on the job would be Proby's fifth since he started to work in the UK in Spring, 1964.

The singer also cancelled previously-booked cabaret dates in London and three provincial cities. A week at Catford's Savoy Club was 'postponed indefinitely' because, according to Proby, 'my new act isn't ready'.

Also imminent is a move from his rented flat in London's Chelsea. 'The neighbours have signed a petition complaining about the noise and parking on the kerb outside,' he told journalists. Proby will move out on December 4 – the same date that his current UK work permit expires.

Proby continued: 'If I haven't got a new manager to straighten out my problems by December 4, I'll probably put on my jeans, borrow the fare home to Hollywood, and get out there and then.

'Right now, things couldn't be much worse – I'm flat broke, penniless, destitute, call it what you like.'

*P.J.: Noise annoys neighbours*

# BEATLES DOUBLE-A? – LENNON SAYS NO

On December 19, 16 days after its release, UK sales of The Beatles' double A-side single 'We Can Work It Out'/'Day Tripper' passed one million, qualifying the group for their fifth gold disc from home sales alone. It has been their fastest seller on home ground since 'Can't Buy Me Love', having reached three-quarters of a million after only five days on sale. The single has also reached No. 1 – and gone gold – in the US.

EMI and John Lennon voiced different opinions about the disc's double-A status just prior to its release. The company announced it as 'We Can Work It Out' coupled with 'Day Tripper', but said there was no preferred A-side. Both tracks would be

Beatles: working it out

promoted equally, being played in rotation on EMI's sponsored Radio Luxembourg shows, for example.

Lennon insisted to the NME that 'Day Tripper' would be the A-side as far as the group were concerned, and George Martin concurred that, after we gave both titles to EMI, the boys decided they preferred "Day Tripper" – but both are extremely good and deserve a lot of plays.'

## 1965 POLL FAVOURITES

The NME's annual Readers Poll produced the following results for 1965:

*World Section*
Male Singer: 1 Elvis Presley; 2 Cliff Richard. Female singer: 1 Dusty Springfield; 2 Brenda Lee. Vocal Group: 1 Beatles; 2 Rolling Stones. Musical Personality: 1 Elvis Presley; 2 John Lennon.

*UK Section*
Male Singer: 1 Cliff Richard; 2 Paul McCartney. Female Singer: 1 Dusty Springfield; 2 Sandie Shaw. Vocal Group: 1 Beatles; 2 Rolling Stones. Vocal Personality: 1 John Lennon; 2 Cliff Richard. TV/Radio Programme: 1 *Top Of The Pops* 2 *Ready Steady Go!* DJ: 1 Jimmy Savile; 2 David Jacobs. New Singer: 1 Donovan; 2 Chris Andrews. New Group: 1 Seekers; 2 Walker Brothers. UK Single: 1 '(I Can't Get No) Satisfaction' – Rolling Stones; 2 'Help' – Beatles.

This, the 14th NME poll, pulled in more votes than any previously held.

## THE GRAPEVINE

- New fathers: Don Everly has a daughter, and Roger Miller a son.

- A pair of Paul McCartney's gloves fetched 22 shillings ($3.50) when auctioned for charity in England.

- Publisher Simon & Schuster has ordered a 13th US printing of John Lennon's book *In His Own Write*, which has now sold 213,000 copies in America; the follow-up *A Spaniard In The Works* has US sales of 95,000 to date.

Tom Wilson (above) to produce Animals

## WILSON TO PRODUCE ANIMALS AFTER DYLAN AND S&G

US Producer Tom Wilson, who produced Bob Dylan's first rock-influenced album 'Bringing It All Back Home' and its hit single 'Subterranean Homesick Blues' earlier this year, and is also responsible for Simon & Garfunkel's current US chart-topper 'The Sound Of Silence', will undertake a UK assignment in the New Year.

Wilson has been engaged as The Animals' producer for their future Decca (UK) and MGM (US) material, following the group's recent split from Mickie Most. He will arrive in London on January 5, to begin work with the Animals on a new single – already set by Decca for an February 11 UK release.

. . . as Mickie Most leaves them

### CHARTS

| | |
|---|---|
| US45 | Turn! Turn! Turn!<br>*Byrds* |
| USLP | Whipped Cream & Other Delights<br>*Herb Alpert & The Tijuana Brass* |
| UK45 | The Carnival Is Over<br>*Seekers* |
| UKLP | The Sound Of Music<br>*Soundtrack* |

— WEEK 2 —

| | |
|---|---|
| US45 | Turn! Turn! Turn!<br>*Byrds* |
| USLP | Whipped Cream & Other Delights<br>*Herb Alpert & The Tijuana Brass* |
| UK45 | We Can Work It Out/Day Tripper<br>*Beatles* |
| UKLP | Rubber Soul<br>*Beatles* |

— WEEK 3 —

| | |
|---|---|
| US45 | Turn! Turn! Turn!<br>*Byrds* |
| USLP | Whipped Cream & Other Delights<br>*Herb Alpert & The Tijuana Brass* |
| UK45 | We Can Work It Out/Day Tripper<br>*Beatles* |
| UKLP | Rubber Soul<br>*Beatles* |

— WEEK 4 —

| | |
|---|---|
| US45 | Over & Over<br>*Dave Clark Five* |
| USLP | Whipped Cream & Other Dlights<br>*Herb Alpert & The Tijuana Brass* |
| UK45 | We Can Work It Out/Day Tripper<br>*Beatles* |
| UKLP | Rubber Soul<br>*Beatles* |

The cause of all the trouble – The Animals, with Alan Price (right) leaving the group

*George and Patti embark on honeymoon*

## CHARTS

|  |  |
|---|---|
| US45 | Sounds Of Silence *Simon & Garfunkel* |
| USLP | Whipped Cream & Other Delights *Herb Alpert & The Tijuana Brass* |
| UK45 | We Can Work It Out/Day Tripper *Beatles* |
| UKLP | Rubber Soul *Beatles* |

— WEEK 2 —

|  |  |
|---|---|
| US45 | We Can Work It Out *Beatles* |
| USLP | Rubber Soul *Beatles* |
| UK45 | We Can Work It Out/Day Tripper *Beatles* |
| UKLP | Rubber Soul *Beatles* |

— WEEK 3 —

|  |  |
|---|---|
| US45 | We Can Work It Out *Beatles* |
| USLP | Rubber Soul *Beatles* |
| UK45 | Keep On Running *Spencer Davis Group* |
| UKLP | Rubber Soul *Beatles* |

— WEEK 4 —

|  |  |
|---|---|
| US45 | Sounds Of Silence *Simon & Garfunkel* |
| USLP | Rubber Soul *Beatles* |
| UK45 | Keep on Running *Spencer Davis Group* |
| UKLP | Rubber Soul *Beatles* |

— WEEK 5 —

|  |  |
|---|---|
| US45 | We Can Work It Out *Beatles* |
| USLP | Rubber Soul *Beatles* |
| UK45 | Keep On Running *Spencer Davis Group* |
| UKLP | Rubber Soul *Beatles* |

# GEORGE HARRISON MARRIES

Beatle George Harrison became the third married member of the group when he wed Pattie Boyd on January 21, in a quiet Friday morning ceremony near his Epsom home.

The wedding was a surprise not only to press and public, but also to most of the bride and groom's friends and relatives. Although the couple (who had first met in 1964 on the set of *A Hard Day's Night*, in which model/actress Pattie had a bit part) had made their decision some four weeks earlier, they kept the date a secret almost until it arrived.

George's parents had four day's notice to travel from Liverpool. The other Beatles were also told, but Paul McCartney was the only one present since both John and Ringo and their families were on holiday.

Asked at the subsequent press conference how they had managed to keep it a secret, George replied: 'Simple – we didn't tell anyone.'

He told the press: 'Just before Christmas, we were in the car and Pattie was driving, and I said "How about getting married, then?", and she said "Yes, okay" without taking her eyes off the road. What a driver!

'We've had some great wedding presents, you know. Things for the house and that. Paul gave us a fantastic Chinaman's head that you hang on the wall. We also had a smashin' antique table from Brian Epstein.'

## MOTOWN SELLS IN MILLIONS

The Detroit-based Motown Record Corporation outpaced all other companies in the US during 1965 in total sales of singles. The label, which describes itself as 'The Sound Of Young America', took the top-selling tag away from Capitol, which led the field in 1964, thanks to its success with The Beatles.

Through the year, Motown had million-selling singles by The Four Tops ('I Can't Help Myself'), The Temptations ('My Girl'), Jr Walker & The All-Stars ('Shotgun'), and no less than three by The Supremes ('Stop! In The Name Of Love', 'Back In My Arms Again' and 'I Hear A Symphony'), while Marvin Gaye, The Miracles and Martha & The Vandellas also enjoyed Top 10 hits.

Remarkable aspects of this success are that Motown has had no share in the flood of British acts which has found US success in 1965, and that the label is an entirely independently run and distributed black-owned record company, with no ties to any of the corporate major US labels.

## THE GRAPEVINE

■ The Merseybeats are now down to two members, Tony Crane and Billy Kinsley, who will continue as vocalists, abbreviating their name to The Merseys. Former group colleagues, John Banks and Aaron Williams, have quit the business.

■ John Carter has left The Ivy League, though he will continue to write songs with Ken Lewis, who remains with the group. The duo are also setting up a production company.

*Motown best-sellers The Supremes in action*

## OLDHAM'S STONES DOCUMENTARY

Manager Andrew Oldham has made an hour-long documentary on the Rolling Stones, entitled *Charlie's My Darling*. It was filmed when the group were touring Ireland in the Autumn, and features both concert footage and backstage interviews.

Brian Jones discusses his fear of marriage, Charlie Watts his limitations as a musician, while Mick Jagger impersonates Elvis Presley! The film is being offered to TV companies.

# CHAD AND JEREMY SEEK US CITIZENSHIP

British duo Chad Stuart and Jeremy Clyde have applied for US citizenship, a radical decision following two years of considerable record and TV success in America, unmatched at home.

Most of the duo's immediate commitments require their availability in the US. The main worry in their minds is that, as US citizens, they would become eligible for military service. They have no wish to end up defending their adopted country in Vietnam.

Jeremy Clyde told reporters in Hollywood: 'We really don't know what to do. If we live in Britain, we pay double taxes, and have to go through so much red tape to come over to the US. But if we move here, we may end up in the army!'

It is thought to be impracticable to arrange constant renewal of work permits to film an ongoing TV series. As currently projected, this will feature the duo as English actors stranded in Texas with a trunkful of costumes but no money.

Various episodes will show them trying to work their way across the US to New York, and thence to the UK, making use of the theatrical outfits.

There is only one Them, as far as the record-buying public is concerned, the original group from Belfast fronted by Van Morrison (second from left)

## THEM AND THEM AGAIN

The existence of two groups called Them has led to a bitter dispute between two agencies, and could also affect record releases.

The first Them is managed by Dorothy Solomon (also manager of The Bachelors), and includes vocalist Van Morrison and guitarist Alan Henderson, both of whom were on the hits 'Baby Please Don't Go' and 'Here Comes The Night'. The namesake group is managed by Ray Henderson who, in January, registered the band as Them Ltd., in an effort to prevent the Morrison-led group using the name.

In retaliation, Dorothy Solomon's husband Phil registered Fortunes Ltd. and Pinkerton's Assorted Colours Ltd. (both names of acts represented by Henderson's Them agency), giving and assigning the names to two little-known Birmingham groups. Solomon then informed Decca's Sir Edward Lewis that unless all records by groups using those names were withdrawn, he would sue for 'substantial damages'.

Solomon said: 'Our Them have lost worldwide bookings because of confusion caused by this other group. I intend to cause similar confusion by booking out duplicate Fortunes and Pinkerton's Colours – after all, I've registered the names. I shall only give way when I have compensation from King's Agency for all the work we have lost, and a promise that they will drop the name.'

The real Pinkerton's Assorted Colours

## CHARTS

| | | |
|---|---|---|
| US45 | USLP | UK45 | UKLP |

| | |
|---|---|
| My Love | *Petula Clark* |
| Rubber Soul | *Beatles* |
| Michelle | *Overlanders* |
| Rubber Soul | *Beatles* |

— WEEK 2 —

| | |
|---|---|
| My Love | *Petula Clark* |
| Rubber Soul | *Beatles* |
| These Boots Are Made For Walkin' | *Nancy Sinatra* |
| Rubber Soul | *Beatles* |

— WEEK 3 —

| | |
|---|---|
| Lightnin' Strikes | *Lou Christie* |
| Rubber Soul | *Beatles* |
| 19th Nervous Breakdown | *Rolling Stones* |
| Rubber Soul | *Beatles* |

— WEEK 4 —

| | |
|---|---|
| These Boots Are Made For Walkin' | *Nancy Sinatra* |
| Rubber Soul | *Beatles* |
| 19th Nervous Breakdown | *Rolling Stones* |
| Rubber Soul | *Beatles* |

## STAR QUOTE

### TOM JONES

on his formative years

'In my teens, we were all very aggressive. Our girls were aggressive, too. They wore a lot of make-up and were very tough. That's the kind of thing I grew up with, and it's left its mark.'

The macho boyo, Tom Jones

# 1966

## WHO SINGLE: A LEGAL MATTER

The Who's single 'Substitute', the first under the group's new deal with the Reaction label via Polydor, was released in the UK on Friday, March 4, and quickly set off a complex chain of events.

Firstly, The Who's previous label Brunswick – marketed by UK Decca – rushed out a Who single of its own, coupling 'A Legal Matter' from their debut LP with 'Instant Party' – a track formerly scheduled as the group's next A-side under the title 'Circles'.

A day later, producer Shel Talmy, responsible for every Who recording prior to their Reaction debut, successfully applied for a temporary injunction to prevent Polydor from marketing 'Substitute'. His complaint was that 'Instant Party' was also on the B-side of the Brunswick single, and his copyright was thus infringed.

Polydor was served with the injunction on March 9, and stopped pressing the record. In the London High Court on the afternoon of the same day, counsel for Polydor told the judge that a sale ban might kill the chances of the record 'which in less than a week has entered the New Musical Express chart (compiled that morning) at No. 19, and is expected to rise to No. 1.'

On Monday 14, Polydor circumvented the injunction by releasing a new pressing of 'Substitute' with a different B-side, an instrumental track titled 'Waltz For A Pig'.

Then on March 18, the injunction on the original pressing was removed by the High Court, and Polydor was able to shift a warehouse stock of 40,000.

*Confusion surrounds The Who as rival record companies wrangle over their rights*

## LULU LOSES LUVVERS

Lulu and her backing group The Luvvers are to split in mid-March after a tour of Poland.

It has been decided that the former romance between the singer and Luvvers' guitarist Alec Bell is likely to hold back their careers if they continue working together, though a split was not originally planned until May.

The group will henceforth record for Decca in their own right, with Bell as lead singer.

## THE GRAPEVINE

■ According to a New York Times article, CBS is close to developing a disc which can reproduce pictures on a TV screen, as well as sound. The price of a disc is likely to be low – around the retail cost of a 45rpm single.

■ Drummer Barry Jenkins has left The Nashville Teens to join The Animals in place of John Steele.

■ Paul McCartney has owned up to writing Peter & Gordon's 'Woman' under the pseudonym of 'Bernard Webb'.

### CHARTS

| | |
|---|---|
| US45 | Ballad Of The Green Berets *Sgt. Barry Sadler* |
| USLP | Going Places *Herb Alpert & The Tijuana Brass* |
| UK45 | 19th Nervous Breakdown *Rolling Stones* |
| UKLP | The Sound Of Music *Soundtrack* |

— WEEK 2 —

| | |
|---|---|
| US45 | Ballad Of The Green Berets *Sgt. Barry Sadler* |
| USLP | Ballads Of The Green Berets *Sgt. Barry Sadler* |
| UK45 | I Can't Let Go *Hollies* |
| UKLP | The Sound Of Music *Soundtrack* |

— WEEK 3 —

| | |
|---|---|
| US45 | Ballad Of The Green Berets *Sgt. Barry Sadler* |
| USLP | Ballads Of The Green Berets *Sgt. Barry Sadler* |
| UK45 | The Sun Ain't Gonna Shine Anymore *Walker Brothers* |
| UKLP | The Sound Of Music *Soundtrack* |

— WEEK 4 —

| | |
|---|---|
| US45 | Ballad Of The Green Berets *Sgt. Barry Sadler* |
| USLP | Ballads Of The Green Berets *Sgt. Barry Sadler* |
| UK45 | The Sun Ain't Gonna Shine Anymore *Walker Brothers* |
| UKLP | The Sound Of Music *Soundtrack* |

## NANCY GETS 'WRONG' GOLD !

Nancy Sinatra was presented with a gold disc to mark over a million US sales of 'These Boots Are Made For Walkin'' in a ceremony at Hollywood's It's Boss Club.

Because the actual gold record of 'Boots' failed to arrive in time from New York, British expatriot dj 'Lord Tim' Hudson actually presented Nancy with the similar award earned by Dean Martin (his prospective father-in-law) for 'Everybody Loves Somebody'.

*Don't drop her – she shouts!*

*Nancy's boots made for dancing?*

# DUSTY DEMANDS NEW US LABEL

Dusty Springfield has announced that she will not record again until her UK record label Philips Records releases her from the American part of her contract, which until now has seen her US releases on the Philips-owned Mercury label.

With 'You Don't Have To Say You Love Me' giving the singer her first UK No. 1, Mercury president Irving Green has flown to London to try to sort out the situation, but Dusty's manager Vic Billings says that she is determined to have a new US label.

It seems likely that Philips will indeed accede to the demand and release her – possibly to Atlantic.

Dusty said: 'I have no real quarrel with the company in Britain, but in the US they have done virtually nothing to promote me or my records. Most of the kids there seem to have no idea when I have a disc on release – in fact, they write telling me how badly I am being promoted in America!

'I've just had an 18-page letter from a fan in Los Angeles about the situation, and it was heartbreaking to read.

*Dusty defects*

'Anyway, I am totally dissatisfied with the whole set-up in the States, and I'm just not going to record again until something is done. Some people might say this attitude is unfair to my fans in Britain, but the present situation is unfair to the fans in the States, too, and I have to think of them as well.'

## BRITISH WALKER BROTHERS!

US hitmaking trio The Walker Brothers, based for a year in Britain and currently topping the UK chart with 'The Sun Ain't Gonna Shine Anymore' are to relinquish their American citzenship and apply for Biritsh nationality.

Manager Maurice King announced that the three individual Walkers – vocalists Scott Engel and John Maus and drummer Gary Leeds – have already begun the complicated procedure of applying for British naturalization, although they will probably have to live in the UK for a further two years to establish the necessary residential qualification.

Scott is quoted as saying: 'It takes a long time for the whole thing to become finalized – but even if we are not still at the top

*Walker Bros to become Brits?*

in Britain when everything is completed, it will make no difference. We like it here, and we intend to stay for good. Once, being American helped an artist in the UK; now it means nothing at all. We are essentially British stars.'

## THE GRAPEVINE

■ Drummer Chris Curtis has left The Searchers, following a five-week absence, suffering from 'overstrain'. He has joined Pye Records as a producer, and label boss Louis Benjamin has given him a virtually free hand to record what he likes – including himself as a soloist or with a new group.

The Searchers' new drummer, meanwhile, is John Blunt, Curtis's recent tour stand-in.

# MAY 1966

# MOON DOWN, BUT NOT OUT

Who drummer Keith Moon has withdrawn a threat to leave the group and take bass player John Entwistle with him, five days after he announced that he was quitting following an onstage incident which left him injured.

On Friday May 20, the group was playing at the Ricky Tick club in Newbury, UK, when Pete Townshend accidentally struck Moon in the face with his guitar as they went through a 'wild' routine on 'My Generation'. The drummer collapsed on his kit, and ended up with a black eye and a knee injury which required three stitches.

In the aftermath, he told a reporter that he and John Entwistle were both getting out of The Who to work as a duo.

A temporary drummer deputized on the next few days' dates while Moon recovered from his injuries at his London home, but by Wednesday he had relented over quitting, and the group's agent Robert Stigwood said: 'Everything has been sorted out. Keith will probably be back for concerts this weekend in Blackpool and Morecambe.'

*Spector, currently in the studio with Ike and Tina Turner*

Col. Parker looking in appropriately expansive mood

## THE GRAPEVINE

■ Colonel Tom Parker's office has categorically denied a report that Elvis Presley has given 22-year old Priscilla Beaulieu – who has been living for some time in Memphis with Presley's grandmother – a diamond engagement ring and a house near Hollywood.

■ Worldwide sales of the *West Side Story* film soundtrack album have topped five million.

■ Frank Sinatra recorded a cover of 'Downtown' with Petula Clark standing in the studio beside him.

## SPECTOR VS RIGHTEOUS BROTHERS

Phil Spector has filed a three and one half million dollar lawsuit against The Righteous Brothers, who have left his Philles label to sign to Verve, a subsidiary of MGM. Spector commented: 'If they can get out of this contract, then no contract in the record business is worth the paper it's written on.'

## STONES TO ACT INDIVIDUALLY IN FILM PLAN

A new film project has been announced for The Rolling Stones. This previously-slated *Back, Behind And In Front*, on which the group were originally to have started work in April, has now been scrapped, and instead they have bought the movie rights to *Only Lovers Left Alive*, a British novel written by teacher David Wallis, which details an imaginary conquest of the country by its violent and rebellious youth.

Andrew Oldham says that The Stones will NOT be portrayed as a group in the film, but that Mick, Charlie, Keith, Brian and Bill will all be playing individual character roles. However, there will be several featured songs penned by Jagger and Richard – who are to write the whole score – and the group will record the soundtrack in Los Angeles at the end of their American tour in late July.

Filming is planned to start in Britain in August, as soon as The Stones return from the US.

# ROY ORBISON'S WIFE DIES IN CRASH

Claudette Orbison, 26-year-old wife of singer Roy (and inspiration behind 'Claudette', the song he wrote for the Everly Brothers in 1958), died on June 7, two hours after her motorcycle was in collision with a truck on the road between Nashville and the Orbisons' home in Hendersonville, Tenn.

Roy and Claudette were riding together on separate machines when the crash occurred, and he witnessed the tragedy. The couple, reunited a few months ago after an earlier separation, had just begun a holiday at home following a lengthy bout of overseas touring.

Roy himself had a minor motorbike injury while performing in Britain last month, and Claudette had flown to join him for the remainder of the tour (including the all-star NME poll winners concert in London) to ensure that all was well. She died exactly four weeks after accompanying him home for a well-earned rest.

## CLIFF'S CLUB CLOSES

Cliff Richard's official fan club, which has been running for nine years and has 42,000 members, is to wind down and close completely in April 1967 — the same month in which Cliff, at the end of a London Palladium season, is expected to semi-retire to undertake a three-year college course in divinity.

Jane Vane (22), who has run the club since its inception, has relinquished her post as secretary, but will oversee the closure.

## CHARTS

| | |
|---|---|
| US45 | **When A Man Loves A Woman** *Percy Sledge* |
| USLP | **What Now My Love** *Herb Alpert & The Tijuana Brass* |
| UK45 | **Strangers In The Night** *Frank Sinatra* |
| UKLP | **Aftermath** *Rolling Stones* |

—— W E E K 2 ——

| | |
|---|---|
| US45 | **Paint It Black** *Rolling Stones* |
| USLP | **What Now My Love** *Herb Alpert & The Tijuana Brass* |
| UK45 | **Strangers In The Night** *Frank Sinatra* |
| UKLP | **Aftermath** *Rolling Stones* |

—— W E E K 3 ——

| | |
|---|---|
| US45 | **Paint It Black** *Rolling Stones* |
| USLP | **What Now My Love** *Herb Alpert & The Tijuana Brass* |
| UK45 | **Strangers In The Night** *Frank Sinatra* |
| UKLP | **Aftermath** *Rolling Stones* |

—— W E E K 4 ——

| | |
|---|---|
| US45 | **Paperback Writer** *Beatles* |
| USLP | **What Now My Love** *Herb Alpert & The Tijuana Brass* |
| UK45 | **Paperback Writer** *Beatles* |
| UKLP | **Aftermath** *Rolling Stones* |

David 'Screaming Lord' Sutch

## MU IN TV MIME BAN

Britain's Musicians' Union has tightened its stranglehold on the country's pop music by successfully ordering an all-out ban on TV shows which allow artists to mime to their records. Both the BBC and Independent Television have given in to the union's 'no miming' demand, and the previously widespread practice will end on July 31.

One immediate effect is that BBC-1's *A Whole Scene Going*, due to return for a new series on September 8 after a summer recess, has been scrapped. *Top Of The Pops*, however, will continue by having artists remake their records in the BBC's studios the day before the show, and mime to the new tapes during transmission.

The union allows this procedure, since accompanying musicians thereby receive additional work, even though it is being recorded.

MU general secretary Hardie Ratcliffe says that the mime ban is something which groups as a whole should welcome, and claims: 'We believe this move will open the door for hundreds of groups who have never had the chance to appear on TV, just because they have not made a record.'

## THE GRAPEVINE

■ The Beatles' LP 'Yesterday And Today' has been delayed in the US because of a last-minute decision by Capitol Records to change the sleeve design. Early reactions to a shot of the group surrounded by chunks of meat and broken dolls convinced the label that controversy might ensue.

■ British singer Geneveve has called off her brief engagement to eccentric rocker Screaming Lord Sutch, to concentrate on her singing career.

# 1966

# HAYDOCK SACKED FROM HOLLIES

Bass guitarist Eric Haydock has left The Hollies, and despite widespread reports that he disliked touring and wanted to spend more time at home, he was actually sacked from the group.

Hollie Graham Nash explained: 'We gave him a month's notice before we went on holiday – it was joint decision. Musically we had no complaint, but his unreliability got to the point where we didn't know whether we were coming or going.

'We had to get an emergency replacement for Eric immediately before our trip to Sweden, and he was also missing from the session for "Bus Stop". The uncertainty had been getting us down, particularly when we knew we were all as tired and overworked as he was. After all, the bass player does the least work in the group.'

Admitting his sacking, Haydock said: 'It's a raw deal, and I'm consulting my lawyers. I wanted a few days off in November, when my wife is expecting a baby. It's true that I've missed a few dates through illness, but on each occasion I've produced a doctor's certificate.'

The new Hollies bassist is 23-year old Bern Calvert from Nelson, Lancashire, who deputized for Haydock on the group's recent European jaunt.

## JONES QUITS MANFREDS TO GO SOLO

Following the announcement of their recording move from EMI's HMV to Philips' Fontana label, Manfred Mann announced at a press conference on July 6 that lead singer Paul Jones would leave the group at the end of the month. His replacement is Michael D'Abo, formerly with A Band Of Angels.

Jones makes his final live appearance with the Manfreds at Blackpool South Pier on July 31, and D'Abo will join the group when they fly to Copenhagen for live work a week later. He has aleady taken over on the first recording sessions for the new label, and sings lead on the group's forthcoming single, a cover of Bob Dylan's 'Just Like A Woman', produced by Shel Talmy.

Jones, meanwhile, remains

*Mike D'Abo, seated centre*

with HMV as a soloist, and will continue to work with producer John Burgess. He has also been signed to co-star with another novice actor – model Jean Shrimpton – in a film for controversial director Peter Watkins (who made *The War Game*), which will go into production on August 1, mostly on location in London and Birmingham, UK.

Titled *Privilege*, it concerns a pop singer who is manipulated into a cultural phenomenon.

*Leaving to do his own thing, ex-Manfred vocalist Paul Jones*

*'Sheila' hitman Tommy Roe*

## THE GRAPEVINE

■ Righteous Brother Bill Medley had an operation on July 12 to remove nodes from his vocal chords. Back home, he explained (via a note): 'I won't be allowed to talk at all for a week, and then I'll be another four weeks gradually getting back to full-time singing'.

■ Tommy Roe has been screen-tested for the movie *The Cool Ones*, which has a Lee Hazlewood score.

# LENNON IN THE WARS

John Lennon is to split from The Beatles for two months – just days after the group return to the UK from their current US tour. He has been offered a part in the Second World War film *How I Won The War*, which is to be made on location in West Germany and Spain during September and October by director Dick Lester, who made The Beatles' *A Hard Day's Night* and *Help!* movies.

Meanwhile, when The Beatles arrived in Chicago at the opening of their 1966 US tour, controversy surrounded them. Remarks made by John Lennon in a UK press interview earlier in the year, to the effect that The Beatles were currently more popular than Jesus, were hardly noticed at home. However, following belated US syndication, the comments have upset many religious-minded Americans, and ignited fury among some who choose to conceal their own bigotry behind religion, notably the Ku Klux Klan, which has leaped in with Beatle record-burning bonfires, denouncing him as the devil's emissary and the group in general as foreign undesirables.

Lennon took the bit between his teeth and, for the sake of good relations on the tour, publicly apologized at a Chicago press conference to those he had offended. He was sorry for having expressed himself poorly, and thus giving mistaken impressions, and added that he would be more guarded in future. He also made clear, however, that he defended his right to hold controversial opinions.

# HOLLIES FOR HOLLYWOOD?

Partly as a result of a chewing gum TV ad. made by The Hollies, currently being seen across the US, the group have been offered a Hollywood movie at the end of the year.

It would feature Graham Nash and Allan Clarke playing the lead parts, with the whole group in acting roles, as well as music by The Hollies.

However, the group's agent Colin Hogg commented: 'I must emphasise it's far from definite, and cannot be agreed until I have approved both terms and script.'

## THE GRAPEVINE

■ The Lovin' Spoonful have revealed that 'Summer In The City' is proving a pain to perform on stage. Zal Yanovsky says: 'It turns out that while Steve is playing organ, poor John has to play piano, which he can only do by concentrating – and not singing. So Joe sings lead when we do it live.

■ Jeff Beck's contraction of severe tonsillitis has caused The Yardbirds to cancel their appearance at the UK's Windsor Jazz & Blues Festival.

*'Summer In The City' during a recent television performance*

*A long way from home Manchester's Hollies are Hollywood bound*

## CHARTS

| | | |
|---|---|---|
| US45 | Wild Thing | *Troggs* |
| USLP | Yesterday & Today | *Beatles* |
| UK45 | With A Girl Like You | *Troggs* |
| UKLP | The Sound Of Music | *Soundtrack* |

--- WEEK 2 ---

| | | |
|---|---|---|
| US45 | Summer In The City | *Lovin' Spoonful* |
| USLP | Yesterday & Today | *Beatles* |
| UK45 | With A Girl Like You | *Troggs* |
| UKLP | Revolver | *Beatles* |

--- WEEK 3 ---

| | | |
|---|---|---|
| US45 | Summer In The City | *Lovin' Spoonful* |
| USLP | Yesterday & Today | *Beatles* |
| UK45 | Yellow Submarine/Eleanor Rigby | *Beatles* |
| UKLP | Revolver | *Beatles* |

--- WEEK 4 ---

| | | |
|---|---|---|
| US45 | Summer In The City | *Lovin' Spoonful* |
| USLP | Yesterday & Today | *Beatles* |
| UK45 | Yellow Submarine/Eleanor Rigby | *Beatles* |
| UKLP | Revolver | *Beatles* |

# NAPOLEON XIV – WHO IS THAT MASKED MAN?

As well as John Lennon, another hitmaker causing controversy is Napoleon XIV, whose surprise smash 'They're Coming To Take Me Away, Ha-Haaa!' takes a comic look at mental illness. Radio stations on both sides of the Atlantic have banned the disc as offensive, but this has done nothing to halt its sales.

The artist is now revealed to be New York recording engineer Jerry Samuels, who made the disc himself and then had its commercial potential spotted by Warner/Reprise's George Lee.

# KINKS: KONTRACTUAL KOMPLICATIONS, AND QUAIFE KWITS

*Ray Davis (top) and the other Kinks look to unsettled times in the immediate future*

A deadlock over The Kinks' recordings between the group, its management and Pye Records may mean an indefinite postponement of their next album and single.

The group are currently in the US Top 20 with 'Sunny Afternoon', which was issued in June in the UK and became a No. 1 hit. However, a new single is not expected before late November, and the 16-track LP 'Kinks', originally scheduled for an August UK release, will not now appear at all until business negotiations are concluded between their US business director Allen Klein and Pye managing director Louis Benjamin.

The deadlock is said to be similar to that currently preventing Pye from releasing new Donovan material in the UK – including his US chart-topper 'Sunshine Superman'.

Meanwhile, The Kinks have also lost an original member. After weeks of rumours, manager Robert Wace confirmed that bass guitarist Pete Quaife, who has been unable to play with the group for three months because of injuries sustained in a road accident, has now left permanently. He seems likely to settle in Copenhagen, and is rumoured to be marrying a Danish girl, Annette Paustian.

Wace says: 'I feel that Pete may have made the wrong decision to leave – but it is his decision. It could be at least six months before he would have been well enough to rejoin the group, and he has decided instead to make his career in other fields.'

John Dalton, who has been deputizing for Quaife, has now joined The Kinks as his permanent replacement. One report suggests that Quaife may be joining British European Airways' advertising department as a designer.

## ORBISON: 'TOO SOON NOT SICK!'

Roy Orbison is unhappy that people are making the wrong connection between new single 'Too Soon To Know' – a ballad about loss – and the recent death of his wife Claudette.

He told the press: 'After the accident, I didn't care what was released . . . there were several possibilities, but the content of others, like "You'll Never Be Sixteen Again", was, under the circumstances, even worse.

'I didn't want to go into the studio to record something new, so I just said "release whatever you think is best" – and that was "Too Soon To Know".

'Every song I do from now on could be subject to misinterpretation, but anyone who thinks that "Too Soon To Know" was released at this time so that I could make sympathy-money, must have a sick mind!'

*The Big 'O' – 'Too Soon' not too soon*

### THE GRAPEVINE

■ Drummer Barry Jenkins will be the only one of the existing Animals to remain with Eric Burdon in the singer's soon-to-be formed 'new' Animals; Hilton Valentine and Chas Chandler are both moving into production.

■ Georgie Fame is parting from his long-time backing group the Blue Flames, following a final gig in Amsterdam on October 1.

*Georgie Fame – extinguishing The Flames?*

# AUSTRALIA AND US CENSOR UK DISCS

Two current UK Top 10 singles are running into difficulties elsewhere in the world. Dozens of US radio stations have banned Dave Dee, Dozy, Beaky, Mick & Tich's 'Bend It' because the lyrics are considreed too suggestive, and the group have responded by recording a new version in London with a different set of words.

The tapes of this have been flown to the US for rush release, while the original single has been withdrawn.

Meanwhile, in Australia, the Commercial Broadcasting Federation is debating whether to approve a total ban on the Troggs' 'I Can't Control Myself' – which, if effected, will mean not only no radio or TV plays, but dealers being prevented from selling it, too.

This would be the first complete state censoring of a pop record in Australia. The Troggs' lead singer Reg Presley commented: 'Naturally we're disappointed, but there's no point in getting angry about it.'

Dave Dee, Dozy, Beaky, Mick and Tich: new version of 'Bend It' to combat suggestive allegations

Moody Blues – on hold pending change of Laine

## WHO RECORDING ROW FINALLY ENDS

The Who have amicably settled their differences with their former producer Shel Talmy, and the group's long-awaited second LP, provisionally titled 'Jigsaw Puzzle', will be released in the UK in December on Track – a new label being launched by Polydor principally for Who recordings.

The Who's next release, the EP 'Ready Steady Who', will appear in the UK on Robert Srigwood's Reaction label (as have their last two singles 'Substitute' and 'I'm A Boy'), and it competes with a same-week release on Brunswick of 'La-La-La Lies', the third single to be extracted from the Talmy-produced 'My Generation' album since The Who left their original label.

## STAR QUOTE

### ERIC CLAPTON

*'If I get any more popular, I shall have to have plastic surgery and get myself a Dr Kildare face, but by that time they'll probably have Scott Engel rubber masks for everyone anyway!'*

## CHARTS

| | | |
|---|---|---|
| US45 | Cherish | Association |
| USLP | Revolver | Beatles |
| UK45 | Distant Drums | Jim Reeves |
| UKLP | The Sound Of Music | Soundtrack |

WEEK 2

| | | |
|---|---|---|
| US45 | Cherish | Association |
| USLP | Revolver | Beatles |
| UK45 | Distant Drums | Jim Reeves |
| UKLP | The Sound Of Music | Soundtrack |

WEEK 3

| | | |
|---|---|---|
| US45 | Reach Out, I'll Be There | Four Tops |
| USLP | Revolver | Beatles |
| UK45 | Distant Drums | Jim Reeves |
| UKLP | The Sound Of Music | Soundtrack |

WEEK 4

| | | |
|---|---|---|
| US45 | Reach Out, I'll Be There | Four Tops |
| USLP | Supremes A GoGo | Supremes |
| UK45 | Distant Drums | Jim Reeves |
| UKLP | The Sound Of Music | Soundtrack |

WEEK 5

| | | |
|---|---|---|
| US45 | 96 Tears | ? & The Mysterians |
| USLP | Supremes A GoGo | Supremes |
| UK45 | Reach Out, I'll Be There | Four Tops |
| UKLP | The Sound Of Music | Soundtrack |

## McCARTNEY TO SCORE HAYLEY MILLS FILM

Paul McCartney is writing the musical score for *Wedlocked*, a new Boulting Brothers film starring Hayley Mills and Hywel Bennett, which has just been completed at England's Shepperton Studios.

Written by Bill Naughton (of *Alfie* fame), it is based on the West End play *All In Good Time*, and concerns the trials of a newlywed couple forced to spend their honeymoon with parents.

Although neither Boulting Brothers nor the Beatles' office will yet provide official confirmation of McCartney's involvement, manager Brian Epstein had already hinted that Paul would soon be undertaking a solo project on the heels of John Lennon's film work in *How I Won The War*.

This will be the first time that McCartney has written officially without his partner, though the duo's exclusive songwriting contract with Northern Songs will still apply to this music.

# MYSTERY OF THE MISSING BOB DYLAN

## ELVIS FIGHTS FLAB

Elvis Presley is reported to have won an important personal battle on November 7 as shooting on his film *Easy Come, Easy Go* wrapped up. He had been concerned about his weight, and while in Hollywood embarked on a programme to trim himself to 170 pounds – his exact weight on leaving the US Army in 1960.

On his last day at the studio, he hit his target.

During filming, Presley was also presented with two awards for being the public figure setting the highest standard for American youth to follow.

*The normally reclusive Bob Dylan has virtually disappeared completely since his mysterious motorcycle smash*

A mystery is deepening over the whereabouts and condition of Bob Dylan, who is now three months into a complete disappearance. In August, he reportedly had an accident on his motorbike, sustaining broken neck vertebrae and concussion, and it was said that a couple of months' convalescence would be necessary before he could resume his normal engagements.

However, Dylan did not simply retreat home to nurse his injuries, but dropped out of sight completely. Many of his closest friends do not know where he is, or even how badly he was hurt.

Such a total absence of news, over such a lengthy period, is now leading to widespread speculation that his accident – and the injuries – were far worse than originally suggested, and that his career is over. His manager Albert Grossman dismisses such suggestions as nonsense, but can give no definite news of Dylan, or of when he is likely to re-emerge.

To further fuel these rumours, the publication of Dylan's book *Tarantula*, previously scheduled for this autumn, has been postponed indefinitely, while a TV special originally slated for mid-November is now cancelled.

It is believed that only two people have known Dylan's whereabouts since the accident – the determinedly silent Grossman, and the singer's close friend, poet Allen Ginsberg. In mid-October, the World Journal Tribune tracked down a hideaway where Dylan had been staying – a rambling old house miles off the beaten track on the Cape Cod peninsula in Massachusetts.

The paper challenged Ginsberg with this information, and he admitted visiting Dylan there and taking him some reading material. However, when a Tribune reporter called at the house, nobody was prepared to say whether or not Dylan was still in residence.

Until this cloak-and-dagger behaviour ends, just what has happened to Dylan will remain a mystery.

## THE GRAPEVINE

■ Pete Quaife has rejoined The Kinks after a five-month absence. John Dalton, whose temporary tenure as bassist was thought permanent, has left. 'Pete thought again, and asked to rejoin' said manager Robert Wace.

■ The Yardbirds are said to be on the verge of splitting as soon as their US tour closes on November 27, with guitarists Jeff Beck (whose health has been suffering) and Jimmy Page likely to leave.

*Elvis's weight – "Easy come, easy go"*

*The Yardbirds, Long plagued by health problems*

# TOM JONES: GOODBYE DECCA, HELLO MOTOWN?

Tom Jones may leave British Decca to accept an offer from Motown chief Berry Gordy Jr to become his Detroit-based company's first white British artist.

Gordy has long cherished an ambition to sign Jones, and the singer in turn is keen to record at the Motown studios in Detroit. A 'substantial offer' has now been made, and Jones is presently seeking to establish whether he is contractually tied to Decca. His lawyer has already begun discussions with the company.

Jones signed to Decca in July 1964, and has subsequently released nine singles and three albums. A spokesman for the label claimed that his contract does not, in fact, expire until 1970. Meanwhile, his current single, 'Green, Green Grass Of Home', is topping the UK chart and has become the biggest-selling British single of 1966. Domestic sales are close to a million, and Jones is expected to become the first British artist in Decca's history to win a gold disc for sales entirely at home.

In fact, only three previous singles released by or through Decca have ever topped the million sale in the UK alone, and all were by Americans: Bill Haley ('Rock Around The Clock'), Harry Belafonte ('Mary's Boy Child') and Elvis Presley ('It's Now Or Never').

## IKE AND TINA IN ROAD CRASH

Soul singer Tina Turner suffered minor head injuries, though husband Ike Turner escaped unhurt, when the tour bus carrying the duo and their backing band crashed outside Topeka, Kansas.

Seven band members were detained in hospital, including bassist Ron Johnson with a broken jaw, and drummer Ed Mosley with a back injury.

All equipment was damaged beyond repair, but thanks to borrowed gear and deputy band members, the Turners managed to avoid missing any tour dates.

## THE GRAPEVINE

■ Scott Engel of The Walker Brothers entered a monastery on the Isle Of Wight for ten days' retreat. However, he left after only seven days at the abbot's request as fans had arrived to besiege the monastery gate.

■ The Supremes have turned down $25,000 and a percentage of the box office of a week at Harlem's Apollo Theatre, because they are too tied up with cabaret dates.

## CHARTS

| | | |
|---|---|---|
| US45 | Winchester Cathedral | New Vaudeville Band |
| USLP | The Monkees | Monkees |
| UK45 | Green Green Grass Of Home | Tom Jones |
| UKLP | The Sound Of Music | Soundtrack |
| | WEEK 2 | |
| US45 | Good Vibrations | Beach Boys |
| USLP | The Monkees | Monkees |
| UK45 | Green Green Grass Of Home | Tom Jones |
| UKLP | The Sound Of Music | Soundtrack |
| | WEEK 3 | |
| US45 | Winchester Cathedral | New Vaudeville Band |
| USLP | The Monkees | Monkees |
| UK45 | Green Green Grass Of Home | Tom Jones |
| UKLP | The Sound Of Music | Soundtrack |
| | WEEK 4 | |
| US45 | Winchester Cathedral | New Vaudeville Band |
| USLP | The Monkees | Monkees |
| UK45 | Green Green Grass Of Home | Tom Jones |
| UKLP | The Sound Of Music | Soundtrack |
| | WEEK 5 | |
| US45 | I'm A Believer | Monkees |
| USLP | The Monkees | Monkees |
| UK45 | Green Green Grass Of Home | Tom Jones |
| UKLP | The Sound Of Music | Soundtrack |

## TOP OF THE POLLS FOR 1966

The results of the annual NME readers' poll for this year produce the following winners in the

### DECEMBER 1966

World Section:

*Male singer* – Elvis Presley; *Female singer* – Dusty Springfield; *Vocal group* – Beach Boys; *Musical personality* – Elvis Presley.

In the British-only section: *Male singer* – Cliff Richard; *Female singer* – Dusty Springfield; *Vocal group* – Beatles; *Instrumental group* – Shadows; *New singer* – Stevie Winwood; *New group* – Spencer Davis Group; *Single* – 'Eleanor Rigby' – Beatles; *Disc jockey* – Jimmy Savile; *TV or radio show*: Top Of The Pops (BBC TV).

The Beatles were surprisingly defeated by The Beach Boys as the world's top vocal group by just 101 votes. However, their lead over the second-placed Rolling Stones in the UK group category was a very comfortable 3,838 votes.

*Beach Boys – beat Beatles*

# THE ROLLING STONES – PLAYIN' WITH FIRE

On the night of 12 February 1967, Chief Inspector Gordon Dineley of the West Sussex police and more than a dozen other officers under his command, drove up to the front door of Redlands, a large mansion house set in the heart of a wooded estate a few miles from the English seaside town of Lewes.

Inside, they could hear the sound of music playing loudly. The owner was at home and, from the snatches of conversation and laughter Dineley could make out, he was not alone.

The house was owned by Keith Richards, guitarist of The Rolling Stones – a group which probably most personified every nightmare the establishment had of youth gone wild. And his guests that night included the Stones' lead singer Mick

Jagger – arguably one of the most formidable symbols of that youth – and Marianne Faithful, the beautiful ex-convent girl singer who was a flagrant example of how far good girls could fall in the wrong company.

By the end of the raid, Keith and Mick had been arrested and charged with a variety of offences: Keith for possession of hash and allowing his home to be used for the consumption of illegal drugs, and Mick for possession of four pep pills he'd purchased quite legally in Italy for himself and Marianne.

There was little doubt in everyone's minds that The Rolling Stones had been targeted for some perceived greater good. By catching them red-handed, and then making an example of them, the powers

that be probably assumed they'd be handing out some great moral lesson – don't play with us, 'cos you're playing with fire. Or words to that effect.

If proof were needed of that theory, the fact that the Stones' other guitarist, Brian Jones, was busted by London police on 10 May – the very same day that Mick and Keith first appeared in court to face their charges – is stretching the law of coincidence way beyond breaking point.

When Mick and Keith finally came to trial on 27 June, few believed they wouldn't have the book thrown at them if they were found guilty. They were, and it was.

Mick was sentenced to three months' jail, despite evidence from his doctor that the pills had been bought legally and that he would have prescribed them in any case, had Mick asked for them.

Keith was given a one-year jail sentence and ordered to pay £500 ($1,000) costs. The establishment had won — or so it thought.

Within days, it became clear that it hadn't.

Setting a complete precedent in legal and journalistic terms, *The Times* newspaper (as Establishment as they come) published an editorial comment headed: 'Who Breaks A Butterfly On A Wheel?'.

That editorial, which slammed the severity of Mick and Keith's sentences, was echoed in the next few days by similar articles in other leading British papers. The two Stones were immediately released from prison, pending the result of their appeals.

On 31 July, before the court of the Lord Chief Justice, Mick and Keith were told that their original sentences had been thrown out. Mick's was commuted to a conditional discharge, while Keith was completely acquitted.

That the British establishment should have focussed so much on The Rolling Stones in their search for sacrificial lambs is not surprising when you consider how much a symbol of youth-in-revolt the group were from the very beginning.

They lived with girlfriends, and swapped girlfriends. They wrote songs about sex with no pretence they were talking about true love. They dressed in drag to promote singles. They were a pain in the establishment's butt, no buts about it.

Jagger's obvious intelligence and

undoubted articulacy made him especially dangerous, and he gave great copy on the subject of politics. He was The Bad Boy incarnate — and we all know what happens to bad boys, don't we?

The Stones rolled on, however. And although they've caused their fair share of shock-horror headlines in the intervening years, age and time — and a new wave of angry younger men coming up behind — have meant a steady erosion of their importance as figureheads, symbols or bad boys.

Maybe the establishment won, after all.

*Left: Mick Jagger being driven to Brixton Prison to begin a three-month sentence*

*Below: Girl in the centre of it all, Marianne Faithfull*

*Fame for The Game – or notoriety? BBC chickens out of drug-taking implications in 'The Addicted Man'*

# NME: HANG THE JURY!

In a rare venture into serious newspaper editorial, the NME has been prompted into the following statement on the drugs-in-pop-lyrics issue.

Last Saturday, seven minutes were cut from the BBC Juke Box Jury. The show – pre-recorded the previous weekend – had included a lengthy discussion on The Game's recording 'The Addicted Man' which the Corporation decided was unsuitable for transmission.

The Game's disc is concerned with drug-taking, and the panel had criticised it mercilessly. Rightly so! BUT IF THE BBC IS GOING TO TURN A COLD SHOULDER TO ALL DRUG-TAKING IMPLICATIONS IN POP MUSIC, IT MIGHT AS WELL SCRUB JBJ IMMEDIATELY.

Directly or indirectly, drugs are playing an increasingly prominent part in pop lyrics, and in last week's show the BBC had a golden opportunity – in the hands of five acknowledged pop authorities – to dismiss this trend as distasteful rubbish. But they funked the chance. The object of introducing the new resident panel on JBJ was to allow discs to be discussed informatively and authoritatively. How pointless, then, that the BBC should insist upon the panel's chat being sugar-coated and whitewashed – at the expense of the most topical pop controversy of the day.

'The Addicted Man' should never have been released. But the fact that it is now available in the shops – even though EMI is belatedly trying to suppress it – makes it a matter of public concern. For this reason, producer Albert Stevenson was right to include it in the programme. The pity is that the corporation bigwigs thought otherwise.

If the panel of four disc-jockeys is only to be allowed to pronounce upon obvious hits, with a veto on any subject which might be construed as slightly offensive, Juke Box Jury might as well revert to its time-honoured formula of comedians and glamour girls.

## GOLDEN 1966: BEATLES MINED THE RICHEST ORE

The RIAA's annual survey reveals that 80 Gold Disc awards were made for US record sales during 1966. 57 of them went to albums (awarded for ½ million sales apiece), and 23 to singles (signifying one million sales). Most-awarded act were The Beatles, who won six golds, while The Beach Boys, The Mamas & The Papas, Bill Cosby and Herb Alpert & The Tijuana Brass all collected four apiece.

Triple winners included The Rolling Stones and new sensation, The Monkees, who have had a 100% gold score with their one LP and two singles to date.

# THE GRAPEVINE

■ Col. Tom Parker is reported to have given Elvis Presley a cup of drinking water for his 32nd birthday. 'Elvis drinks more water than anyone else I know; he figures it keeps him healthy'.

■ Donovan has been invited to write music for the British National Theatre production of Shakespeare's *As You Like It* at the Old Vic, to star Laurence Olivier.

*80 Gold Discs – four such for The Beach Boys (pictured) The Mamas & The Papas, Bill Cosby and Herb Alpert & The Tijuana Brass*

# EPSTEIN SHOWS THREATENED BY STRIKE

Beatles manager Brian Epstein has run into trouble with the National Association of Theatrical and Kine Employees, following his sacking of London's Saville Theatre house manager Michael Bullock, which in turn led to a strike threat by the rest of the backstage staff. The union has now ordered its members to boycott Epstein's Sunday concerts at the Saville. This could in turn cause the loss of his NEMS Enterprises' Sunday licence for the venue.

The trouble arose at a Sunday night concert by Chuck Berry, during which two fans climbed on to the stage. Bullock, following local safety regulations,

lowered the curtain while Berry continued to play – to the intense displeasure of the audience, who proceeded to near-riot.

Epstein, a witness to all from his box seat, said after the show that he sided with the audience, and dismissed Bullock.

The union has subsequently called for a withdrawal of Epstein's 'irresponsible attack on his staff', while the promoter himself has said that, if his licence for the Saville should be withdrawn at any time, he would 'simply move the shows to another theatre'. A follow-up Berry concert the next Sunday was scheduled to go ahead as planned.

## MOVIE PLANS FOR BEATLES AND MONKEES

The Beatles have approved a basic script by writer Owen Holder for their third – as yet untitled – film, and await a final screenplay before setting a shooting date. The movie will feature the group in comedy character roles, with a minimum of singing. The main musical element will be the incidental score, penned by Lennon and McCartney.

The Monkees are scheduled to make a full-length feature in Hollywood for Columbia Pictures, probably in the spring. It is suggested that the quartet might not necessarily be playing their TV series characters in the movie.

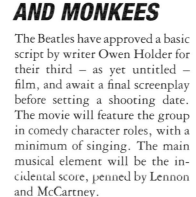

## THE GRAPEVINE

■ P. J. Proby has filed for bankruptcy in Los Angeles, listing debts of £180,000, including £50,000 to the UK Inland Revenue.

■ Girl drummer Honey Lantree has left The Honeycombs to work solo, and is planning a cabaret act. The group is seeking a replacement (preferably female) drummer.

■ The Beatles have been nominated for eight of this year's Grammy Awards.

*Beatles: Acting naturally. Their third movie is planned though the title is not yet confirmed and they are awaiting the final screenplay*

## JOE MEEK GUN DEATH TRAGEDY

Joe Meek, the songwriter/producer who created international smashes like 'Telstar' and hits by artists like The Honeycombs, Heinz, John Leyton and Mike Berry from a home-built and equipped studio in his flat (nicknamed 'The Bathroom') in London's Holloway Road, has been found dead from gun wounds to the head on the floor of that same studio.

The evidence suggests suicide, and it was known that Meek had been depressed for some time as

he fought to come to terms with the rapidly changing styles that have taken over pop music since his 'Telstar' heyday in 1962. His last major successes were with The Honeycombs in 1964 and 1965.

One of Meek's abiding musical inspirations was Buddy Holly, and it has already been suggested as being no coincidence that February 3 – the day on which he apparently chose to take his own life – was the eighth anniversary of Holly's death.

# 1967

*Alpert – Grammy for 'What Now My Love'*

# HENDRIX TO REPRISE

A deal concluded in Los Angeles on March 14 between Warner-Reprise Records and the Jimi Hendrix Experience's co-manager Mike Jeffrey, will give Reprise the North American release rights to Hendrix's recordings, and guarantee the guitarist a signing fee stated to be 'in excess of $50,000'.

Warner-Reprise president Mo Ostin claims that this is the highest advance the company has ever paid for a new artist.

A major publicity campaign, the details of which were being worked out in further discussions between Jeffrey and Ostin, is to promote Hendrix in his native US as 'the greatest talent since The Rolling Stones'.

Said a record company spokesman: 'We shall introduce a com-

pletely new conception in promotion, which should put Jimi right at the top in a very short time.'

## GRAMMIES LIST

The National Academy Of Recording Arts And Sciences' Grammy Awards for 1966, just announced in New York, include the following:

Song Of The Year – 'Michelle' by John Lennon and Paul McCartney.

Record Of The Year – Frank Sinatra's 'Strangers In The Night' (also Best Male Vocal Performance, Best Engineered Record, and Best Accompanying Arrangement).

Album Of The Year – Sinatra again, with 'A Man And His Music'.

Best R&B Record – Ray Charles's 'Crying Time' (also Best R&B Solo Vocal).

Best Contemporary Group Performance – The Mamas & The Papas with 'Monday Monday'.

Best Instrumental Performance – Herb Alpert's 'What Now My Love'.

Best Instrumental Theme – 'Batman' by Neal Hefti.

Best Contemporary Recording – New Vaudeville Band's 'Winchester Cathedral'.

Best Contemporary Solo Vocal – Paul McCartney, on The Beatles 'Eleanor Rigby'.

*The New Vaudeville Band*

# VIETNAM INSPIRES CLIFF & SHADOWS MOVIE DRAMA

The war in Vietnam is the inspiration behind a major film drama featuring Cliff Richard and The Shadows.

As yet untitled, this will be the first dramatic cinema project undertaken by singer and group together, although Cliff did have a (supporting) dramatic role in his movie debut *Serious Charge*, eight years ago.

He is already signed for another in the production he's agreed to make for the Billy Graham Organization during the spring and early summer – also, as yet, untitled. Tentatively scheduled to begin shooting in September, a month or so after the Graham film is completed, the new movie is expected to have acting roles for all the group.

Cliff has said: 'I particularly wanted to make this war story. I hope it will be a believable production showing how a group of young people can become easily involved in warfare, even though they do not want to be. The movie will not actually be *about* Vietnam, but it has been inspired by it, and it will project a similar situation.

'The story will be about the moral issues involved. Four songs will be featured, but the movie won't be a musical by any means – and we don't intend to play up the comedy angle as we did with the H-bomb in *Finders Keepers*.'

## THE GRAPEVINE

■ Rolling Stone Brian Jones has written the incidental soundtrack music for a short, independently-produced feature film, as yet untitled, starring his girlfriend Anita Pallenberg,

■ The Dave Clark Five will have acting roles in a thriller to be produced by Clark's own company in the Autumn; no songs will be featured, but the group will record all the incidental music.

## THE WORLD WANTS SANDIE AFTER EUROVISION WIN

Sandie Shaw won the 1967 Eurovision Song Contest, held in Vienna on April 8, with the Bill Martin/Phil Coulter-penned UK entry 'Puppet On A String'.

It collected 147 votes out of a possible 160, more than double the score of the runner-up Irish entry, Sean Dunphy's 'If I Could Choose'.

Manager Eve Taylor told journalists that offers for Sandie flooded in from all over the world as soon as the contest — watched by an estimated 200 million TV viewers via Eurovision — was over. Bookings worth in excess of £250,000 were currently being considered, but taking up all the offers from places as far apart as Argentina and Czechoslovakia would be impossible, partly because of existing UK and European live commitments.

A co-starring role with Peter Noone of Herman's Hermits in the MGM film *Mrs Brown You've Got A Lovely Daughter* had also been rejected.

Sandie: 'Puppet' winner

# IF DAVY IS DRAFTED, WILL ROONEY'S SON BE A MONKEE?

*Jones: a GI?*

Unconfirmed reports have suggested that Monkee Davy Jones, having earlier been passed A-1 by the US Medical Board, has already received his draft papers, and will shortly be leaving the group.

However, Jones' business representative Hal Cone, speaking to journalists during a London visit, said: 'Davy can't be called up until he has undergone further tests — and in any case, he is seeking reclassification or deferment. He still has to undergo various educational and psychological tests, and cannot be drafted until these are completed.

'We think it probable he will be deferred under a hardship case, as his father is a dependent relative. Davy's appeal is certain to take several weeks, and even if it fails, the draft board will probably allow him to complete existing commitments. If the govern-

ment insists on his drafting, we shall make every effort to ensure it does not take place until 1968.'

Another US report states that 20-year old Tim Rooney, son of actor Mickey and his second wife Betty Jane Rase, is standing by to become Jones' Monkee replacement if he leaves.

The group's UK publicist commented: 'Obviously there is a possibility of Davy being drafted, and they would be foolish not to prepare for this contingency, but we have had no valid confirmation of this story from The Monkees or their management.

'The Monkees would, of course, carry on as a group even if Davy were drafted; the TV series would continue in the same way. There is absolutely no question of them not coming to Britain in June, and we are certain Davy will be with them.'

## THE GRAPEVINE

■ The Move have offered a £200 reward for the recovery of the master tapes of ten songs intended for the group's June LP. The tapes were stolen from their agent's car when it was parked in London's 'Tin Pan Alley', Denmark Street.

■ Reports that Monkee Davy Jones is to play the title role in the film version of *Oliver* have been dismissed as 'rubbish' by the producers.

# ELVIS WEDS HIS ARMY SWEETHEART

Elvis Presley married his long-time girlfriend, 23-year old Priscilla Beaulieu, on May 1 in Las Vegas.

The civil ceremony at the Aladdin Hotel, before 100 invited guests, was conducted by Nevada Supreme Court Justice David Zenoff. Elvis' personal assistant Joe Esposito was his best man, while Priscilla's sister Michelle was her maid of honour.

A reception was held at the hotel, after which the couple left for a Palm Springs honeymoon.

The two first met during Elvis' US Army service in West Germany, late in 1959. Priscilla was the 15-year old stepdaughter of a US Air Force officer. Elvis dated her regularly, and was quoted as saying at the time: 'She is very mature and intelligent.'

For some years since Elvis'

demob, Priscilla has lived at his Graceland mansion with his grandmother. She completed her schooling in Memphis, and on her 18th birthday was given a scarlet Chevrolet and $3000-worth of clothes by Elvis.

Rumours around Memphis suggested that the couple had been married for some time. Colonel Tom Parker denied the rumours.

## WALKER BROTHERS SPLIT TO GO SOLO

Hit-making UK-based American trio The Walker Brothers announced on May 3 – three days after completing a four week tour with a final show at Tooting Granada, London – that they have broken up the team.

Each member is to pursue a solo career. Individual recording contracts are under negotiation, and new backing groups are being formed.

As individuals, Scott Engel, John Maus and Gary Leeds will continue with management company Capable, which – in a joint statement with agent Harold Davidson – said of the split: 'This decision results from an agreed opinion that they have accomplished as much as possible as a group, and that their future pro-gress lies in the freedom to exploit their individual talents. They part on the best of terms, and will continue to work in Britain.'

Carl Wilson still wearing his hat after a late arrival on the Beach Boys current trek of Europe

## BEACH BOY PLAYS TOUR ON BAIL

Carl Wilson of The Beach Boys paid $5000 for a private trans-atlantic jet flight to Dublin, Ireland, to join the rest of the group for the first night of a European tour.

The others had arrived a day earlier, but Wilson had been in custody for five days charged with avoiding the draft and refusing to take the Oath of Allegiance.

At a court hearing in LA, he was released on bail but will face the court again when the group returns to California after the rest of its European dates.

Scott, John and Gary – together for the last time?

| | | CHARTS |
|---|---|---|
| US45 | | Somethin' Stupid *Frank & Nancy Sinatra* |
| USLP | | More Of The Monkees *Monkees* |
| UK45 | | Puppet On A String *Sandie Shaw* |
| UKLP | | The Sound Of Music *Soundtrack* |
| | | WEEK 2 |
| US45 | | The Happening *Supremes* |
| USLP | | More Of The Monkees *Monkees* |
| UK45 | | Puppet On A String *Sandie Shaw* |
| UKLP | | The Sound Of Music *Soundtrack* |
| | | WEEK 3 |
| US45 | | Groovin' *Young Rascals* |
| USLP | | More Of The Monkees *Monkees* |
| UK45 | | Silence Is Golden *Tremeloes* |
| UKLP | | The Sound Of Music *Soundtrack* |
| | | WEEK 4 |
| US45 | | Groovin' *Young Rascals* |
| USLP | | More Of The Monkees *Monkees* |
| UK45 | | Silence Is Golden *Tremeloes* |
| UKLP | | The Sound Of Music *Soundtrack* |

# A LOOK AT SERGEANT PEPPER

The Beatles' eagerly-awaited LP 'Sergeant Pepper's Lonely Hearts Club Band' was released simultaneously around the world on June 1st. NME album reviewer Allen Evans (alter ego of editor Andy Gray) made one of his rare breaks from one-paragraph reviews to appraise it more deeply:

'Trust The Beatles to come up with something different! Their latest LP is a sort of concert, starting with 'Sergeant Pepper's Lonely Hearts Club Band' and ending with it, except for a finale piece called 'A Day In The Life'. In between, we get 10 other tunes, all varied and interesting, with George's sitar-and-song startler 'Within You, Without You' the most memorable.

'But I must admit I also liked Paul's amusing 'When I'm 64' and 'Getting Better', his melo-drama-in-song 'She's Leaving Home', and Ringo's homely 'With A Little Help From My Friends' very much.

'John Lennon and Paul McCartney have written all the songs, except for 'Within You', which is by George Harrison. Whether the album is their best yet, I wouldn't like to say after one hearing. Whether it was worth the five months it took to make, I would also argue. But it is a very good LP, and will sell like hot cakes.'

## MONKEE JONES WILL NOT BE DRAFTED

## BEACH BOYS CUT MONTEREY, BUT FESTIVAL IS A HUGE SUCCESS

The Beach Boys withdrew from the Monterey pop festival, at which they were to have headlined the Saturday evening programme (the first to be sold out), at almost the last minute. The group cited pressure from Capitol for a new single and album as being overwhelming, while Carl Wilson felt that with his trial regarding the draft being due on June 20, he would not be able to concentrate fully on giving a good performance.

The three-day event, with a stellar line-up (including Simon and Garfunkel, Eric Burdon, Johnny Rivers, Lou Rawls and the Association on Friday, Otis Redding, Jefferson Airplane, the Byrds and Big Brother & The Holding Company on Saturday, and the Who, Jimi Hendrix, Ravi Shankar, Buffalo Springfield and organisers the Mamas & Papas on Sunday) attracted a huge audience. By the Friday opening at 9.15pm. it was estimated that there were at least 10,000 people in the auditorium, a similar number of fans around the grounds and booths, and some 20,000 ticketless milling outside.

*Who's a lucky girl?*

### THE GRAPEVINE

- John Entwistle of the Who married former schoolfriend Alison Wise on June 23.
- Steve Winwood has been asked by his local vicar in Birmingham, UK, to write music for two psalms.
- Larry Page's bid to retain his former 10% interest in the Kinks has been dismissed by London's high court.
- Byrd David Crosby filled in with Buffalo Springfield at Monterey.

*Hendrix holds Monterey*

Davy Jones of the Monkees will now definitely not be drafted into the US Army, having just been officially notified of his exemption from service with the Armed Forces. It is understood that the draft board – in a much earlier decision than anticipated – has agreed to Jones' reclassification into the 2A group, which makes him unacceptable for active military service. This ruling has been made on the grounds that he is responsible for supporting his father: a possible alternative plea based on Jones' insufficient height is now no longer necessary. Although he is a British citizen, Jones was liable for US military service in common with all who work and are currently resident in America.

# THE WHO SALUTE JAGGER AND RICHARDS ON IMPROMPTU SINGLE

## CHARTS

## THE GRAPEVINE

■ In an attempt to lure Elvis Presley back to long-neglected live performance, Gary Singler – responsible for artist bookings at the Statler Hilton Plaza in Miami – has offered a $85,000 fee for Presley to appear in cabaret at the hotel. No response is reported from Col. Parker's office, but should the deal be accepted, it would be Elvis' first stage appearance since early 1961.

*Townshend and Co. lend support to jailed Stones, Mick 'n' Keef*

With Rolling Stones Mick Jagger and Keith Richards both convicted on drug charges, with appeals to be heard before the Lord Chief Justice and two other judges on July 31, The Who, in a move of solidarity, have recorded two Jagger/Richards songs, and will use their royalties to assist the two Stones with legal costs.

Recorded at a rapidly-convened session on the afternoon of Friday June 30 – the day after The Who held an 'emergency meeting' to discuss the situation – 'The Last Time' and 'Under My Thumb' were available as a UK single within five days, with the label crediting 'The Who in support of Mick and Keith'.

Kit Lambert and Chris Stamp co-produced the session, which was originally booked to cut a follow-up to the group's hit 'Pictures Of Lily'. This project was postponed until a New York session eight days later. Because bassist John Entwistle was out of the country at the time, honeymooning aboard the Queen Elizabeth, the bass guitar part was overdubbed by Pete Townshend.

A statement from the group noted: 'There was no time to consider production or arrangements, and what has emerged is a straightforward and very rough cover version of the two songs. The Who intend to continue recording Jagger/Richard compositions for as long as they are in jail, in order to keep their work before the public.'

## YANOVSKY QUITS THE SPOONFUL

Zal Yanovsky, guitarist with The Lovin' Spoonful, has left the group to pursue a solo career. His final live appearance with them was at the Forest Hills Music Festival in New York, on June 24, since when his replacement, 24-year-old Jerry Yester (brother of Jim Yester of The Association), has already stepped into Yanovsky's shoes.

Yanovsky's departure was said to be 'on the most amicable terms', and The Spoonful's John Sebastian was well forewarned, enabling him to recruit Yester with a minimum of disruption. Yanovsky, who has immediate plans for solo recording sessions, said: 'I was getting bored. I want to look around and see what's been happening for the past two years. I feel I've lost touch, and there are so many things I want to do alone.'

Expected to sign a record deal within a couple of weeks, he does not intend to form a group of his own in the forseeable future.

A report that Yanovsky's split had precipitated a complete break-up of The Spoonful is thought to be inaccurate.

*Zal: 'Getting bored'*

# HENDRIX: DID HE GO OR WAS HE PUSHED?

After playing only seven dates as support act on The Monkees' US tour, The Jimi Hendrix Experience have quit the package. Conflicting reports suggest that Hendrix either quit in anger because he resented having to open the shows, or that he was sacked after protests from the conservative women's league, The Daughters Of The American Revolution, that his act was 'too erotic'.

Co-manager/producer Chandler announced that Jimi left 'by mutual agreement with The Monkees', after being asked to tone down his act but refusing to do so.

Said Chandler: 'There had been many protests and a lot of parents were up in arms because the audiences which The Monkees draw are primarily in the 7-12 age group. So they moved Jimi to the opening spot and

asked him to cool his act. He felt he could not co-operate, as it was like asking him to play with one hand. He talked it over with The Monkees and decided to quit.'

Hendrix decided to stay on in the US to undertake recordings and play club dates – including an unexpected few days at the Whisky A-Go-Go in New York's Greenwich Village.

'There is no problem about him getting work,' said Chandler. 'He has been offered plenty of dates following his success at the Monterey Festival, and 'The Wind Cries Mary' is now shooting up the US singles chart.'

A total of 42 studio hours in New York produced 'The Burning Of The Midnight Lamp', which Hendrix plans as his new single. 'The Wind Cries Mary', was cut in one take lasting all of six minutes!

*Hendrix and the Experience: too wild for teenybop Monkees fans, pull out of tour and opt for club dates*

*Hippy hypster McKenzie recalls re-run of Reagan role*

## STAR QUOTE

### SCOTT McKENZIE

'I played a 50-year old general in John Loves Mary, which was a hit on Broadway back in 1949. . . . In the original production, Ronald Reagan played the role I had!'

## THE SUPREMES: NUNS WITH TARZAN!

The Supremes have been signed for their first dramatic acting roles – not in a feature film, but in a guest appearance on the next season of NBC's *Tarzan* TV series, starring Ron Ely.

The group are cast as three American nuns working in Africa, and will wear the appropriate habit throughout. They will also do some singing – of hymns!

## THE GRAPEVINE

■ Marianne Faithfull has been signed for a starring part opposite French actor Alain Delon in a film to be shot in Europe this Autumn. Titled *Girl On A Motor Cycle*, it is being made by Mid-Atlantic films, whose directors include Radio Caroline boss Ronan O'Rahilly. Last month, Marianne failed a screen test for the new British movie *The Magus*.

## RADIO CAROLINE WAVES THE JOLLY ROGER

*Good lolly on the pop ship*

As the UK government's legislation to ban offshore broadcasting took effect after midnight on August 14, the pirate stations which had ruled the airwaves for three years shut up shop.

The most powerful, Radio London, shut down at 3pm on the 14th. Radios Scotland, 390 and 270 also closed before the law made them illegal, but the original UK pirate, Radio Caroline – broadcasting a northern service from a ship off the Isle Of Man, and a southern service from a vessel off the Essex coast – continued defiantly into illegality. The station has announced that it will defy the UK ban by moving its offices from London to Amsterdam and Paris.

The company would continue to take internationally-based advertising, supplemented, it says, by 'fake adverts, to confuse the police should they consider prosecuting advertisers!'

# 'BE SURE TO WEAR SOME FLOWERS IN YOUR HAIR'

San Francisco was the centre of the musical universe in 1967, the year of Flower Power, LSD and psychedelic music. The very first rock festival of note was held in 1967 at Monterey, and many feel that it remains the best ever event of its type, because it featured a star-studded bill and took place before the record industry had any real idea that rock music was more than a passing fad and should be regarded as an asset with long-term profit potential. Monterey Pop, as it was known, was where many world famous stars first emerged internationally. Located just south of San Francisco, Monterey's rural setting was the perfect location for a celebration of the burgeoning youth culture. Featuring established top acts from Los Angeles like The Mamas & The Papas and The Byrds, plus notable newcomers like Buffalo Springfield (with Neil Young and Stephen Stills) and The Association, Monterey also provided the platform for the emergence of the best San Francisco groups, like Big Brother & The Holding Company (featuring Janis Joplin), Jefferson Airplane, The Grateful Dead, Quicksilver Messenger Service and Country Joe & The Fish, as well as many other unknown quantities who became superstars, such as Jimi Hendrix and Otis Redding.

The bill included many dynamic performers, but especially the Bay Area bunch, who had developed a local scene involving music designed to appeal to those who took drugs, particularly acid (LSD). Country Joe McDonald (who was named after Stalin!) later said that 'Electric Music For The Mind and Body', his first album with his group, The Fish, was specifically designed as the perfect soundtrack for an acid trip. It was more artistically successful than

Pioneers of folk/rock and country/rock The Byrds (left to right) Chris Hillman, David Crosby, Jim McGuinn, Michael Clark, Gene Clark.

San Francisco's psychedelic Grateful Dead (standing left to right) Bob Weir, Phil Lesh, Bill Kreutzmann, Ron 'Pigpen' McKernan, (seated left to right) Jerry Garcia, Mickey Hart

the debut album by The Grateful Dead, whose inclination to extend songs (sometimes to ludicrous proportions) was not allowed free reign in the studio. The Dead, as personified by mercurial guitar hero Jerry Garcia, only became hugely successful when they could stretch out on tracks like 'Dark Star', and were clearly late developers as they are more popular in 1991 than ever before, and fans travel literally around the world to attend their concerts. Country Joe, on the other hand, had retreated into cult status by the mid-1970s.

The Grateful Dead's philosophy gained them much early popularity. They lived communally and became the focal point for the emergent hippie tribes, who regarded The Dead as their local band, and turned out in large numbers to drop acid and listen to the music. There can be little doubt that the group's philosophy remains sincere – where the vast majority of bands discourage bootlegging of their live concerts, a special area is set aside alongside the Dead's mixing desk (where the optimum sound balance ought to be available) for 'Deadheads', the group's faithful followers, to set up microphones and tape recorders to provide fresh material for the international network in tape trade (not sale) which has become an obsession for many.

Jefferson Airplane did not provoke such adoration, although they have remained active for as long as The Dead, give or take the odd name change (to Jefferson Starship, then to Starship, then back to Jefferson Airplane), with key members leaving and re-joining. The Airplane's most commercially successful era under that name came at the start, after ex-model Grace Slick left The Great Society and became their vocalist. 'Surrealistic Pillow', her first album with the band, included two US Top 10 hits, the anthemic 'Somebody To Love' and the surreal Alice In Wonderland allegory, 'White Rabbit', both of which Slick had previously performed with The Great Society. As Lewis Carroll was allegedly a drug taker, why not? Slick married the group's singer/rhythm guitarist Paul Kantner, and they called their daughter China. The later 1970s saw Jefferson Starship release six consecutive gold albums and in 1991, the Airplane once again took off for a new flight, with reasonable results.

Quicksilver Messenger Service was an archetypal psychedelic group name, and with lead guitarists John Cippolina (who died in 1990) and Gary Duncan, can be bracketed musically with The Dead, although commercially speaking, they didn't last much longer than The Fish. The biggest star of the era from San Francisco was Janis Joplin, a white R&B singer from Texas with a spine-tingling voice, who soon outgrew Big Brother & The

*Psychedelic chartbusters Jefferson Airplane (left to right) Jorma Kaukonen, Jack Casady, Grace Slick, Paul Kantner, Marty Balin, Spencer Dryden*

*Purveyors of heavenly hippy harmonies The Mamas & Papas (left to right) John Phillips, (top) 'Mama' Cass Elliot, (bottom) Michelle Phillips, Denny Doherty*

Holding Company and embarked on a solo career. After her disappointing solo album, 'I Got Dem Ole Kozmic Blues Again, Mama', she had virtually completed a follow-up, 'Pearl', in 1971 when she overdosed on heroin and became a legend.

The irony of the San Francisco musical revolution was that its anthem, 'San Francisco (Be Sure To Wear Some Flowers In Your Hair') was written by Hollywood superstar John Phillips of The Mamas & Papas, and sung by a folk singer who lived in Los Angeles, Scott McKenzie. It was probably partly inspired by what was happening in San Francisco, where the acid-tripping hippies made a point of enjoying flowers, but the enduring interest in wearing flowers has not approached the continuing passion for psychedelic music and its associated drug culture.

*Superstar-siring Buffalo Springfield, named after a steamroller (left to right) Dewey Martin, Richie Furay, Stephen Stills, Bruce Palmer (bottom), Neil Young (top)*

# 1967

## THE GRAPEVINE

■ Herman's Hermits have been invited to play at the Shah of Persia's coronation in Teheran next month. They will fly to Persia on October 23 and stay at the royal palace for five days. Although the group had intended to be on holiday during this period, they are likely to accept the invitation – particularly as it came from the Shah personally.

# McCARTNEY: 'NO EPSTEIN REPLACEMENT'

*Epstein, architect of the Beatles success and Merseybeat manager supreme*

Following the sudden death of Brian Epstein at his London home, The Beatles have decided NOT to appoint another manager. Paul McCartney, speaking for the group, explained: 'No one could possibly replace Brian.'

The group were under a personal management contract to Epstein, but have now decided to manage themselves. Their agency contract with NEMS Enterprises is due to expire in October, but is likely to be renewed.

Epstein's brother Clive has been elected by directors as the NEMS chairman, and Robert Stigwood becomes managing director. The company has announced that it will continue to pursue Brian Epstein's policies and projects.

NEMS ownership remains in doubt, since Epstein owned 70 per cent of the shares, with the rest being split between his brother and The Beatles. In the absence of a will, Epstein's majority holding passes to his widowed mother, who may sell if death duty taxes prove exorbitant.

A spokesman for The Beatles stated: 'They would be willing to put money into NEMS if there was any question of a takeover from an outsider. The Beatles will not withdraw their shares from NEMS. Things will go on just as before.'

Epstein was buried at Long Lane Cemetery, Liverpool. A memorial service is likely to be held in London in the near future.

## MAGICAL BEATLES TOUR

The Beatles and a cast of extras have been touring Devon and Cornwall in a 60-seater coach, filming their TV movie *Magical Mystery Tour* at a variety of England's West Country locations.

Three further weeks will be spent in studio editing and soundtrack recording when the two-week jaunt on the road is complete.

# MOTHER WOULDN'T LIKE IT

*Mothers: 'mind shattering'*

NME's assistant editor John Wells witnessed the first-ever UK performance by Frank Zappa and The Mothers Of Invention. These are his comments:

'The 40-year-old flower children in The Royal Albert Hall's half-full audience for the British stage debut of America's Mother Of Invention last Saturday hung on every word of leader Frank Zappa, applauded every mind-shattering sound (even when it was a mistake), and laughed at the crudest of jokes.

'This was the greatest send-up (or down) of pop music, the audience, America and the group themselves I've ever witnessed. As musicians they were fantastically good, and the entire act was unbelievably professionally presented.

'But, frankly, what was the point of it all? An entire concert of biting ridicule, both verbal and musical – however well done – is just a bore.'

# MAMAC AND PAPAC: CHANGES IN THE FAMILY?

*Their career currently in crisis, Mamas and Papas take a break*

With The Mamas & The Papas 'on indefinite leave of absence', in the words of their producer and label boss Lou Adler, speculation is rife concerning their future, after cancelled live dates in London and Paris were followed by John Phillips and his wife Michelle Gilliam moving on to West Germany, and Cass Elliott and Denny Doherty returning unexpectedly to the US.

The group's new album is a compilation of earlier tracks, titled (some would suggest ominously) 'Farewell To The First Golden Era'.

However, they have signed a new long-term deal with Adler's Dunhill Records, while Phillips has also signed to Dunhill as record producer.

Adler announced: 'They were halfway through cutting another album when they decided to take a break for an indefinite period to seek inspiration. They will not record again until they feel more creative, and are able to come up with the right product.'

Current speculation concerns likely changes in the group's personnel, and suggests that Doherty is to be replaced by 'San Francisco' hitmaker Scott McKenzie, who once sang with John Phillips in The Journeymen and is presently produced by him. McKenzie's close association with the group – he travelled to Europe with them – lends plausibility to a tie-up, notwithstanding his current chart success as a soloist.

*Cliff changes mind on Christian career, opting for pop after all*

## OCTOBER 1967

## THE GRAPEVINE

■ Cliff Richard has now decided not to quit show business to become a teacher of religion, and explained: 'I shall continue with my religious studies, but I now realize that I can be an entertainer as well as a Christian. Provided that the public continues to accept me, I am quite prepared to remain in the business for another 20 years. On reflection, it was foolish even to think of quitting.'

## JONES THE BREAD

Tom Jones will become a millionaire on the strength of a 13-week cabaret booking at the Las Vegas Flamingo. The million-dollar fee, negotiated by Jones' agent and manager Colin Berlin and Gordon Mills and US agent Lloyd Greenfield, is believed to be the highest ever guaranteed to a British singer in the US.

Under the deal, Jones will play three separate Flamingo engagements spread over 18 months, the first being a four-week season opening on March 19, immediately after a month-long stint at the Copacabana in New York.

## PROCUL NIX MOVIE

Procul Harum have turned down an offer for the group to star in the film *Seventeen Plus*, to be produced by the makers of Paul Jones' *Privilege*. The main reason for this refusal is that work on the movie would have meant curtailing a vital US promotional visit, regarded as a key part of the campaign to solidly establish Procul Harum in the States.

Following this decision, the group have announced that they are to write their own film, for shooting late next spring. Coincidentally, ex-members Ray Royer and Bobby Harrison have announced that their group Freedom has been signed to appear in the movie *The Attraction*.

## MARTIN TO SCORE BEATLES CARTOON FILM

The Beatles' producer George Martin has been appointed musical director for the film *Yellow Submarine*, a full-length cartoon based on the group and their music. Produced by King Features and Subafilms, the movie is said to incorporate the most advanced techniques in animation ever used.

The drawings, influenced by pop and psychedelic art, are in a style reflective of the 'mod world of the Beatles'. *Yellow Submarine* is a musical chase and rescue comedy written by Al Brodax, Jack Mendelsohn and Erich Segal, and will feature all The Beatles in animated form – though not with their own speaking voices. These will be dubbed by actors.

George Martin will produce a musical score to complement the Beatles' songs heard on the soundtrack, which – in addition to the title number – will include three new and previously-unreleased Lennon/McCartney numbers, and eight tracks taken from the 'Sergeant Pepper' LP. The group have recently completed recording the new numbers, and a soundtrack album is planned for release in the spring of 1968.

*Musical mentor Martin*

## BAILED STONE AWAITS TRIAL APPEAL RESULT

Rolling Stone Brian Jones has been resting at a friend's home after being released on bail pending his appeal against a sentence of nine months' imprisonment for drug offences. He was released 'in the light of further medical evidence, and on condition that he undertakes to have medical treatment'.

It is likely that Jones' case will take up to six weeks to come before the appeal court. In the meantime, stressed a spokesman for The Rolling Stones, the group WILL continue in any eventuality. Business manager Allan Klein commented: 'There is absolutely no question of bringing in a replacement'.

Klein is currently having discussions in New York with Mick Jagger and Keith Richards regarding the probable late-November release of the recently completed new LP by The Stones.

Asked how Brian Jones' position affects the group's future plans, their publicist Les Perrin said: 'They have not appeared in concert since April, and have not played a British date since October last year, so you will see that they are not very interested in touring.

'There are no tour plans whatsoever. We will meet all other obstacles as they present themselves – but if necessary The Stones can continue for an interim period as a four-man group.'

*''Mining Disaster' Bee Gees almost hit by real tragedy*

### THE GRAPEVINE

■ Robin Gibb of The Bee Gees escaped shaken but unhurt from the rail crash at Hither Green, South London, in which several passengers died.

■ In Argentina, the annual international record festival Mar Del Plata has acclaimed The Troggs as 'the new interpreters of youthful rhythm in international dancing music'; they received gold diplomas, and now plan an in-person visit.

# OTIS REDDING DIES IN PLANE CRASH

Soul star Otis Redding, aged 26, died with four members of his backing group, The Bar-Kays, when their plane crashed into Lake Monoma in Wisconsin.

Also killed were the twin-engined light plane's pilot, and Redding's 17-year-old valet Matthew Kelly. The only survivor of the crash was Bar-Kay Ben Cauley, who was found by rescuers in the icy water.

Eddie Floyd, Redding's friend and Stax label-mate, told the NME: 'The last time I spoke to Otis was in the States. I was joking with him about training for his pilot's licence. Now I will never forget that day – he wasn't flying himself, but he died in his own plane.

'I can only say that I've lost my brother. We as soul brothers are as one; he wasn't the only one . . . there was the great Sam Cooke . . . I don't know my own destiny, either.'

## CHARTS

| | |
|---|---|
| US45 | Daydream Believer *Monkees* |
| USLP | Pisces, Aquarius, Capricorn & Jones Ltd. *Monkees* |
| UK45 | Let The Heartaches Begin *Long John Baldry* |
| UKLP | The Sound Of Music *Soundtrack* |

—— WEEK 2 ——

| | |
|---|---|
| US45 | Daydream Believer *Monkees* |
| USLP | Pisces, Aquarius, Capricorn & Jones Ltd. *Monkees* |
| UK45 | Hello Goodbye *Beatles* |
| UKLP | The Sound Of Music *Soundtrack* |

—— WEEK 3 ——

| | |
|---|---|
| US45 | Daydream Believer *Monkees* |
| USLP | Pisces, Aquarius, Capricorn & Jones Ltd *Monkees* |
| UK45 | Hello Goodbye *Beatles* |
| UKLP | The Sound Of Music *Soundtrack* |

—— WEEK 4 ——

| | |
|---|---|
| US45 | Daydream Believer *Monkees* |
| USLP | Pisces, Aquarius, Capricorn & Jones Ltd. *Monkees* |
| UK45 | Hello Goodbye *Beatles* |
| UKLP | The Sound Of Music *Soundtrack* |

—— WEEK 5 ——

| | |
|---|---|
| US45 | Hello Goodbye *Beatles* |
| USLP | Pisces, Aquarius, Capricorn & Jones Ltd. *Monkees* |
| UK45 | Hello Goodbye *Beatles* |
| UKLP | The Sound Of Music *Soundtrack* |

## THE GRAPEVINE

- Lulu's 'To Sir With Love' has sold over two million copies in the US, making it the biggest-ever American hit by a British female singer.

- The Bee Gees have written a Christmas carol titled 'Thank You For Christmas', to be performed by the group in a televised Christmas Eve carol service from Liverpool Cathedral.

## YARDBIRDS BALLET STAGED IN PARIS

An hour-long ballet written by The Yardbirds and with all music played by the group, is premiered at the Paris Olympia on December 13 and 14. Still untitled, it is being presented by French impresario Bruno Coquetrix, and the initial performance will be filmed for subsequent TV screening in France and Sweden.

The ballet will be danced by BBC-TV dance team Pan's People, choreographed by Flick Colby, and the director is Sean Murphy. The Yardbirds will perform the music from a vantage point at the side of the stage.

Discussions are taking place with regard to the group recording an LP of the ballet music, primarily for the French market. There are no present plans for the production to be staged elsewhere, although promoters are being sounded out on the possibility of a UK presentation.

*One-time raw blues blowers the Yardbirds branch into ballet*

*'Pops' prancers Pans People prepare for Paris premier*

## NME READERS' FAVOURITES OF 1967

The annual NME popularity poll, based on the votes of its readers, included the following results:

*World Section*
**Male singer**
1 Elvis Presley; 2 Tom Jones.
**Female singer**
1 Dusty Springfield; 2 Lulu.
**Vocal group**
1 Beatles; 2 Beach Boys.
**Musical Personality**
1 Elvis Presley; 2 John Lennon.

*UK Section*
**Male singer**
1 Tom Jones; 2 Cliff Richard.
**Female singer**
1 Lulu; 2 Dusty Springfield.
**Vocal group**
1 Beatles; 2 Rolling Stones.
**Instrumental group**
1 Shadows; 2 Sounds Incorporated.
**UK single**
1 'A Whiter Shade Of Pale' – Procul Harum; 2 'All You Need Is Love' – Beatles.

**TV or radio programme**
1 *Top Of The Pops*; 2 *Dee Time*.

**DJ**
1 Tie between Jimmy Savile and Tony Blackburn.

# 1968

## PRESLEY RETURNS TO TV

Elvis Presley has been signed to make his first TV appearance for nearly eight years. He will star in a one-hour spectacular for NBC, to be filmed in New York in the summer, for probable US screening on the network in December. The producer will be Bob Finkel, who is currently responsible for NBC's *Jerry Lewis Show* series.

Presley last appeared on TV in 1960 soon after leaving the US Army, in a 'welcome home' show hosted by Frank Sinatra, which included duets between the two singers. At present, it is not known whether any guests will be added to the planned NBC show.

### CHARTS

| | | |
|---|---|---|
| US45 | Hello Goodbye | *Beatles* |
| USLP | Magical Mystery Tour | *Beatles* |
| UK45 | Hello Goodbye | *Beatles* |
| UKLP | Sgt. Pepper's Lonely Hearts Club Band | *Beatles* |

—— W E E K 2 ——

| | | |
|---|---|---|
| US45 | Hello Goodbye | *Beatles* |
| USLP | Magical Mystery Tour | *Beatles* |
| UK45 | Hello Goodbye | *Beatles* |
| UKLP | Sgt. Pepper's Lonely Hearts Club Band | *Beatles* |

—— W E E K 3 ——

| | | |
|---|---|---|
| US45 | Judy In Disguise (With Glasses) | *John Fred & His Playboy Band* |
| USLP | Magical Mystery Tour | *Beatles* |
| UK45 | The Ballad Of Bonnie And Clyde | *Georgie Fame* |
| UKLP | Val Doonican Rocks, But Gently | *Val Doonican* |

—— W E E K 4 ——

| | | |
|---|---|---|
| US45 | Judy In Disguise (With Glasses) | *John Fred & His Playboy Band* |
| USLP | Magical Mystery Tour | *Beatles* |
| UK45 | Everlasting Love | *Love Affair* |
| UKLP | The Sound Of Music | *Soundtrack* |

# GROUP CHANGES, TEMPORARY AND OTHERWISE

Shadows drummer Brian Bennett is temporarily out of the group, recuperating after an appendix operation.

His stand-in – who has already deputized for Bennett on an ATV *Showtime* TV slot, and is expected to do so again for the telerecording of a Cliff Richard & The Shadows TV spectacular for Rediffusion in February – is Tony Meehan, the drummer Bennett replaced in 1961.

Kink Dave Defects

Gilmour joins Floyd

Meehan back in Shadows

Bassist John Rostill, who suffered a nervous breakdown shortly after Christmas, was declared fit after two weeks and rejoined The Shadows just before Bennett's enforced absence.

Another temporary group absence involves Dave Davies of The Kinks, who is to play his first-ever solo concerts on a tour of Germany, Sweden, Belgium and France, between late February and the end of April.

Auditions have been held to select a band to accompany Dave, but it is stressed by Kinks manager Robert Wace that this is purely a temporary arrangement between Kinks live commitments, and there is no question of Dave actually leaving The Kinks.

Meanwhile, Pink Floyd has grown to a five-piece with the addition of 21-year-old David Gilmour, who has been rehearsing with the group for several weeks, and is currently recording with them. The Floyd are quoted as saying that the augmentation is to 'explore new instruments and add further experimental dimensions to our sound.'

Finally, Freddie & The Dreamers are set to split – but only on new singles to be released shortly. The Freddie-less Dreamers debut will be 'The Maybe Song' at the end of January, while the singer's solo, scheduled for early February, will either be the Reg Presley-penned 'Little Red Donkey' or an Italian song with English lyrics by Mitch Muray.

The group reunites for cabaret work in February, and a tour of Australia in April.

## THE GRAPEVINE

■ Georgie Fame is to sing the theme song, written by Don Black and Johnny Dankworth, for the Elizabeth Taylor/Richard Burton film *Goforth*.

■ Cat Stevens has split with producer Mike Hurst, and will produce himself in future.

■ Former hitmaker Bobby Rydell has signed a long-term contract with Reprise Records.

■ Johnny Rivers has been taking sitar lessons from Ravi Shankar.

More fame for Georgie with Burton/Taylor film song

# SUPREMES RECORD LIVE IN LONDON

*Supremes – the talk of the town*

The Supremes' one-hour cabaret act at London's Talk Of The Town nitespot has been recorded for a projected Motown album. It is only the second time the trio have recorded outside Detroit, the earlier occasion being a similar live recording in 1966 at New York's Copacabana.

EMI producer Tony Palmer (who has worked with The Yardbirds, Georgie Fame and The Scaffold), supervised tapings of The Supremes' performances over three nights from 1 to 3 February. They were backed by the resident Burt Rhodes Orchestra, augmented to a 28-piece unit for this season.

Items likely to be included on the LP which will be edited down from the three shows, are show tunes like 'Mame' and 'Thoroughly Modern Millie', a Sam Cooke tribute selection, and a medley of the group's own biggest hit singles.

Diana Ross commented: 'We want to come back to Britain. The response from everybody has been fantastic, though next time we feel we really must try and get closer to the fans. Concert dates would be the ideal thing next time.'

## NON-MONKEE BUSINESS: NESMITH'S ROCK/JAZZ SYMPHONY

Mike Nesmith of The Monkees has written and produced, in collaboration with jazz trumpeter Shorty Rogers, a full-length rock'n'roll symphony, believed to be the first work of its kind. Nesmith and Rogers have recorded the piece, titled 'The Wichita Train Whistle', with over 50 jazz musicians from the Duke Ellington, Woody Herman, Stan Kenton, and other major bands.

Nesmith has worked on the project independently of The Monkees and their label, Colgems. Having sunk $70,000 of his own money into it, he intends to lease the masters of the recording to the record company offering the most favourable deal, and hopes for a rush US release in March, once a label is finalized.

Nesmith has also written 'Tapioca Tundra' for the B-side of the next Monkees single 'Valleri'. The song was inspired by the group's summer 1966 tour.

### THE GRAPEVINE

■ Cliff Richard has accepted an invitation to preach three sermons during May at Kensington Temple in Notting Hill, London, as part of a series of special guest speaker sevices at the church. He will talk on the Christian faith and its relationship to the world of show business.

■ Secretly married Roger Daltrey of The Who is being sued for divorce.

## ARETHA'S GOLD

Aretha Franklin's single 'Chain Of Fools' has been certified by the RIAA as having sold a million copies in the US within six weeks of release, which makes it Atlantic Records' fastest million seller of all time.

Aretha has now collected four gold singles (previous ones being for 'I Never Loved A Man', 'Respect' and 'Baby I Love You') and one gold album within one year – an achievement unequalled by any other female singer.

She has also topped five polls as the best female singer of 1967.

*Soul queen Aretha, poll-winner and Atlantic best-seller*

*Preacherman Cliff*

*Daltrey – on and off marriage*

## BROTHERS: DIFFERENT BUT STILL RIGHTEOUS

With Bill Medley about to launch a solo recording career, the original Righteous Brothers are no more, but the act continues.

Bobby Hatfield is now being partnered by Jimmy Walker, former singer with The Knickerbockers (of 'Lies' fame), in a similar blue-eyed-soul style.

### CHARTS

| | | |
|---|---|---|
| US45 | Love Is Blue | Paul Mauriat |
| USLP | Blooming Hits | Paul Mauriat |
| UK45 | Cinderella Rockefella | Esther & Abi Ofarim |
| UKLP | The Supremes' Greatest Hits | Supremes |

— W E E K  2 —

| | | |
|---|---|---|
| US45 | Love Is Blue | Paul Mauriat |
| USLP | Blooming Hits | Paul Mauriat |
| UK45 | Cinderella Rockefella | Esther & Abi Ofarim |
| UKLP | The Supremes' Greatest Hits | Supremes |

— W E E K  3 —

| | | |
|---|---|---|
| US45 | (Sittin' On) The Dock Of The Bay | Otis Redding |
| USLP | Blooming Hits | Paul Mauriat |
| UK45 | Cinderella Rockefella | Esther & Abi Ofarim |
| UKLP | John Wesley Harding | Bob Dylan |

— W E E K  4 —

| | | |
|---|---|---|
| US45 | (Sittin' On) The Dock Of The Bay | Otis Redding |
| USLP | Blooming Hits | Paul Mauriat |
| UK45 | Cinderella Rockefella | Esther & Abi Ofarim |
| UKLP | John Wesley Harding | Bob Dylan |

— W E E K  5 —

| | | |
|---|---|---|
| US45 | (Sittin' On) The Dock Of The Bay | Otis Redding |
| USLP | Blooming Hits | Paul Mauriat |
| UK45 | Lady Madonna | Beatles |
| UKLP | John Wesley Harding | Bob Dylan |

# GRAMMYS: FOUR EACH FOR BEATLES AND 5TH DIMENSION

*Four live Beatles take their place on the set for the 'Sergeant Pepper' album cover*

The National Academy of Recording Arts and Sciences' Grammy Awards for 1967 saw the Beatles' 'Sergeant Pepper's Lonely Hearts Club Band' album win in four categories: Album of the Year, Best Contemporary Album, Best Engineered Recording, and Best Album Cover Graphic Art.

The Fifth Dimension also collected four Grammys for their first hit 'Up, Up And Away', which was voted Record of The Year, Best Contemporary Single, Best Performance by a Vocal Group up to Six Persons, and Best Contemporary Group Peformance, Vocal or Instrumental.

'Up, Up And Away' then went further still, winning Song of the Year for its writer Jim Webb, and even a Grammy to the Johnny Mann Singers for their cover version of the song: Best Performance by a Chorus of Seven or More Persons.

Other Grammy winners included Bobbie Gentry (Best New Artist, Best Female Vocal Performance for 'Ode To Billy Joe', and Best Performance of a Contemporary Song for the same record), Glen Campbell (Best Male Vocal Performance and Best Country Solo Vocal for 'By The Time I Get To Phoenix').

Lou Rawls won his Grammy Award for Best Male R&B Performance for 'Dead End Street', while Aretha Franklin won hers for the Best Female R&B Performance (for 'Respect'), Elvis Presley winning the Best Sacred Performance Award for 'How Great Thou Art'.

### THE GRAPEVINE

■ Sandie Shaw secretly married fashion designer and boutique owner Jeff Banks on 6 March at Greenwich Register Office, London.

■ Jimmie Rodgers, found unconscious with a fractured skull in Hollywood in December, is sueing LA City Council for $10 million, accusing police of assault and battery. He claims he is now unable to play the guitar, and has lost his senses of balance, taste and smell.

*Sandie banks on Jeff*

*Troggs for the troops?*

## TROGGS TO PLAY IN VIETNAM?

The Troggs may be the first British group to perform in Vietnam. The group has applied through the Australian and New Zealand authorities for permission to entertain their troops in the country after completing a US tour in April.

A previous request had been made to entertain US forces based in Vietnam, but the group's management were told that responsibility could not be accepted by the US authorities for the safety of non-American artists.

Manager Stan Phillips told the NME: 'We are still hopeful that Australia and New Zealand will help us – so far they have been very co-operative.'

The Troggs' vocalist Reg Presley, says that the group's motive in going to Vietnam is 'strictly as entertainers – it must be dreadful out there, and we would just like to provide a few hours' music for the troops.'

# PRESLEY AND JONES MEET IN LAS VEGAS

Tom Jones: standing ovation

Elvis the Pelvis takes time out to take in Jones the Voice

On 6 April Elvis Presley, his wife Priscilla and a party of eight friends journeyed 400 miles from LA to Las Vegas to watch Tom Jones's cabaret act at the Flamingo. Presley took a bow when Jones introduced him to the audience, and led a standing ovation at the end of the show as Jones encored with 'Land Of 1000 Dances'.

The Presleys then went backstage, and the two singers chatted for an hour. Jones had previously visited Presley on a film set in 1965, but he is the first UK singer that the American has ever seen performing live.

As they talked over a cigar and a glass of champagne apiece, Presley recalled his own less-than-wonderful memories of performing in Vegas: 'I was at the Frontier Hotel about ten years ago, and I died a terrible death. When I came out with those hip movements (demonstrating) – man, they just weren't ready for me!'

The two also discussed song-

writer Jerry Reed, who wrote the most recent Presley hit, 'Guitar Man'. 'Glad you had a hit with that – I publish the song in Britain through my company, Valley Music!' said Jones.

Presley mentioned that he rated Jones's 'Delilah': 'A great record – I see it was a smash in Britain.' To Jones's observation that it was moving less quickly in the US, he countered: 'Man, I want to make a prediction – it'll be a smash here, too.'

On the subject of Jones's 'Green Green Grass Of Home', Presley recalled, 'When it was issued here, the boys and I were on the road, driving in our mobile home. Man, that record meant so much to us boys from Memphis, we just sat there and cried. Then we called the radio station and asked them to play it again – they did, four times! We just sat there and sobbed our hearts out.'

## CHARTS

| | | |
|---|---|---|
| US45 | (Sittin' On) The Dock Of The Bay | Otis Redding |
| USLP | The Graduate | Soundtrack |
| UK45 | Lady Madonna | Beatles |
| UKLP | John Wesley harding | Bob Dylan |

### WEEK 2

| | | |
|---|---|---|
| US45 | Honey | Bobby Goldsboro |
| USLP | The Graduate | Soundtrack |
| UK45 | Congratulations | Cliff Richard |
| UKLP | John Wesley Harding | Bob Dylan |

### WEEK 3

| | | |
|---|---|---|
| US45 | Honey | Bobby Goldsboro |
| USLP | The Graduate | Soundtrack |
| UK45 | What A Wonderful World | Louis Armstrong |
| UKLP | John Wesley Harding | Bob Dylan |

### WEEK 4

| | | |
|---|---|---|
| US45 | Honey | Bobby Goldsboro |
| USLP | The Graduate | Soundtrack |
| UK45 | What A Wonderful World | Louis Armstrong |
| UKLP | John Wesley Harding | Bob Dylan |

Congratulations Cliff, runner-up in this year's Eurovision Song Contest

## TOP EURO-SONGS SUED OVER COPYRIGHT

Irish songwriters Shay O'Donoghue and Aiden Magennis of The Debonaires Showband are sueing British writers Bill Martin and Phil Coulter for breach of copyright, claiming that the latter's Cliff Richard-sung 'Congratulations' – the UK's second-placed song in the Eurovision Song Contest – has 'the same chord sequence' as their 'Far Away From You', which was recorded 18 months ago by Doc Carroll & The Royal Blues, and reached No. 8 in the Irish charts.

A writ has also been issued in connection with the winning Eurovision song, Spain's 'La La La', which is alleged to infringe on the copyright of Ray and Dave Davies's 'Death Of A Clown'.

## THE GRAPEVINE

■ Chris 'Ace' Kefford has, after a period of absence due to illness, now permanently left The Move, who will continue as a four-piece.

■ Zoot Money has disbanded his group Dantalian's Chariot and joined Eric Burdon's Animals, though he will also continue to record as a soloist for CBS; he is likely to have an acting role alongside Burdon in the forthcoming film The Death of Harry Farmer.

# BEACH BOYS – MAHARISHI TOUR FLOP

An apathetic reaction has greeted the opening of the joint US tour by the Transcendental Meditation guru Maharishi Mahesh Yogi with The Beach Boys, leading to two weeks of dates being cancelled.

Arriving in the US a day late and missing a New York press conference, the Maharishi joined the group for the low-key opening concert at Georgetown University in Washington on 3 May. The next afternoon's show at New York's Singer Bowl was cancelled after The Beach Boys had already set up to play, because only 300 people had turned up. Philadelphia that night attracted a healthier 5,000 – but half of them walked out following the group's set, before the guru's lecture.

After two more moderately successful dates, the Maharishi dropped out, probably displeased by his ultra-lukewarm reception, but ostensibly to honour a movie contract he had signed with Four Star Productions in Hollywood; this project should have been made earlier, but illness had prevented it.

The upset and somewhat angry Beach Boys decided not to press cancellation charges, 'since the tour was all in the cause of love, friendship and peace', and in return the Maharishi has promised to join them again from 17 May, for the final scheduled bookings in Denver, Col. and several venues in California.

## JAGGER ACTING DEBUT (AND STONES FILM?)

Mick Jagger is to make his dramatic acting debut in a film which goes into production in London in July. He will play opposite James Fox in Warner/7 Arts' *Performance*, directed by Donald Cammell and Nicolas Roeg from an original screenplay by Cammell.

The movie tells of a pop musician (Jagger) who is a 'drop-out from the social stream of contemporary life' until he meets a vicious gangster (Fox). Though Jagger's role is dramatic, he will sing one song within the context of the script, and has also written the musical score for the project.

Meanwhile, it is understood that The Rolling Stones as a whole are to start making their own feature film almost immediately, subject to contracts being signed. If, as expected, production on this starts within two or three weeks, it will be completed in time for Jagger to make his solo debut. The group also has a new LP scheduled for June, completed with producer Jimmy Miller.

*Diversifying: Jagger and the Stones pursue movies, solo album, new group LP later*

### THE GRAPEVINE

■ Dave Mason, who left Traffic at the end of last year to work as a soloist and producer, has rejoined the group in New York, where he worked on recording sessions for their next album, on which he has several songs.

■ Resting on Cream's US tour, Eric Clapton went to see The Mothers Of Invention at LA's Shrine Auditorium, and ended up guesting on stage with them.

*Currently Stateside, Clapton, Baker and Bruce*

*Return of Dave Mason*

# STONES IN STUDIO BLAZE DRAMA

The Rolling Stones were involved in a fire drama at London's Olympic Sound studios in the early morning of 11 June. At 4.15 am, while the group were filming a sequence for their movie *One By One* with French director Jean Luc Godard, the roof of the building was seen to be ablaze, and the fire brigade were called.

The film crew, ironically, were following the Stones recording a new number called 'Sympathy For The Devil' at the time. Their performance of this song, in gradual development from sketchy beginnings to full studio production, is their key part in the movie, being described as a 'musical embroidery' to the plot's parallel themes of 'construction and destruction'.

Mick Jagger commented: 'The fire brigade was so thorough in extinguishing the blaze that our Hammond organ and all the electronic equipment was completely drenched. The sequence will have to be re-taken.'

*Stones extinguished*

## MANFREDS' 'JACK' IS CHANGED TO AVOID RACE PROTEST

*Manfred's struggle with a lyrical problem*

All first pressings in the UK of the new Manfred Mann single 'My Name Is Jack' have been scrapped after being recalled by the distributor just days before the scheduled release date. Mercury Records in the States had complained about a phrase in the lyric (by US writer John Simon) which might antagonize race relations.

The group returned to the studio on Wednesday, 5 June (only two days before the original scheduled UK release date) to re-record the track with the potentially offending phrase changed.

A spokesman told the NME: 'We were told that the record could not possibly be released in the States in its original form, so rather than re-record the disc specially for the US market, we decided to maintain consistency by changing the lyric for Britain too. It should only hold up UK release by a week.'

## HUMPERDINCK TOPS ON US JUKEBOXES

A cross-section survey by *Billboard* magazine of America's 480,000 jukeboxes – covering the 12 months between March 1967 and February 1968 – reveals that Engelbert Humperdinck was the most-played artist, followed by Nancy Sinatra and then The Monkees.

Humperdinck's 'Release Me' was also the most-played individual jukebox record of the period.

*Jukebox giant Engelbert*

## ROSSI TO WRITE FILM MUSIC

Mike Rossi of Status Quo, who wrote the group's 'Pictures Of Matchstick Men' and it's follow-up, has been invited to write the title song and incidental music for *Je*, a French feature film which starts production in August.

Status Quo will be seen in the movie's opening credits, performing the title number.

### CHARTS

| | |
|---|---|
| US45 | Mrs. Robinson *Simon & Garfunkel* |
| USLP | Bookends *Simon & Garfunkel* |
| UK45 | Young Girl *Union Gap* |
| UKLP | This Is Soul *Various* |
| **WEEK 2** | |
| US45 | Mrs. Robinson *Simon & Garfunkel* |
| USLP | Bookends *Simon & Garfunkel* |
| UK45 | Young Girl *Union Gap* |
| UKLP | This Is Soul *Various* |
| **WEEK 3** | |
| US45 | Mrs. Robinson *Simon & Garfunkel* |
| USLP | The Graduate *Soundtrack* |
| UK45 | Young Girl *Union Gap* |
| UKLP | This Is Soul *Various* |
| **WEEK 4** | |
| US45 | This Guy's In Love With You *Herb Alpert* |
| USLP | The Graduate *Soundtrack* |
| UK45 | Jumpin' Jack Flash *Rolling Stones* |
| UKLP | This Is Soul *Various* |
| **WEEK 5** | |
| US45 | This Guy's In Love With You *Herb Alpert* |
| USLP | Bookends *Simon & Garfunkel* |
| UK45 | Jumpin' Jack Flash *Rolling Stones* |
| UKLP | This Is Soul *Various* |

## THE GRAPEVINE

■ Cream have recorded a series of commercials for the Falstaff Brewing Company in California.

■ The Monkees are fighting Screen Gems over ownership of the group name.

■ Glen Campbell has been signed by Paramount to co-star with John Wayne in a Western.

■ The sight of Elvis Presley chatting to Paul Revere (of The Raiders) on a Sunset Boulevard sidewalk brought traffic to a standstill.

## JULY 1968

### CHARTS

| | |
|---|---|
| US45 | This Guy's In Love With You *Herb Alpert* |
| USLP | Bookends *Simon & Garfunkel* |
| UK45 | Baby Come Back *Equals* |
| UKLP | Ogdens Nut Gone Flake *Small Faces* |

— W E E K 2 —

| | |
|---|---|
| US45 | This Guy's In Love With You *Herb Alpert* |
| USLP | Bookends *Simon & Garfunkel* |
| UK45 | Baby Come Back *Equals* |
| UKLP | Ogdens Nut Gone Flake *Small Faces* |

— W E E K 3 —

| | |
|---|---|
| US45 | Grazin' In The Grass *Hugh Masakela* |
| USLP | Bookends *Simon & Garfunkel* |
| UK45 | Baby Come Back *Equals* |
| UKLP | Ogdens Nut Gone Flake *Small Faces* |

— W E E K 4 —

| | |
|---|---|
| US45 | Grazin' In The Grass *Hugh Masakela* |
| USLP | The Beat Of The Brass *Herb Alpert* |
| UK45 | Mony Mony *Tommy James & The Shondells* |
| UKLP | Ogdens Nut Gone Flake *Small Faces* |

*A poster poser for Immediate trio The Nice as they look to sales across the Atlantic*

# PRESLEY TALKS TO THE PRESS!

As part of the pre-publicity build-up for his NBC television special, now in production at the company's Burbank studios, Elvis Presley held his first press conference for many years. Asked why he was doing the TV show, he said: 'We figured it was about time. Besides, I thought I had better do it before I got too old!' he chuckled.

Asked about the content of the show, Presley quipped: 'Well, I insisted that the cameras keep on me most of the time! What I do is sing, almost exclusively. And I sing the songs I'm known for.'

'Hell, if he sang the songs he's known for, that would take hours,' butted in Col. Tom Parker. 'NBC only gave us an hour. He is going to sing *some* of the songs he's famous for.'

On fans, Presley thought that

*Elvis relaxes – TV special soon*

his had probably changed a little through the years: 'A lot of them are now young mothers, or girls about to get married.'

Did he ever write songs? 'All

I've written is two lines of "Love Me Tender", and that was a while ago.'

---

*Blonde Tom: Tommy James of the Shondells and jukebox that doubtless contains their latest hit*

## NOT NICE AT ALL, CLAIM GROUP

The Nice have asked their label, Andrew Oldham's Immediate Records, to withdraw a controversial poster advertising their single 'America', claiming that bookings and even record sales are suffering as a result of the poster's 'adverse effect' on the public.

It pictures the group members with small boys on their knees, but superimposed on the children's heads are the faces of the assassinated John F. Kennedy, Robert Kennedy and Dr Martin Luther King.

A spokesman for The Nice says: 'Several record stores in the UK have refused to stock our current single, and some promoters will not book the group because of this poster.

'The Nice feel that if the posters are issued in America, they will do considerable harm. The group has been offered a US college and TV tour in September, and has no wish to create ill-will from the outset.'

## THE GRAPEVINE

- Scott Walker has had to withdraw from a tour of Japan on doctor's orders; he has been certified as suffering from 'psycho-neurosis', and is forbidden to travel.
- On 12 July, Mickey Dolenz of The Monkees married Samantha Juste – the British girl he met 16 months ago on BBC-TV's *Top of the Pops* – in a secret ceremony performed by his clergyman father, at Dolenz's Hollywood home.

## LIGHTS INSPIRE JAMES

Tommy James has described how he and songwriting partner Richard Cordell found the inspiration for 'Mony Mony', Tommy James & The Shondells' biggest international success to date:

'We were writing one night at my apartment, and we happened to look out of the window. Across the street is a neon sign for "Mutual Of New York", and when it's lit up, it spells out M-O-N-Y. That was just the type of title we wanted!'

# RECORD US GOLD DISC TALLY

*Sellers supreme in the growing album market, folk-rock duo Simon and Garfunkel*

*Gold disc Goldsboro*

More gold discs were awarded in America during the first six months of this year than for any similar period in the past. The RIAA, certification of 54 awards (21 singles and 33 albums) is eight more than the previous all-time-high six-month tally – a clear sign that record sales continue to climb steadily.

Million-selling singles included Bobby Goldsboro's 'Honey', The Monkees' 'Valleri', The Beatles' 'Lady Madonna', Simon & Garfunkel's 'Mrs Robinson', Otis Redding's '(Sittin' On) The Dock Of The Bay' and The 1910 Fruitgum Company's 'Simon Says'.

The Union Gap scored two in a row with 'Woman, Woman' and 'Young Girl' (and have subsequently made it a hat-trick with 'Lady Willpower').

In the LP field, where discs need to sell half a million within the US to qualify, Dean Martin picked up four golds, while Elvis Presley, Ray Charles, Bob Dylan and Andy Williams collected two apiece.

The biggest album sellers of the period were Simon & Garfunkel's 'Bookends', and the soundtrack from 'The Graduate', which also showcases the duo.

## CHARTS

| | | |
|---|---|---|
| US45 | Hello I Love You | *Doors* |
| USLP | The Beat of The Brass | *Herb Alpert* |
| UK45 | Mony Mony | *Tommy James & The Shondells* |
| UKLP | Bookends | *Simon And Garfunkel* |

**WEEK 2**

| | | |
|---|---|---|
| US45 | Hello I Love You | *Doors* |
| USLP | Wheels Of Fire | *Cream* |
| UK45 | Mony Mony | *Tommy James & The Shondells* |
| UKLP | Delilah | *Tom Jones* |

**WEEK 3**

| | | |
|---|---|---|
| US45 | People Got To Be Free | *Rascals* |
| USLP | Wheels Of Fire | *Cream* |
| UK45 | Mony Mony | *Tommy James & The Shondells* |
| UKLP | Bookends | *Simon And Garfunkel* |

**WEEK 4**

| | | |
|---|---|---|
| US45 | People Got To Be Free | *Rascals* |
| USLP | Wheels Of Fire | *Cream* |
| UK45 | Help Yourself | *Tom Jones* |
| UKLP | Bookends | *Simon And Garfunkel* |

**WEEK 5**

| | | |
|---|---|---|
| US45 | People Got To Be Free | *Rascals* |
| USLP | Wheels Of Fire | *Cream* |
| UK45 | Help Yourself | *Tom Jones* |
| UKLP | Bookends | *Simon And Garfunkel* |

## SHADOWS TO LOSE BENNETT – AND WELCH TOO?

Despite wildly exaggerated UK media reports, The Shadows are not breaking up.

However, drummer Brian Bennett intends to leave in December - after the group's London Palladium season with Cliff Ricahrd – and founder-member Bruce Welch is considering quitting at the same time, probably to go into music publishing and management.

Manager Peter Gormley said: 'Bruce has been talking about settling down for some time, and now that Brian is going and the group is having to be reshaped, he feels this might be an opportune time for him to leave, too.

'But nothing will be decided until the boys' return from holiday at the end of the month – and I must stress that Bruce may equally well decide to stay on. Whatever happens, The Shadows will continue – both Hank Marvin and John Rostill are quite determined about that.'

## THE GRAPEVINE

■ Fleetwood Mac now have three lead guitarists since adding Danny Kirwen (a protégé of group leader Peter Green and manager Clifford Davis) alongside Green and Jeremy Spencer.

■ Honeybus lead singer Pete Dello, who wrote the group's hit 'I Can't Let Maggie Go', has left to concentrate on writing and production.

■ The Beatles have closed down their Apple boutique in London's Baker Street.

*Apple crumbles*

## STONES' GRAFFITI SLEEVE DISPUTE

The sleeve illustration for the new Rolling Stones album 'Beggars Banquet' is the subject of a dispute between the group and Decca Records, their British label.

It depicts a lavatory wall, inscribed with such slogans as 'John Loves Yoko' and 'Mao Loves Lyndon', and Decca is concerned that these and other scrawlings may cause offence in the US.

Mick Jagger, though, is adamant that nothing will be altered on the LP sleeve despite its controversial photograph.

# 1968

## DUSTY IN MEMPHIS

Dusty Springfield is in Memphis to make her first recordings for Atlantic Records. Producer Jerry Wexler said prior to the sessions: 'Everybody expected us to go the Aretha Franklin route with Dusty, but we're not: I've lined up the same rhythm and string sections that The Box Tops and Merilee Rush use in Memphis. Tom Dowd and Arif Mardin will also be on the session.

'I've taken Dusty to Memphis because it's important that she gets away from the sound we've been producing in New York. She's tough in the studio – very picky and choosey with material, and highly critical – but I wouldn't have it any other way.

'We're loaded with songs,' he added. 'For the past few weeks we've done nothing but send stuff to London. I just hope she likes them.'

# THE NEW YARDBIRDS

*Plant (left) Page (back to camera) and Jones*

The Yardbirds have now completed the re-shaping of their personnel, and have formulated their plans for the next four months.

Leader Jimmy Page, in partnership with group manager Peter Grant, has formed a company called Super-Hyp Recording, which will now be responsible for the production of all Yardbirds records, ending their recording link with producer Mickie Most.

It is also likely that the group will no longer appear on their current labels (EMI in the UK, Epic in the US), since it is understood that four major British record companies are currently negotiating for the rights to Super-Hyp's output, while Warner-Reprise is tipped as the likely US licencee.

The new line-up teams Page (lead and steel guitar) with John Paul Jones (bass guitar and organ), John Bonham (drums), and Robert Plant (vocals). A six-week US tour of one-nighters and college dates will begin on November 14.

The group are currently in Scandinavia, fulfilling bookings made on behalf of the previous line-up earlier in the year.

## US DISC SALES AT ALL-TIME PEAK

Record sales in America reached an all-time peak in 1967, according to industry figures. Over $1,000 million were spent on records, and for the first time ever, more albums were sold than singles in the US: 192 million against 187 million. In terms of dollar value, LP sales represented 82 per cent of total turnover.

Total annual revenue from US record sales has almost doubled in the last decade – from 511 million dollars in 1958 to 1967's 1,051 million dollars.

There were 7,231 singles released in the US during 1967 (against 7,086 in 1966), and 4,328 albums (3,752 in 1966).

## CHARTS

| | |
|---|---|
| US45 | People Got To Be Free *Rascals* |
| USLP | Waiting For The Sun *Doors* |
| UK45 | I've Gotta Get A Message To You *Bee Gees* |
| UKLP | Bookends *Simon And Garfunkel* |

— WEEK 2 —

| | |
|---|---|
| US45 | People Got To Be Free *Rascals* |
| USLP | Waiting For The Sun *Doors* |
| UK45 | Hey Jude *Beatles* |
| UKLP | Bookends *Simon And Garfunkel* |

— WEEK 3 —

| | |
|---|---|
| US45 | Harper Valley PTA *Jeannie C. Riley* |
| USLP | Waiting For The Sun *Doors* |
| UK45 | Hey Jude *Beatles* |
| UKLP | The Hollies' Greatest Hits *Hollies* |

— WEEK 4 —

| | |
|---|---|
| US45 | Hey Jude *Beatles* |
| USLP | Time Peace *Rascals* |
| UK45 | Hey Jude *Beatles* |
| UKLP | The Hollies' Greatest Hits *Hollies* |

## THE GRAPEVINE

■ The Doors' third LP 'Waiting For The Sun' became a gold record on the day of release, with over a million dollars'-worth of advance orders.

■ Mixed and confused audience reactions to advance screenings of The Monkees' feature film *Head* have prompted Screen Gems to re-edit it and put back the opening.

■ The Beach Boys lost 300-400,000 dollars touring with the Maharishi.

*Financial vibes not good as transcendental trek bombs for the Beach Boys*

# SPENCER'S NEW MEN

Spencer Davis has engaged two new musicians to replace drummer Pete York and organist Eddie Hardin, both of whom quit his group on October 26, due to 'differences over musical policy'.

The newcomers – both formerly in a group named Mirage – are Dave Hynes (drums) and Dee Murray (bass), and both will join Davis for concerts in West Germany before undertaking a five-week tour of the US and Canada from November 1.

Prior to the personnel switch, on October 9, Davis himself collapsed from what was described in the music press as 'exhaustion and hypertension', while in Berlin completing work on a version of the song 'Aquarius' (from the musical *Hair*) which is planned as a Germany-only single. He was ordered to convalesce for two weeks, and his wife flew to join him in Berlin.

*Left: Outpacing even 'Pepper, The Sound of Music remains in the album charts after more than three years*

*Right: Cream to call it a day at London finale*

## THE GRAPEVINE

■ The last Yardbirds performance was at Liverpool University on October 20: Jimmy Page has now decided to rename the new line-up Led Zeppelin.

■ Cream will play their farewell concert at London's Royal Albert Hall on 26 November, and the BBC intend to film it as a TV special.

■ The Beatles' 'Hey Jude' has sold 4,738,000 copies worldwide in eight weeks.

## THE BRITISH HILLS ARE ALIVE WITH THEM

This month, the soundtrack album from the film *The Sound of Music* became the biggest-selling LP in British record history.

Its UK sales hit two million on October 2, and an RCA Records spokesman estimated that one out of every four homes in the country with a record player also own a copy of this disc.

The soundtrack is still in the top ten of the NME album chart after over 180 weeks, and its sales gross is said to have now exceeded £3,225,000.

It has also been estimated that if all the copies of the album so far sold in Britain were stacked up together, they would reach fifteen times the height of the Empire State Building!

## MASON QUITS TRAFFIC AGAIN AFTER ABORTIVE TOUR

Dave Mason has left Traffic for the second time, to concentrate on record production.

He departed after the group's US tour, which was planned to last six weeks, but was called off after only 10 days because 'venues which had been hoped for did not materialize', and because Steve Winwood became plagued by a throat infection.

Traffic returned to the UK to start recording work on another LP, but without Mason, who went to Los Angeles to discuss business deals. A Traffic spokesman said: 'Dave is too individual to be part of a group, and he feels he will be happier working alone, producing records.'

## CHARTS

| | | |
|---|---|---|
| US45 | Hey Jude | *Beatles* |
| USLP | Waiting For The Sun | *Doors* |
| UK45 | Those Were The Days | *Mary Hopkin* |
| UKLP | The Hollies' Greatest Hits | *Hollies* |

**WEEK 2**

| | | |
|---|---|---|
| US45 | Hey Jude | *Beatles* |
| USLP | Cheap Thrills | *Big Brother & The Holding Company* |
| UK45 | Those Were The Days | *Mary Hopkin* |
| UKLP | The Hollies' Greatest Hits | *Hollies* |

**WEEK 3**

| | | |
|---|---|---|
| US45 | Hey Jude | *Beatles* |
| USLP | Cheap Thrills | *Big Brother & The Holding Company* |
| UK45 | Those Were The Days | *Mary Hopkin* |
| UKLP | The Hollies' Greatest Hits | *Hollies* |

**WEEK 4**

| | | |
|---|---|---|
| US45 | Hey Jude | *Beatles* |
| USLP | Cheap Thrills | *Big Brother & The Holding Company* |
| UK45 | Those Were The Days | *Mary Hopkin* |
| UKLP | The Hollies' Greatest Hits | *Hollies* |

## DJs: THE YARD GOES OFF FOREVER!

Richard Harris's new single 'The Yard Went On Forever', written (like his 'MacArthur Park') by Jim Webb, is causing controversy on US radio, where some DJs are refusing to play it.

Though its lyrics are oblique, it is an anti-Vietnam war song, based on a speech by the late Robert Kennedy.

# MELOUNEY TO QUIT BEE GEES

Vince Melouney's departure from The Bee Gees has been confirmed by the group's manager Robert Stigwood, who said: 'For some time there has been a musical disagreement between the Gibb brothers and Vince, who wanted to play more blues-based material. We have decided it would be better for him to leave, though we have not yet decided about his future.'

The guitarist's final concert with the group will be on December 1, at the end of the current German tour. He will not then be replaced; instead, Maurice Gibb will move to take over his lead guitar slot.

There will now be a delay in the production of The Bee Gees' film *Lord Kitchener's Little Drummer Boys*, as Melouney has to be written out of the script. Filming originally due to start in December will now take place in February, and the group will complete the recording of the January-scheduled double album 'Masterpiece' before Christmas.

## CHARTS

| | | |
|---|---|---|
| US45 | Hey Jude | *Beatles* |
| USLP | Cheap Thrills | *Big Brother & The Holding Company* |
| UK45 | Those Were The Days | *Mary Hopkin* |
| UKLP | The Hollies' Greatest Hits | *Hollies* |

### WEEK 2

| | | |
|---|---|---|
| US45 | Hey Jude | *Beatles* |
| USLP | Cheap Thrills | *Big Brother & The Holding Company* |
| UK45 | With A Little Help From My Friends | *Joe Cocker* |
| UKLP | The Hollies' Greatest Hits | *Hollies* |

### WEEK 3

| | | |
|---|---|---|
| US45 | Hey Jude | *Beatles* |
| USLP | Electric Ladyland | *Jimi Hendrix Experience* |
| UK45 | The Good, The Bad & The Ugly | *Hugo Montenegro* |
| UKLP | The Hollies' Greatest Hits | *Hollies* |

### WEEK 4

| | | |
|---|---|---|
| US45 | Hey Jude | *Beatles* |
| USLP | Electric Ladyland | *Jimi Hendrix Experience* |
| UK45 | Eloise | *Barry Ryan* |
| UKLP | The Hollies' Greatest Hits | *Hollies* |

### WEEK 5

| | | |
|---|---|---|
| US45 | Love Child | *Diana Ross & The Supremes* |
| USLP | Cheap Thrills | *Big Brother & The Holding Company* |
| UK45 | Eloise | *Barry Ryan* |
| UKLP | The Beatles | *Beatles* |

## MAMA CASS VOCAL UNCERTAINTY

*Mama Cass (left) in more carefree days with the Mamas and Papas*

Mama Cass Elliott faces grave uncertainty over her future singing career. She collapsed with a throat haemorrhage on the opening night of a six-week season at Las Vegas's Caesar's Palace – an engagement which would have earned her $250,000 – and is now awaiting a major throat operation.

At present, Cass cannot sing at all, and, assuming the operation is successful, it would be many months before she could resume recordings or concerts. More seriously, there is a risk that surgery could adversely affect her vocal chords, and thus place her whole career in jeopardy.

## NASH TO LEAVE HOLLIES

Graham Nash is to split from The Hollies following their December 8 appearance in the all-star 'Save Rave' charity concert at the London Palladium – which Nash himself is organizing.

It is understood that Nash is tired of live performance, and is anxious to develop some new ideas he has been formulating for several months, but which group commitments have prevented him from pursuing.

Most of his future career is likely to be in songwriting and record production, though he will also probably record as an artist in the US.

A spokesman for The Hollies told the NME: 'We are in the process of sorting out a replacement for Graham, and have two or three names on our shortlist. Meanwhile, the group are already recording backing tracks for a new album, which will be completed after the newcomer is selected.'

*Herman with DJ Stuart Henry*

# THE GRAPEVINE

■ Peter Noone – Herman of The Hermits – married Mireille Strasser on November 5 (his 21st birthday), at the Church of the Immaculate Conception in Mayfair, London.

■ Cream's farewell US tour grossed over $700,000.

■ Aretha Franklin has broken a leg following a fall at a Honolulu hotel; expected to be in plaster for six weeks, she is currently making live appearances in a wheelchair.

# STONES' ROCK'N'ROLL' CIRCUS

Left to right, Clapton, Lennon, Mitchell and Richards jam in front of the TV cameras

The Rolling Stones filmed their *Rock'n'Roll Circus* TV special on 11 December, at Wembley's Intertel TV studios in London, before an invited audience of fans.

One of the highlights of the day was the formation of a one-off 'supergroup' comprising John Lennon, Keith Richard, Eric Clapton (late of Cream), and drummer Mitch Mitchell from The Jimi Hendrix Experience. They performed two numbers, including Lennon's 'Yer Blues', a song from the new Beatles double LP.

As well as the Stones' own show-closing spot, other sections of the special included a solo by Marianne Faithfull, a classical contribution from Julius Katchen, and various circus acts – including Keith Richard and Mick Jagger in a knife-throwing interlude!

Other groups on the bill were Jethro Tull and special guests The Who – the latter replacing the previously scheduled Traffic, who have now split up.

No plans have yet been announced for the screening of the special.

## CHARTS

| | | |
|---|---|---|
| US45 | Love Child | *Diana Ross & The Supremes* |
| USLP | Cheap Thrills | *Big Brother & The Holding Company* |
| UK45 | Lily The Pink | *Scaffold* |
| UKLP | The Beatles | *Beatles* |

### WEEK 2

| | | |
|---|---|---|
| US45 | I Heard It Through The Grapevine | *Marvin Gaye* |
| USLP | Cheap Thrills | *Big Brother & The Holding Company* |
| UK45 | Lily The Pink | *Scaffold* |
| UKLP | The Beatles | *Beatles* |

### WEEK 3

| | | |
|---|---|---|
| US45 | I Heard It Through The Grapevine | *Marvin Gaye* |
| USLP | Wichita Lineman | *Glen Campbell* |
| UK45 | Lily The Pink | *Scaffold* |
| UKLP | The Beatles | *Beatles* |

### WEEK 4

| | | |
|---|---|---|
| US45 | I Heard It Through The Grapevine | *Marvin Gaye* |
| USLP | The Beatles | *Beatles* |
| UK45 | Lily The Pink | *Scaffold* |
| UKLP | The Beatles | *Beatles* |

## A TRIO OF MONKEES

Jones, Nesmith and Dolenz

The Monkees are now reduced to a trio, following the departure of Peter Tork to pursue a solo career.

The others have already filmed a Christmas TV appearance on NBC's *Hollywood Squares* as a threesome, and it seems that they will continue this way rather than recruit a replacement for Tork – who is understood to be currently negotiating a recording contract and considering forming a backing group.

## PRESLEY TRIUMPHS IN TV SPECIAL

Elvis Presley's return to TV in his own one-hour NBC special (with the unlikely sponsorship of Singer Sewing Machines) was screened on December 3.

It proved to be an artistic and commercial triumph, pulling in big ratings and finding acclaim not only from fans, but also from critics who had written off Presley's ability to generate musical excitement after a string of increasingly minor movies.

NME's New York correspondent June Harris commented: 'Elvis, at 33, with his weight tapered down, and moving his body with all the sex that resulted in waist-upward-only shots on the Ed Sullivan TV show in 1956, is sensational . . . he still sings those Memphis blues like they've just been written, and "Jailhouse Rock", "Hound Dog" and others didn't sound dated at all – they sounded like new rock.

'Elvis's second career, after closing a twelve-year rock gap, starts off from the top. A personal appearance tour now seems like the next logical move to make.'

## THE GRAPEVINE

- Dave Edmunds' Love Sculpture have signed a US deal with London Records guaranteeing £250,000.
- Mary Hopkin is 'sympathetically considering' a lead acting role in Stanley Baker's forthcoming film *The Rape of the Fair Country*.
- Mark Volman of The Turtles has insured his distinctive frizzy hair for $100,0000 against fire, theft(!) or loss due to illness.

Turtle vocalist Volman

# WOODSTOCK: ROCK MUSIC COMES OF AGE

It wasn't the first of its kind, despite what convenient omissions history may have passed down. But Woodstock reigns supreme in most people's memory as *the* rock festival – the quintessence of that peculiar urge huge numbers of people have to make their way to some fairly remote spot, grab a few square feet of land and sit in various states of discomfort for days on end while a steady line of performers do their best to make the brief time they've been given to perform as memorable as possible.

Woodstock's pre-eminence undoubtedly stems from the fact that – with the recent exceptions of Live Aid and the Nelson Mandela birthday celebrations of 1989 (known as Freedom Fest in the USA), and the Maysles Brothers' excellent *Gimme Shelter* movie of The Rolling Stones' tragic Altamont fiasco – the Woodstock Music and Arts Festival (to give it its correct name) is the most chronicled and quoted example of its genre.

It started, as most music business events do, as a great and relatively simple plan to make a lot of money. Attendance figures from previous festivals suggested there was an almost unlimited audience out there who'd be more than happy to fork out between five and ten dollars for 'Three days of peace and music'.

A site was found – 600 acres of land near Bethel, in upstate New York, owned by farmer Max Yasgur – and a date set: 15-17 August 1969. Work began on assembling the biggest and best list of rock's top names, and of putting together the infrastructure of what would be an ad hoc

township with a population of around 200,000, all of whom would need feeding, watering and washing, and some of whom (for sure) would require medical help after over-indulging on the many and varied substances which would undoubtedly be on sale.

In the event, there were three deaths, two births and four miscarriages – what you'd expect from a town that size.

What you wouldn't expect – and the organizers certainly didn't – was the complete chaos the festival would cause in the surrounding countryside as more than 400,000 people tried to make it to Yasgur's farm. There were traffic jams of 20 or more miles all round, including freeways. On-site security, including ticket booths and official entrances, became swamped so quickly and comprehensively that the gates were simply thrown open and the festival was designated 'free'.

Musically the commitment and passion which comes out of the Michael Wadleigh movie, and from the grooves of the ten album sides Atlantic Records released, more than compensate for the flaws.

Among those who battled through the traffic and rain to fulfil their debt of honour by playing Woodstock were The Band, The Who, Jimi Hendrix (pictured bottom left), Jefferson Airplane, Crosby Stills, Nash & Young, Creedence Clearwater, Tim Hardin, Country Joe & The Fish, The Grateful Dead, Sly & The Family Stone, Joe Cocker (pictured bottom right), Blood Sweat & Tears, Joan Baez, Mountain and Canned Heat.

Johnny Winter was there, too. Alvin Lee became a superstar via his appearance with Ten Years After, Ravi Shankar probably doubled sitar sales in America with his set, and Joni Mitchell (who didn't play) was inspired enough by the instant mythology to write a hit song.

Woodstock was the birthday party to celebrate rock 'n' roll music's coming of age. Nothing would ever be the same.

# JANUARY

## 1969

### CHARTS

| | |
|---|---|
| US45 | I Heard It Through The Grapevine *Marvin Gaye* |
| USLP | The Beatles *Beatles* |
| UK45 | Lily The Pink *Scaffold* |
| UKLP | The Beatles *Beatles* |

——— W E E K 2 ———

| | |
|---|---|
| US45 | I Heard It Through The Grapevine *Marvin Gaye* |
| USLP | The Beatles *Beatles* |
| UK45 | Ob-La-Di, Ob-La-Da *Marmalade* |
| UKLP | The Beatles *Beatles* |

——— W E E K 3 ———

| | |
|---|---|
| US45 | I Heard It Through The Grapevine *Marvin Gaye* |
| USLP | The Beatles *Beatles* |
| UK45 | Ob-La-Di, Ob-La-Da *Marmalade* |
| UKLP | The Beatles *Beatles* |

——— W E E K 4 ———

| | |
|---|---|
| US45 | I Heard It Through The Grapevine *Marvin Gaye* |
| USLP | The Beatles *Beatles* |
| UK45 | Albatross *Fleetwood Mac* |
| UKLP | The Beatles *Beatles* |

*Dusty – stitched up cheek, broken nose*

# ATLANTIC'S BEST-EVER YEAR

Atlantic Records enjoyed the greatest year in its history in 1968, with sales up by 85 per cent over 1967, and a tally of 23 certified gold records – more than any other company has ever achieved in one year.

The label's top-selling artist was Aretha Franklin, who had four million-selling singles and two gold albums. Since joining Atlantic in 1967, Franklin has amassed 10 gold trophies in all, more than any other female singer in pop history.

Rock groups, once not regarded as an Atlantic strength, also scored well for the label, notably its UK signings: Arthur Brown and Cream had US million-selling singles with 'Fire' and 'Sunshine Of Your Love'. Cream also scored three gold albums, including one for their 'Wheels of Fire' double set.

## HENDRIX AND DUSTY: BASE OVER APEX

Jimi Hendrix and Dusty Springfield both saw in the New Year with injuries from falls. Hendrix has been resting in New York, obliged to cancel an appearance at the Utrecht Pop Festival in Holland, after he fell very awkwardly in a heavy snowstorm at Christmas, tearing several ligaments in his leg.

Dusty, meanwhile, tripped over a paving stone on the balcony of her parents' home in Richmond, England, where she was spending Christmas. She had to have two stitches in her cheek, and was later discovered to have also broken her nose. She had to cancel her New Year's Eve cabaret date at London's Hilton hotel, though was fit to appear at Atlantic Records' Bahamas convention on 16 January.

*The Herd: Frampton (top) to go solo*

*Aretha: a solid gold soul star*

### THE GRAPEVINE

■ Three of The Troggs – Ronnie Bond, Reg Presley and Chris Britten – are to have solo records released by Page One in February or March.

■ Lead singer Peter Frampton is to leave The Herd for a solo career; the remaining members have already recorded without him for a new single.

■ 120 gold disc awards were made in the US during 1968 – 25 more than the previous record figure in 1967.

# NEW-LOOK CREAM HAS WINWOOD IN BRUCE'S PLACE!

The recently-split Cream are to re-form, though under a different name, and with Steve Winwood, former leader of Traffic, replacing Jack Bruce.

The trio have spent early February living and rehearsing together in Winwood's Berkshire (England) cottage, and intended to start recording on the 8th. However, suitable studio time was not available, so the initial sessions were postponed. A suitable name for the group is currently being sought, as well as a permanent bass player to augment them as a quartet.

Clapton said that initial intentions were to get an album together, and that live performances would probably then commence within about a month. The group's attitude to singles would be similar to that of Cream: 'We will not set out with the principal object of making them, but if any track stands out as an obvious single, we'll release it.'

On the rapid reunion with Baker, Clapton adds: 'We haven't really picked each other – we simply floated back together. I don't anticipate any contractual difficulties for the new group, because anyone who stood in the way of a project like this would be mad!'

## CHARTS

| | | |
|---|---|---|
| US45 | Crimson & Clover | Tommy James & The Shondells |
| USLP | The Beatles | Beatles |
| UK45 | Albatross | Fleetwood Mac |
| UKLP | The Best Of The Seekers | Seekers |

WEEK 2

| | | |
|---|---|---|
| US45 | Crimson & Clover | Tommy James & The Shondells |
| USLP | TCB | Diana Ross & Supremes and Temptations |
| UK45 | Albatross | Fleetwood Mac |
| UKLP | Diana & Supremes Join The Temptations | Diana Ross & Supremes and Temptations |

WEEK 3

| | | |
|---|---|---|
| US45 | Everyday People | Sly & The Family Stone |
| USLP | The Beatles | Beatles |
| UK45 | Blackberry Way | Move |
| UKLP | Diana & Supremes Join The Temptations | Diana Ross & Supremes and Temptations |

WEEK 4

| | | |
|---|---|---|
| US45 | Everyday People | Sly & The Family Stone |
| USLP | The Beatles | Beatles |
| UK45 | (If Paradise Is) Half As Nice | Amen Corner |
| UKLP | Diana & Supremes Join The Temptations | Diana Ross & Supremes and Temptations |

## THE GRAPEVINE

■ Jim Morrison of The Doors has had a black suit made from the hide of an unborn pony.

■ Doubleday books has advance orders for 80,000 hardback copies of Tiny Tim's biography.

■ Guitarist Trevor Burton has left The Move, to be replaced by Rick Price, previously with Sight & Sound.

■ Art Garfunkel has taken a straight acting role in the film *Catch 22*, with location shooting in Mexico.

*Mr. & Mrs. Tiny Tim*

*Garfunkel the movie star*

*Morrison and the unborn pony (puke!)*

## BEATLES CALL IN KLEIN; GIVE ROOFTOP PERFORMANCE

The Beatles have called in American business negotiator Allen Klein – who has previously handled the financial affairs of other major UK groups like The Rolling Stones and The Animals – to advise them on the running of their Apple Enterprises.

He flew to London for a preliminary business conference with the group on 3 February, and took over the reins of Apple a week later.

Meanwhile, rehearsals for the much-announced Beatles London concert have now definitely become the basis of a TV documentary film. Several new, specially written songs were heard by startled passers-by in London's Savile Row on the afternoon of Thursday, 30 January, when the group gave a spontaneous performance on the Apple roof, and were filmed and recorded for the programme.

Almost all 12 tracks of the new Beatles album, centred around the documentary, are now complete, with final recordings to take place before the end of February. An April or May release is slated for the LP.

## PRESLEY RECORDS IN MEMPHIS

Elvis Presley has recorded in Memphis for the first time since leaving Sun REcords in 1955.

At American Studios, with the resident band, he has cut over 30 new tracks, including a version of the Beatles' 'Hey Jude'.

## MARCH 1969

### CHARTS

| | |
|---|---|
| US45 | Everyday People<br>*Sly & The Family Stone* |
| USLP | The Beatles<br>*Beatles* |
| UK45 | Where Do You Go To My Lovely<br>*Peter Sarstedt* |
| UKLP | Diana & Supremes Join The Temptations<br>*Diana Ross & Supremes and Temptations* |

—— WEEK 2 ——

| | |
|---|---|
| US45 | Everyday People<br>*Sly & The Family Stone* |
| USLP | Wichita Lineman<br>*Glen Campbell* |
| UK45 | Where Do You Go To My Lovely<br>*Peter Sarstedt* |
| UKLP | Diana & Supremes Join The Temptations<br>*Diana Ross & Supremes and Temptations* |

—— WEEK 3 ——

| | |
|---|---|
| US45 | Dizzy<br>*Tommy Roe* |
| USLP | Wichita Lineman<br>*Glen Campbell* |
| UK45 | Where Do You Go To My Lovely<br>*Peter Sarstedt* |
| UKLP | Diana & Supremes Join The Temptations<br>*Diana Ross & Supremes and Temptations* |

—— WEEK 4 ——

| | |
|---|---|
| US45 | Dizzy<br>*Tommy Roe* |
| USLP | Wichita Lineman<br>*Glen Campbell* |
| UK45 | Where Do You Go To My Lovely<br>*Peter Sarstedt* |
| UKLP | Goodbye<br>*Cream* |

—— WEEK 5 ——

| | |
|---|---|
| US45 | Dizzy<br>*Tommy Roe* |
| USLP | Blood, Sweat & Tears<br>*Blood, Sweat & Tears* |
| UK45 | I Heard It Through The Grapevine<br>*Marvin Gaye* |
| UKLP | Goodbye<br>*Cream* |

### THE GRAPEVINE

■ Motown vice-president Barney Ales has visited London in a bid to sign The Pretty Things as the US label's first British act.

■ Ex-Shadow Brian Bennett is to be Tom Jones's drummer on his world tour.

■ Mason, Capaldi, Wood & Frog, the group formed out of Traffic after Steve Winwood's departure, has split after just 60 days together, without recording.

# MORRISON IN TROUBLE

Jim Morrison of The Doors was arrested on March 1 in Miami on multiple charges, including lewd and lascivious behaviour in public, indecent exposure, and public profanity and drunkenness — which could land him with a total three and a half year jail sentence.

During a concert at Dinner Key Auditorium, Morrison (who has had previous brushes with the law in New York, New Haven and Phoenix) apparently appeared drunk, screamed obscenities, and exposed himself in full view of the sold-out 10,000-strong audience.

Miami and Dade County police did not arrest him on the spot, for fear that it would cause a riot. They sought him immediately after the concert, but he had left the auditorium. The Doors then left for the Caribbean the next morning.

Morrison's felony charge has made him liable to arrest and extradition anywhere within the US. Joe Durant, an assistant to the Florida State Attorney, comments: 'I was extremely shocked at the facts in this case as to what this man did. The State Attorney's office will prosecute, and ask for the maximum sentence on each count to run consecutively.'

*Pretties to Motown*

*With Tom Jones: Shadow Brian Bennett*

## DYLAN RECORDS WITH CASH

Bob Dylan has completed the sessions for his next album in Nashville, using the same trio (Charlie McCoy, Pete Drake and Kenny Buttrey) who played with him 18 months ago on 'John Wesley Harding', plus three further session men.

An unexpected development at the sessions was a series of duets with country star Johnny Cash — according to reports, the two of them 'just went into the studio and jammed', producing some 15 tracks.

Some of these may make it on to the new LP, but there is speculation that a whole album of Dylan-Cash duets may now follow later.

## LENNON AND McCARTNEY BOTH WED

Paul McCartney and John Lennon have married within days of each other. On March 12, McCartney wed American photographer Linda Eastman at Marylebone Registry Office in London, while on March 20, Lennon tied the knot with Japanese avant-garde artist Yoko Ono in Gibraltar.

*Mr. & Mrs. Macca*

Meanwhile, no date has yet been set for the next Beatles LP because they still have to select the tracks from at least two dozen recent recordings. Among likely candidates are 'Maxwell's Silver Hammer', 'Polythene Pam', 'All I Want Is You', 'Teddy Boy'. 'Jubilee', 'Octopus's Garden' (a Ringo solo), George Harrison's 'Not Guilty' and John's solo 'What's The New Mary Jane'.

# ALBUMS OVERTAKE SINGLES IN UK

In 1968, for the first time ever, production of albums in the UK exceeded that of singles. A total of 49,184,000 LPs (an increase of 11 million over 1967) were manufactured during the year, compared with 49,161,000 singles.

UK record sales as a whole also hit a new high peak in 1968, with revenue topping £30 million – over £2 million more than in the previous year.

The grand total of 98,345,000 records produced in 1968 is second only to 1964's all-time peak figure of 101,257,000. However, singles accounted for almost three-quarters of the 1964 total, and the subsequent spectacular growth in LP sales means the revenue from 1968 sales was greater than that of 1964.

Barry Ryan celebrates three million sales

## THE GRAPEVINE

■ Rolling Stone Bill Wyman and his wife are divorcing.

■ Marital breakup is also strongly rumoured for John and Michelle Phillips of The Mamas & The Papas, though the group are recording again, without the now-solo Cass Elliott.

■ The Kinks' Ray Davies has produced the next Turtles single.

■ Barry Ryan's 'Eloise' has sold over three million worldwide, and topped charts in 17 countries.

Wyman – divorce

# FOUR EUROVISION WINNERS!

The 1969 Eurovision Song Contest, held in Madrid, produced the most amazing result in the competition's history, when four entries tied for first place with (unsurprisingly) the lowest-ever winning totals of 18 points apiece.

The joint winning songs were Holland's 'De Troubadour', sung by Lennie Kuhr, Spain's 'Vivo Cantata', sung by Salome, France's 'Un Jour Un Enfant', sung by Frida Boccara, and the UK's 'Boom Bang-A-Bang', sung by Lulu.

Lulu – first equal

Lulu, who departed soon afterwards for a belated honeymoon in Acapulco with Bee Gee husband Maurice Gibb, as her agent was being inundated with overseas offers on the strength of her win, told the NME: 'I don't mind sharing the prize, as long as I'm one of the firsts. It's better this way, because we're all happy.'

However, a week later, Sweden (whose entry finished ninth) declared 'We have taken part in a mediocre programme long enough,' and announced that it would not participate next year. Yugoslavia (which finished 13th) is also having 'second thoughts' about next year, while Austria and Denmark did not compete this year because of similar feelings about the quality of this supposedly presitigious musical event.

## TORK FINDS RELEASE

Former Monkee Peter Tork is now working with his own group, named Release. He told the NME's Hollywood correspondent: 'Three is the quorum for our group. We sometimes have four members, and are thinking of having a rotating fourth – at the moment it's a girl that I'm promoting, named Judy Mayhan.'

The other three are Tork himself on vocals and lead guitar, Ripley Wildflower on bass and vocals, and Tork's girlfriend Reine Stewart on drums.

'I'd rather work with friends,' says Tork, 'because that makes much better music.'

## CHARTS

| | | |
|---|---|---|
| US45 | Dizzy | Tommy Roe |
| USLP | Wichita Lineman | Glenn Campbell |
| UK45 | I Heard It Through The Grapevine | Marvin Gaye |
| UKLP | Goodbye | Cream |

— WEEK 2 —

| | | |
|---|---|---|
| US45 | Aquarius/Let The Sunshine In | Fifth Dimension |
| USLP | Blood, Sweat & Tears | Blood, Sweat & Tears |
| UK45 | I Heard It Through The Grapevine | Marvin Gaye |
| UKLP | Goodbye | Cream |

— WEEK 3 —

| | | |
|---|---|---|
| US45 | Aquarius/Let The Sunshine In | Fifth Dimension |
| USLP | Blood, Sweat & Tears | Blood, Sweat & Tears |
| UK45 | The Israelites | Desmond Dekker |
| UKLP | Goodbye | Cream |

— WEEK 4 —

| | | |
|---|---|---|
| US45 | Aquarius/Let The Sunshine In | Fifth Dimension |
| USLP | Hair | Original Cast |
| UK45 | The Isrealites | Desmond Dekker |
| UKLP | Goodbye | Cream |

# BLIND FAITH

*Steve Winwood, Rick Grech, Ginger Baker, Eric Clapton – Blind Faith*

It was announced on May 6 that the Eric Clapton-Steve Winwood-Ginger Baker 'supergroup' is to be called Blind Faith.

The fourth member has also now been chosen: on bass (and also possibly electric violin) will be Rick Grech from Family. He joined the others at Winwood's Berkshire cottage on May 3 to begin rehearsals, and has played in the studio sessions which completed the group's debut LP, scheduled for June release.

They are said to have 14 hours of tape in the can, though not all of it is suitable for release.

Blind Faith begin a US tour on July 11, for which manager Robert Stigwood has negotiated them a minimum of $25,000 a concert against a percentage (60-70 per cent) of the gross. One date alone is known to be worth $60,000.

Grech has been replaced in Family by John Weider, formerly with Eric Burdon's Animals.

## STAR QUOTE

JIMMY PAGE

on Led Zeppelin's instant conquest of the US

*'I was anxious to get to America; we came as soon as we could. I didn't have any confidence in English audiences at all. That's because The Yardbirds had their biggest success in the US, and I just assumed it would be the same with us.'*

## US VISA BAN ON LENNON

John Lennon is no longer able to visit America. An official of the US Embassy in London told the NME that Lennon's 'standing visa' was revoked at the time of his recent drug conviction, and that 'very serious consideration' would have to be given before it could be renewed.

The Embassy also suggested that any immediate application by Lennon would almost certainly be turned down, but he is known to have subsequently (on May 5) reapplied for a visa to visit the US on a business trip.

It is understood that any American visit would be for Lennon to join in talks on The Beatles' bid for Northern Songs, or discussions on Apple's US interests – and not for a tour by the group.

## FAIRPORT DRUMMER IS KILLED IN CRASH

Martin Lamble, 19-year old drummer with UK folk-rock group Fairport Convention, was killed in the early hours of Monday, May 12, when the group's van crashed on the M1 motorway as they returned to London from a gig in Birmingham.

Also killed in the crash was American stage clothing designer Jeannie Franklin, while Fairport guitarists Richard Thompson and Simon Nicol, bassist Ashley Hutchings, and road manager Harvey Bramham, were all injured.

The group's lead singer Sandy Denny was travelling separately by car, and was not involved.

*Mickie Most: splitting with Lulu*

## THE GRAPEVINE

■ Lulu has split from producer Mickie Most after a two-year association.

■ The Rolling Stones may launch their own Pear label, patterned after The Beatles' Apple, when their Decca/London contract runs out next February.

■ Peter Green and Jeremy Spencer of Fleetwood Mac plan an orchestral-choral LP telling the life story of Christ.

*Fleetwood Mac get religion?*

# THE BALLAD OF JOHN AND YOKO

John and Yoko Lennon were joined in their hotel room in Toronto, Canada, by more than 40 friends, to record Lennon's anthemic composition 'Give Peace A Chance', which is to be released as a single by Apple, credited to The Plastic Ono Band.

Among the group were Tom Smothers of The Smothers Brothers, and a Montreal Jewish religious leader, Rabbi Feinberg.

Meanwhile, The Beatles' single 'The Ballad Of John And Yoko' has been banned by many US radio stations, and by the Australian Broadcasting Corporation, because of alleged blasphemy.

Lennon sings the phrase, 'Christ, you know it ain't easy' several times on the disc, which has caused no similar upset in the UK. An Apple spokesman commented that the words were 'a natural expression within the context of the song.'

## KING: ROBBERY AND CURRY VANDALISM

Thieves broke into the unoccupied Marble Arch, London, home of recording artist, producer and TV presenter Jonathan King on the night of 7 June. They stole a collection of albums, a white fur coat, and some tapes of a musical score composed by King.

In an eccentric act of vandalism, the thieves also disposed of a large amount of chicken curry: when King returned home some hours later to discover the burglary, he also found this uneaten meal liberally covering the floor of his house.

## STEWART GOES SOLO

Rod the Mod Stewart (second left) leaves The Jeff Beck Group

Rod Stewart, lead singer with The Jeff Beck group, has been signed to a solo recording contract by Mercury — although it is stressed that this will be a parallel independent venture, and that he will not be leaving Beck.

Stewart begins recording for a single and album in mid-June, with producer Lou Reizner. Former Manfred Mann vocalist Mike D'Abo (whose own group announced its split this month) is handling arrangements on some of the tracks.

## THE GRAPEVINE

■ Cilla Black has had plastic surgery to remodel her nose; this puts her in a club with Tom Jones, Dave Clark, Connie Francis, Herb Alpert, Paul Anka and many more.

■ John Sebastian is writing the music for the Peter Sellers/Ringo Starr film The Magic Christian.

■ Davy Jones of The Monkees has revealed a secret 18-month marriage to 24-year old Linda Haines.

Cilla — a new hooter

## TOMMY ROE FILM MUSICAL

Tommy Roe, whose 'Dizzy' has now topped both the US and UK charts and is the biggest-selling single of his seven-year hitmaking career, is to make his starring film debut later this year.

The movie, titled Tommy Who, will begin production for Roe's own independent film company in October. Location shooting will take place in Florida and parts of California.

Roe told the NME: 'It will be a musical comedy in colour, and will include about eight songs. It should take about a month to shoot, but we haven't cast it yet. We don't expect it to be shown before mid-1970.'

131

# JULY 1969

## REDDING QUITS HENDRIX

Bassist Noel Redding has quit The Jimi Hendrix Experience, following a dispute with Hendrix in the US. Redding flew home to London for discussions about his future with the group's former manager Chas Chandler.

It is understood that Redding's decision was prompted by Hendrix's failure to consult him about future plans. The guitarist is believed to be considering dropping the name 'Experience' in order to augment his group into a 'creative commune', which would include both writers and musicians.

Redding has already been running his own part-time outfit known as Fat Mattress since the beginning of the year, and now intends to devote his full-time energy to this group.

Rumours suggest that the third Experience member, drummer Mitch Mitchell – who also flew home to London a few days after Redding – may also decide to leave Hendrix and form his own band.

Redding: leaving the Experience to devote full-time energy to his Fat Mattress

# BRIAN JONES TRAGEDY; STONES TRIUMPH

The Stones In The Park

The Rolling Stones played a highly successful Saturday afternoon outdoor free concert in front of an estimated 250,000 fans in London's Hyde Park on July 5, though the joy of the event was inevitably muted by the death of former group member Brian Jones only two days before.

Jones had left the group to pursue his divergent musical interests (a return to R&B basics) during June; the Stones recruited a replacement, former John Mayall Bluesbreakers guitarist Mick Taylor, in time to prepare for Hyde Park.

Brian died at his home, Cotchford Farm in Hartfield, Sussex, after taking a midnight swim in his pool. He was found floating by house guests who tried to revive him, but was pronounced dead by a doctor at around 3am on July 3.

The Stones dedicated their Hyde Park concert to Jones's memory. Mick Jagger opened the performance with words of tribute and a poem by Shelley, after which a host of butterflies were released into the air.

The Stones' 75-minute act was filmed by Granada TV, which plans a documentary of the event.

## CHARTS

| | | |
|---|---|---|
| US45 | Love Theme From Romeo & Juliet | Henry Mancini Orchestra |
| USLP | Hair | Original Cast |
| UK45 | Something In The Air | Thunderclap Newman |
| UKLP | This is Tom Jones | Tom Jones |

### WEEK 2

| | | |
|---|---|---|
| US45 | In The Year 2525 | Zager and Evans |
| USLP | Hair | Original Cast |
| UK45 | Something In The Air | Thunderclap Newman |
| UKLP | This Is Tom Jones | Tom Jones |

### WEEK 3

| | | |
|---|---|---|
| US45 | In The Year 2525 | Zager and Evans |
| USLP | Hair | Original Cast |
| UK45 | In The Ghetto | Elvis Presley |
| UKLP | This Is Tom Jones | Tom Jones |

### WEEK 4

| | | |
|---|---|---|
| US45 | In The Year 2525 | Zager and Evans |
| USLP | Blood, Sweat & Tears | Blood, Sweat & Tears |
| UK45 | Honky Tonk Women | Rolling Stones |
| UKLP | This Is Tom Jones | Tom Jones |

Stills, Crosby, Nash & Young

## THE GRAPEVINE

■ Crosby, Stills & Nash have recruited Stills's former Buffalo Springfield colleague Neil Young as their fourth member; he will join their first US concert tour in August.

■ Controversy over the sleeve of Blind Faith's debut LP, which pictures a naked teenage girl, has forced Atlantic Records to design a replacement; many US dealers have cancelled orders, claiming it is 'salacious'.

## ROCK TAKES NEWPORT

The 16th annual Newport Jazz Festival at Rhode Island included heavy rock for the first time, and attracted a record three-day audience of over 80,000.

Bands like Jethro Tull, John Mayall, Ten Years After and Jeff Beck played alongside an extensive jazz line-up, and R&B/blues acts James Brown, Johnny Winter and B.B. King. Led Zeppelin played the final night, despite requests from local authorities that they should not appear, 'in the interest of public safety'!

# WOODSTOCK: DISASTROUSLY GREAT

The three-day Woodstock Music and Art Fair, held in rural upstate New York, attracted an enormous audience, estimated at around half a million, to a piece of farmland which stood little chance of catering adequately for such a vast horde – particularly when torrential rain turned the whole area into a quagmire.

However, despite being declared an official disaster area, the festival developed a tribal spirit of its own, focused by an array of some of the world's top rock talent.

Acts who performed (and were filmed and recorded for hoped-for albums and a movie) included Jimi Hendrix, The Who, Creedence Clearwater Revival, Santana, Jefferson Airplane, Crosby, Stills, Nash & Young, Ritchie Havens, Ten Years After, Joan Baez, Sly & The Family Stone, and many more.

## GOLD ZEPPELIN

Led Zeppelin, currently on a record-breaking seven-week US tour, have won a gold disc for over a million dollars' worth of sales of their debut album. The award was presented to the group by Atlantic vice-president Jerry Wexler at a special luncheon in New York.

Meanwhile, work on the group's second LP is almost complete, and US advance orders already total over 200,000.

*(l to r) Jones, Plant, Page – Zep go gold*

*Kiki for Motown*

## CHARTS

| | |
|---|---|
| US45 | In The Year 2525 — *Zager and Evans* |
| USLP | Blood, Sweat & Tears — *Blood, Sweat & Tears* |
| UK45 | Honky Tonk Women — *Rolling Stones* |
| UKLP | Flaming Star — *Elvis Presley* |

### WEEK 2

| | |
|---|---|
| US45 | In The Year 2525 — *Zager and Evans* |
| USLP | Blood, Sweat & Tears — *Blood, Sweat & Tears* |
| UK45 | Honky Tonk Women — *Rolling Stones* |
| UKLP | Stand Up — *Jethro Tull* |

### WEEK 3

| | |
|---|---|
| US45 | In The Year 2525 — *Zager and Evans* |
| USLP | Blood, Sweat & Tears — *Blood, Sweat & Tears* |
| UK45 | Honky Tonk Women — *Rolling Stones* |
| UKLP | Stand Up — *Jethro Tull* |

### WEEK 4

| | |
|---|---|
| US45 | Honky Tonk Women — *Rolling Stones* |
| USLP | At San Quentin — *Johnny Cash* |
| UK45 | Honky Tonk Women — *Rolling Stones* |
| UKLP | Stand Up — *Jethro Tull* |

### WEEK 5

| | |
|---|---|
| US45 | Honky Tonk Women — *Rolling Stones* |
| USLP | At San Quentin — *Johnny Cash* |
| UK45 | In The Year 2525 — *Zager and Evans* |
| UKLP | Stand Up — *Jethro Tull* |

## FRAMPTON AND PIE FREE TO RECORD

A dispute between Peter Frampton and Steve Roland's Double-R Productions, which had forced Frampton's recording career with his new group Humble Pie on to ice, is over.

A statement announced: 'As the result of a substantial settlement from Immediate Records, the courts have lifted the injunction which prevailed on recordings by Peter Frampton.'

Roland had claimed that Frampton was still under contract to Double-R from his Herd days. An ex-parte injunction stopped Immediate from releasing any Humble Pie product until this dispute was revolved.

*Frampton – full steam ahead*

## ELVIS: VIVA LAS VEGAS!

Elvis Presley has made a triumphant return to live work after nearly a decade performing only for the movie cameras.

His four-week cabaret season at Las Vegas's new International Hotel has been critically acclaimed, with all agreeing he had lost little of the stage fire that made him famous. The show mixed Presley classics with rock standards, Beatles covers and new material including his next single 'Suspicious Minds'.

Asked at the pre-opening press conference if he now felt it was a mistake to have done so many film soundtrack LPs, Presley replied: 'I think so. When you do ten songs in a movie, they can't all be good songs. Anyway, I got tired of singing to turtles!'

# LIVING FAST AND DYING PRETTY

Jim Morrison, Jimi Hendrix, Janis Joplin – all died within the same twelve months, and each has enjoyed a posthumous popularity shared with other rock stars who have died while comparatively young. It's a secondary success which seems to bear out the apocryphal words of an unnamed RCA executive who is rumoured to have exclaimed 'Best career move he's made in fifteen years' when told of Elvis Presley's death in 1977. From a marketing point of view, a dead legend is far less trouble and far more profitable than an ego-tripping, insecure erstwhile star whose career is on a rollercoaster to oblivion; and ultimately more romantic, especially when they appear to have had a hand in their own premature demise.

There was nothing new in performers pressing the old self-destruct button of course. While a few like Bill Haley died of more of less natural causes, and the ghostly gremlins of Plummet Airlines hurtled Glenn Miller, Buddy Holly and Otis Redding towards an early entry in the hip Hall of Fame, personal abuse took a regular toll including Billie Holliday (with a big H), Hank Williams, who drank himself to death, and Nat King Cole literally chain-smoking his way to the graveyard.

But it was at the end of the 1960s that seemingly indestructible icons of the youth revolution began dropping like flies.

Brian Jones, late of the 'Stones, said goodbye to the goodlife in 1969 when he was found face down in his swimming pool, but by all the post-mortem accounts he was already floating long before he hit the water. He'd just been given the order of the elbow by his blues blowin' buddies, so who knows what drove him to the edge?

Similarly, Janis, Jimi and Jim all died as a direct or indirect result of drug abuse, although the reasons for their final release were not identical. Janis Joplin had apparently kicked her habit, and to all intents and purposes seemed to be heading for even more glorious success than she had previously enjoyed as lead vocalist with Big Brother & The Holding Company. Joplin had a desperate need to be loved, however, and frequently felt used – that her trust in those around her had been betrayed. Despite being admired, almost worshipped, for her unique voice, she was lonely and depressed. As she completed the classic 'Pearl' album, bedecked in the gladrags of some bygone movie queen, she returned to the chemical crutch she thought she'd learned to live without. Janis died of a heroin overdose in October 1970.

Jimi Hendrix had enjoyed three years of mega-stardom, but by 1970 was finding it harder and harder to live up to his own 'superstud' image while at the same time venturing into uncharted musical areas increasingly distant from the territory of his original fans. Simultaneously, he was discovering that those he had trusted to take care of his financial affairs had become considerably more wealthy than he had himself. He died just a month before Joplin in a singularly unglamorous fashion, choking on his own vomit. The immediate reasons for his death were obvious, less so the complex ramifications of the monetary legacy of his work, still a legal minefield twenty years later.

Jim Morrison, vocalist and focal point of The Doors, has generated more interest (and money of late) since he ended his days in his Paris flat, than he did in his lifetime. When he was found dead in the bath after a heart attack in July '71, he was trying to maintain a low profile after his conviction for obscenity for allegedly exposing himself onstage in Florida. Confirming some critics' views of his career as wimp-to-wally-to-weirdo, Jim announced he was giving up music to be a poet and film maker; however, eight gold albums with The Doors and the looks of a Greek God ensured his place in the pantheon of pop forever.

Over the next decade death stalked the 'Sixties survivors, rock's grim reaper claiming The Who's Keith Moon, Beach Boy Dennis Wilson, Bob Hite of Canned Heat, Sandy Denny, Free's Paul Kossoff. Yet despite their own part in their eventual passing, mistakes are easily forgotten, achievements continually glorified; and who can argue with Ultimate Immortality via the book, the biopic and the boxed set?

Janis Joplin 1943-1970

Jimi Hendrix 1942-1970

Jim Morrison 1943-1971

# 1969

*Mary Hopkin – for Eurovision*

# DYLAN ON ISLE OF WIGHT

Bob Dylan and The Band topped the bill of the UK's 1969 Isle of Wight Festival, drawing an open-air crowd of over 200,000 – including rock celebrities like John Lennon, George Harrison, Ringo Starr, Steve Winwood, Keith Richards and others.

Dylan presented mainly familiar material, all of it well-received, but there was some disappointment in the audience that his act only lasted for an hour. This, it seems, was mainly the fault of poor organization.

As Dylan said afterwards: 'I was here at five-thirty, ready to go on, but I was kept waiting until eleven. I played long enough – I didn't want to go on much later.' Indeed, the NME was told earlier that Dylan would take the stage at 9pm, probably to play until midnight, but organizers' estimates kept changing through the evening.

The Band's own set preceded him, and focussed on their 'Music From Big Pink' LP.

Other acts highlighting the three-day event included The Who, The Moody Blues, The Nice, Joe Cocker, Julie Felix, Richie Havens and Fat Mattress.

*Dylan – well received at the concert but inconvenienced by organizers*

## BEE GEES SACK THEIR DRUMMER

*The Bee Gees with departing drummer Colin Peterson (right)*

The Bee Gees, who have already lost original lead guitarist Vince Melouney and currently-soloing Gibb brother Robin over the last year, have now parted company with drummer Colin Petersen.

The official group statement announced: 'Barry and Maurice Gibb have terminated their association with Colin, who will cease to be a member of the Bee Gees.'

Barry Gibb commented that Petersen's departure is 'all part of our natural progression . . . he has been spending an increasing amount of time on his management activities, and we have been aware for some time that he would eventually leave.'

Peterson disagrees, claiming an agreement exists whereby he is an equal partner in the group for five years from July 4, 1967. Alleging breach of obligation, he has served writs asking for the affairs of the partnership to be wound up in court.

As well as claiming damages, Peterson seeks to restrain the Gibb brothers from performing as The Bee Gees without his participation.

## THE GRAPEVINE

■ All five members of The Equals have been injured in Germany, where their car ran off an autobahn in a gale.

■ James Taylor has broken an arm and a leg in a motorbike crash.

■ Mary Hopkin is to be the UK's representative in the 1970 Eurovision Song Contest.

■ Deep Purple guitarist Ritchie Blackmore has married German dancer Barbel Hardie.

## NASH KEEPS QUIET

Graham Nash, who fell ill shortly after his first major shows with Crosby, Stills & Nash, has recovered, but has been ordered to rest his throat or threaten his singing voice.

He whispered to the NME's New York correspondent: 'My doctor told me that if I don't overdo talking, I won't need an operation - so I'm keeping mum.'

*Nash's vow of silence*

# MOODIES ON THE THRESHOLD

Moody Blues: On The Threshold Of A Label

## THE GRAPEVINE

■ Cliff Richard has signed a three-year deal with Warner Bros. for US releases, starting with current UK hit single 'Throw Down A Line'.

■ Tyrannosaurus Rex – Marc Bolan and Steve Took – are to split, though Bolan will retain the name.

■ Christine Perfect, singer with Chicken Shack and wife of Fleetwood Mac's John McVie, to form her own group, yet unnamed.

## OCTOBER 1969

Christine Perfect (centre) to leave the Shack

The Moody Blues have launched their own record label, named Threshold Records after their worldwide hit album 'On The Threshold Of A Dream'.

Owned jointly by The Moodies and their producer Tony Clarke, the label's intention is 'to provide a small company atmosphere with major company facilities'. The group has signed a five-year deal with Decca for marketing and distribution of Threshold, leaving the Moodies with 'complete artistic control'.

The label will concentrate on LPs, among the first of which will be by a new Liverpool singer named Timon, whom Justin Hayward is producing, and Wolverhampton group Trapeze, with whom John Lodge has been working.

The Moody Blues will launch Threshold themselves, however, with their LP 'Dedicated To Our Children's Children's Children', in November.

## CLAPTON WITH DELANEY & BONNIE

Despite frequent denials of a Blind Faith split, Eric Clapton is booked to tour Europe as a member of Delaney & Bonnie & Friends, the husband-and-wife-led group he met when they supported Blind Faith's US tour.

'This group is incredible – the best group in the world,' commented Clapton.

## BATTERY-POWERED BOWIE

David Bowie has revealed that the electronic astral effects on his hit single 'Space Oddity' were made on a Stylophone. This is a pocket-sized electronic organ, powered by batteries and operated by touching a metal stylus tip to its keyboard – hence the name.

The portable instrument was introduced to UK TV in 1968 by Australian singer Rolf Harris, who made frequent demonstrations of its use.

Bowie now apparently does all his composing on a stylophone, while sales of the instrument are also spreading among teenagers - frequently for use in playing along with groups on disc!

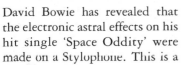

Bowie's stylophone oddity

## DIANA TO LEAVE SUPREMES

It has been officially announced that lead singer Diana Ross will leave The Supremes in January 1970. She will spend February rehearsing her new act, and make her solo cabaret debut in Framingham, Massachusetts, on March 8.

Mary Wilson will take over as The Supremes leader, and Ross will be replaced in the group by Jean Terrell, who is the sister of former heavyweight boxer Ernie Terrell, and former vocalist in his sideline vocal group Ernie & The Heavyweights, which broke up when he retired from the ring.

The group are likely to be renamed The New Supremes, and both they and Ross will continue to record separately for Motown.

## CHARTS

| | |
|---|---|
| US45 | Sugar Sugar *Archies* |
| USLP | Green River *Creedence Clearwater Revival* |
| UK45 | Bad Moon Rising *Creedence Clearwater Revival* |
| UKLP | Abbey Road *Beatles* |
| **WEEK 2** | |
| US45 | Sugar Sugar *Archies* |
| USLP | Green River *Creedence Clearwater Revival* |
| UK45 | I'll Never Fall In Love Again *Bobbie Gentry* |
| UKLP | Abbey Road *Beatles* |
| **WEEK 3** | |
| US45 | I Can't Get Next To You *Temptations* |
| USLP | Green River *Creedence Clearwater Revival* |
| UK45 | I'll Never Fall In Love Again *Bobbie Gentry* |
| UKLP | Abbey Road *Beatles* |
| **WEEK 4** | |
| US45 | I Can't Get Next To You *Temptations* |
| USLP | Green River *Creedence Clearwater Revival* |
| UK45 | I'll Never Fall In Love Again *Bobbie Gentry* |
| UK LP | Abbey Road *Beatles* |

*Flaming Youth – Dutch TV Special*

# ELVIS RETURNS TO CONCERTS; TV WITH RINGO?

Elvis Presley, back atop the US singles chart for the first time since 1962 with 'Suspicious Minds', is to return to the concert arena in the New Year, when he takes his own two-hour package to the Houston Astrodome in Texas (the world's largest indoor arena, with a capacity of 72,000) for three nights from February 27.

Presley's last concert appearance was a charity one-off in Hawaii in 1961, and he last toured regularly in 1956!

The new initiative is seen as a logical step on from his return to the live stage in Las Vegas this summer. He is also booked for a return four-week engagement at the city's International Hotel, which will this time guarantee him one million dollars – 25 per cent more than his first-time fee.

Meanwhile, US press reports suggest that Ringo Starr, along with his *Magic Christian* co-star Raquel Welch, has been invited

*Starr and Sellers*

to join Presley in a second TV spectacular, planned for US screening shortly before Christmas. Apple's press office in the UK, however, could make no comment about such a projected link-up.

## STONES ON THE SCREEN

The film *Michael Kohlhaas*, in which Rolling Stone Keith Richards plays a character role, opens in London on November 13, with a general UK release in December.

Richard's cameo appearance marks his dramatic debut in the cinema, and caused him to have his first haircut for two years! Stars of the film are David Warner, Anna Karina, and Richard's girlfriend Anita Pallenberg.

Meanwhile, the long-awaited film *Performance*, in which fellow Stone Mick Jagger made his starring dramatic debut opposite James Fox (and – again – Anita

Pallenberg), has been reprieved by Warner Bros.

It had originally been planned to scrap the movie after studio executive had declared it 'unintelligible', but Warner now says it can be salvaged, and will be a 1970 cinema release.

*Jagger as Turner*

## PURPLE CONCERTO FOR HOLLYWOOD

Deep Purple are to perform their rock/classical work 'Concerto For Group And Orchestra', written by keyboard player Jon Lord, at the Hollywood Bowl in March next year, during the group's more conventional tour of the United States.

Other performances of the work in Vienna and Zurich will similarly be slotted into a European tour in January.

The concerto was first performed at London's Royal Albert Hall on September 24, when the group played with the Royal Philharmonic Orchestra conducted by Malcolm Arnold. This was recorded by EMI, and will be released as a live album in the UK in December.

### CHARTS

| | | |
|---|---|---|
| US45 | Suspicious Minds | *Elvis Presley* |
| USLP | Abbey Road | *Beatles* |
| UK45 | Sugar Sugar | *Archies* |
| UKLP | Abbey Road | *Beatles* |
| **WEEK 2** | | |
| US45 | Wedding Bell Blues | *Fifth Dimension* |
| USLP | Abbey Road | *Beatles* |
| UK45 | Sugar Sugar | *Archies* |
| UKLP | Abbey Road | *Beatles* |
| **WEEK 3** | | |
| US45 | Wedding Bell Blues | *Fifth Dimension* |
| USLP | Abbey Road | *Beatles* |
| UK45 | Oh Well | *Fleetwood Mac* |
| UKLP | Abbey Road | *Beatles* |
| **WEEK 4** | | |
| US45 | Wedding Bell Blues | *Fifth Dimension* |
| USLP | Abbey Road | *Beatles* |
| UK45 | Sugar Sugar | *Archies* |
| UKLP | Abbey Road | *Beatles* |
| **WEEK 5** | | |
| US45 | Come Together/Something | *Beatles* |
| USLP | Abbey Road | *Beatles* |
| UK45 | Sugar Sugar | *Archies* |
| UKLP | Abbey Road | *Beatles* |

# HENDRIX: NEW GROUP AND FAREWELL TOUR WITH OLD?

### CHARTS

| | |
|---|---|
| US45 | Na Na Hey Hey Kiss Him Goodbye *Steam* |
| USLP | Abbey Road *Beatles* |
| UK45 | Yester-Me Yester-You Yesterday *Stevie Wonder* |
| UKLP | Abbey Road *Beatles* |
| **WEEK 2** | |
| US45 | Na Na Hey Hey Kiss Him Goodbye *Steam* |
| USLP | Abbey Road *Beatles* |
| UK45 | Ruby Don't Take Your Love To Town *Kenny Rogers & The New Edition* |
| UKLP | Abbey Road *Beatles* |
| **WEEK 3** | |
| US45 | Leaving On A Jet Plane *Peter, Paul & Mary* |
| USLP | Abbey Road *Beatles* |
| UK45 | Two Little Boys *Rolf Harris* |
| UKLP | Abbey Road *Beatles* |
| **WEEK 4** | |
| US45 | Someday We'll Be Together *Diana Ross & The Supremes* |
| USLP | Led Zeppelin II *Led Zeppelin* |
| UK45 | Two Little Boys *Rolf Harris* |
| UKLP | Abbey Road *Beatles* |

Jimi Hendrix is planning what he describes as a 'farewell tour' of the US, Britain and Europe, and has asked the two former members of The Experience, Noel Redding and Mitch Mitchell, to rejoin him for six weeks of concerts in the spring.

Several reports that Fat Mattress – Redding's current group - have broken up may leave him in a position to accept this offer, although the bassist is currently convalescing after a nervous breakdown.

Hendrix is also reported to be putting together a larger group for future work, possibly in a new direction. He has named drummer Buddy Miles as a definite member, but has not selected the other musicians.

Until recently, Hendrix has been unable to travel because he was due to face drugs charges in Canada which could have given him a maximum of seven years in prison. However, a Toronto court has acquitted him, and he is now free to tour abroad.

He has devoted much of the last three months to recording with session musicians, and now has a large stockpile of tracks available for future release.

## AND THEN THERE WAS ONE BEE GEE . . .

Barry Gibb has quit The Bee Gees, leaving his brother Maurice (currently holidaying in Australia with wife Lulu) as the sole remaining member of a group which was once a quintet!

Barry gave his reasons for leaving as being that he is 'fed up, miserable and completely disillusioned'. He now intends to embark on a solo career, following in the steps of brother Robin, whose fractious split last year has involved the Gibbs in a legal wrangle which has only just been amicably settled.

Discussions are now necessary between manager Robert Stigwood, Barry and Maurice regarding several projects which may not now take place – including their own Bee Gee record label, and a proposed TV series. Meanwhile, speculation is growing in music business circles that Maurice himself will now drop the Bee Gees name, and concentrate on working with Lulu.

## UNHEARD BEATLES TRACK FOR CHARITY

'Across The Universe', a John Lennon song recorded in 1968 by The Beatles but never released, is to be included in an EMI mid-priced all-star charity album to be issued in the New Year. All profits from the release will go to the World Wildlife Fund.

Meanwhile, the proposed Plastic Ono Band single 'You Know My Name', due for release by Apple on December 5, has been cancelled.

---

## THE GRAPEVINE

■ UK group The Peddlers have been booked for a three-week Las Vegas cabaret season at Caesar's Palace.

■ Pink Floyd are writing the score for Antonioni's next movie *Zabriski Point*.

■ Rumours (and aural evidence) suggest that the lead singers of The Archies ('Sugar Sugar') and The Cuff Links ('Tracy') are one and the same person.

■ George Harrison is another on-stage guest with Delaney & Bonnie.

*Floyd: to score Zabriski Point*

# SIXTIES CHARTBUSTERS

These top records and artist listings have been calculated from the peak chart positions they reached and the number of weeks they spent on the chart. In cases where a record is by two artists, i.e. 'Something Stupid' by Frank and Nancy Sinatra, then both artists receive full credit. In calculating the Top Album acts no various artist albums (including original casts or soundtracks) are included. Since these lists are chart-based rather than sales-based they tend to favour records that spent a long time on the charts over those that may have sold more but did so in a shorter period of time. The 'One-Hit Wonders' lists include all artists whose only Top 50 UK or Top 40 US single hit made the Top 5.

## US ONE-HIT WONDERS OF THE '60s

| | Artist | Title |
|---|---|---|
| 1960 | JEANNE BLACK | He'll Have To Stay |
| | JIMMY CHARLES | A Million To One |
| | MARK DINNING | Teen Angel |
| | FENDERMEN | Mule Skinner Blues |
| | HOLLYWOOD ARGYLES | Alley-Oop |
| | JOE JONES | You Talk Too Much |
| | LOLITA | Sailor (Your Home Is The Sea) |
| | MAURICE WILLIAMS & THE ZODIACS | Stay |
| | LARRY VERNE | Mr. Custer |
| 1961 | CAPRIS | There's A Moon Out Tonight |
| | JORGEN INGMANN | Apache |
| | ERNIE K-DOE | Mother-In-Law |
| | CHRIS KENNER | I Like It Like That (Pt.1) |
| | ARTHUR LYMAN | Yellow Bird |
| | MAR-KEYS | Last Night |
| | ROSIE & THE ORIGINALS | Angel Baby |
| 1962 | MARCIE BLANE | Bobby's Girl |
| | BRUCE CHANNEL | Hey! Baby |
| | CLAUDINE CLARK | Party Lights |
| | CONTOURS | Do You Love Me |
| | BARBARA GEORGE | I Know (You Don't Love Me No More) |
| | FRANK IFIELD | I Remember You |
| | KETTY LESTER | Love Letters |
| | SENSATIONS | Let Me In |
| | TORNADOS | Telstar |
| 1963 | CARAVELLES | You Don't Have To Be A Baby To Cry |
| | CASCADES | Rhythm Of The Rain |
| | CHANTAYS | Pipeline |
| | JAYNETTS | Sally, Go 'Round The Roses |
| | KYU SAKAMOTO | Sukiyaki |
| | SINGING NUN (SOEUR SOURIRE) | Dominique |
| | SURFARIS | Wipe Out |
| | JOHNNY THUNDER | Loop De Loop |
| | VILLAGE STOMPERS | Washington Square |
| 1964 | GALE GARNETT | We'll Sing In The Sunshine |
| | LORNE GREEN | Ringo |
| | HONEYCOMBS | Have I The Right? |
| | MURMAIDS | Popsicle And Icicles |
| | RIVIERAS | California Sun |
| | DANNY WILLIAMS | White On White |
| | J. FRANK WILSON & THE CAVALIER | Last Kiss |
| 1965 | GENTRYS | Keep On Dancing |
| | BARRY McGUIRE | Eve Of Destruction |
| 1966 | COUNT FIVE | Psychotic Reaction |
| | BOB LIND | Elusive Butterfly |
| | LOS BRAVOS | Black Is Black |
| | NAPOLEON XIV | They're Coming To Take Me Away Ha-Haaa! |
| | NEW VAUDEVILLE BAND | Winchester Cathedral |
| | STATLER BROTHERS | Flowers On The Wall |
| | T-BONES | No Matter What Shape (Your Stomach's In) |
| 1967 | BLUES MAGOOS | (We Ain't Got) Nothin' Yet |
| | BILL COSBY | Little Ole Man |
| | MUSIC EXPLOSION | Little Bit O' Soul |
| 1968 | CRAZY WORLD OF ARTHUR BROWN | Fire |
| | RICHARD HARRIS | MacArthur Park |
| | LEMON PIPERS | Green Tambourine |
| | HUGH MASEKELA | Grazing In The Grass |
| | PAUL MAURIAT | Love Is Blue |
| | HUGO MONTENEGRO & HIS ORCHESTRA | The Good, The Bad & The Ugly |
| | CLIFF NOBLES & CO. | The Horse |
| | O'KAYSIONS | Girl Watcher |
| | JEANNIE C. RILEY | Harper Valley P.T.A. |
| | MASON WILLIAMS | Classical Gas |
| 1969 | BROOKLYN BRIDGE | Worst That Could Happen |
| | FLYING MACHINE | Smile A Little Smile For Me |
| | JOHN FRED & HIS PLAYBOY BAND | Judy In Disguise (With Glasses) |
| | MERCY | Love (Can Make You Happy) |
| | SMITH | Baby It's You |
| | STEAM | Na Na Hey Hey Kiss Him Goodbye |
| | YOUNGBLOODS | Get Together |
| | ZAGER & EVANS | In The Year 2525 (Exordium & Terminus) |

*Zager & Evans or Evans & Zager? Maybe we'll know in 2525...*

## UK ONE-HIT WONDERS OF THE '60s

| | Artist | Title |
|---|---|---|
| 1960 | ELMER BERNSTEIN | Staccato's Theme |
| | PERCY FAITH | Theme From 'A Summer Place' |
| | RICKY VALANCE | Tell Laura I Love Her |
| 1961 | LAURIE JOHNSON | Sucu-Sucu |
| 1962 | B. BUMBLE & THE STINGERS | Nut Rocker |
| 1963 | CASCADES | Rhythm Of The Rain |
| | WINK MARTINDALE | Deck of Cards |
| | SINGING NUN | Dominique |
| 1964 | MARY WELLS | My Guy |
| 1965 | BURT BACHARACH | Trains And Boats And Planes |
| | HEDGEHOPPERS ANONYMOUS | It's Good News Week |
| | HORST JANKOWSKI | A Walk In The Black Forest |
| | BARRY McGUIRE | Eve Of Destruction |
| 1966 | BOB LIND | Elusive Butterfly |
| | NAPOLEON XIV | They're Coming To Take Me Away Ha-Haaa! |
| | OVERLANDERS | Michelle |
| 1967 | FLOWERPOT MEN | Let's Go To San Francisco |
| | WHISTLING JACK SMITH | I Was Kaiser Bill's Batman |
| 1968 | BONZO DOG DOO-DAH BAND | I'm The Urban Spaceman |
| | CRAZY WORLD OF ARTHUR BROWN | Fire |
| | JULIE DRISCOLL, BRIAN AUGER & TRINITY | This Wheel's On Fire |
| | JOHN FRED & HIS PLAYBOY BAND | Judy In Disguise (With Glasses) |
| | RICHARD HARRIS | MacArthur Park |
| | 1910 FRUITGUM CO | Simon Says |
| | OHIO EXPRESS | Yummy Yummy Yummy |
| | PLASTIC PENNY | Everything I Am |
| 1969 | ARCHIES | Sugar Sugar |
| | JANE BIRKIN & SERGE GAINSBOURG | Je T'Aime... Moi Non Plus |
| | EDWIN HAWKINS SINGERS | Oh Happy Day |
| | HUMBLE PIE | Natural Born Bugie |
| | UPSETTERS | The Return Of Django |
| | ZAGER & EVANS | In The Year 2525 (Exordium & Terminus) |

## US TOP SINGLES OF THE '60s

| | Title | Artist | Label | Year |
|---|---|---|---|---|
| 1 | TWIST | Chubby Checker | PARKWAY | 1960/2* |
| 2 | HEY JUDE | Beatles | APPLE | 1968 |
| 3 | THEME FROM 'A SUMMER PLACE' | Percy Faith | COLUMBIA | 1960 |
| 4 | TOSSIN' AND TURNIN' | Bobby Lewis | BELTONE | 1961 |
| 5 | I WANT TO HOLD YOUR HAND | Beatles | CAPITOL | 1964 |
| 6 | I HEARD IT THROUGH THE GRAPEVINE | Marvin Gaye | TAMLA | 1968 |
| 7 | I'M A BELIEVER | Monkees | COLGEMS | 1966 |
| 8 | AQUARIUS/LET THE SUNSHINE IN | Fifth Dimension | SOUL CITY | 1969 |
| 9 | ARE YOU LONESOME TONIGHT? | Elvis Presley | RCA | 1960 |
| 10 | IN THE YEAR 2525 | Zager & Evans | RCA | 1969 |
| 11 | IT'S NOW OR NEVER | Elvis Presley | RCA | 1960 |
| 12 | LOVE IS BLUE | Paul Mauriat | PHILIPS | 1968 |
| 13 | BIG GIRLS DON'T CRY | Four Seasons | VEE JAY | 1962 |
| 14 | I CAN'T STOP LOVING YOU | Ray Charles | ABC PARA | 1962 |
| 15 | SUGAR SHACK | Jimmy Gilmer & The Fireballs | DOT | 1963 |
| 16 | CATHY'S CLOWN | Everly Brothers | WARNER | 1960 |
| 17 | BIG BAD JOHN | Jimmy Dean | COLUMBIA | 1961 |
| 18 | TO SIR WITH LOVE | Lulu | EPIC | 1967 |
| 19 | PEOPLE GOT TO BE FREE | Rascals | ATLANTIC | 1968 |
| 20 | HONEY | Bobby Goldsboro | UA | 1968 |

*Appeared in Top 20 in both years

## UK TOP SINGLES OF THE '60s

| | Title | Artist | Label | Year |
|---|---|---|---|---|
| 1 | WONDERFUL LAND | Shadows | COLUMBIA | 1962 |
| 2 | IT'S NOW OR NEVER | Elvis Presley | RCA | 1960 |
| 3 | CATHY'S CLOWN | Everly Brothers | WARNER | 1960 |
| 4 | I REMEMBER YOU | Frank Ifield | COLUMBIA | 1962 |
| 5 | SUGAR SUGAR | Archies | RCA | 1969 |
| 6 | GREEN GREEN GRASS OF HOME | Tom Jones | DECCA | 1966 |
| 7 | HELLO GOODBYE | Beatles | PARLOPHONE | 1967 |
| 8 | TWO LITTLE BOYS | Rolf Harris | COLUMBIA | 1969 |
| 9 | APACHE | Shadows | COLUMBIA | 1960 |
| 10 | FROM ME TO YOU | Beatles | PARLOPHONE | 1963 |
| 11 | RELEASE ME (AND LET ME LOVE AGAIN) | Engelbert Humperdinck | DECCA | 1967 |
| 12 | THOSE WERE THE DAYS | Mary Hopkin | APPLE | 1968 |
| 13 | THE YOUNG ONES | Cliff Richard | COLUMBIA | 1962 |
| 14 | I WANT TO HOLD YOUR HAND | Beatles | PARLOPHONE | 1963 |
| 15 | A WHITER SHADE OF PALE | Procol Harum | DERAM | 1967 |
| 16 | TEARS | Ken Dodd | COLUMBIA | 1965 |
| 17 | GET BACK | Beatles | APPLE | 1969 |
| 18 | THE LAST WALTZ | Engelbert Humperdinck | DECCA | 1967 |
| 19 | TELSTAR | Tornados | DECCA | 1962 |
| 20 | LOVESICK BLUES | Frank Ifield | COLUMBIA | 1962 |

## US TOP ALBUMS OF THE '60s

| | Title | Artist | Label | Year |
|---|---|---|---|---|
| 1 | WEST SIDE STORY | Soundtrack | COLUMBIA | 1962 |
| 2 | BLUE HAWAII | Elvis Presley | RCA | 1961 |
| 3 | MORE OF THE MONKEES | Monkees | COLGEMS | 1967 |
| 4 | DAYS OF WINE AND ROSES | Andy Williams | COLUMBIA | 1963 |
| 5 | THE SOUND OF MUSIC | Original Cast | COLUMBIA | 1960 |
| 6 | SGT. PEPPER'S LONELY HEARTS CLUB BAND | Beatles | CAPITOL | 1967 |
| 7 | THE BUTTON DOWN MIND OF BOB NEWHART | Bob Newhart | WARNER | 1960 |
| 8 | MARY POPPINS | Soundtrack | BUENA VISTA | 1965 |
| 9 | MODERN SOUNDS IN COUNTRY AND WESTERN MUSIC | Ray Charles | ABC PARA | 1962 |
| 10 | EXODUS | Soundtrack | RCA | 1961 |
| 11 | A HARD DAY'S NIGHT | Beatles | UA | 1964 |
| 12 | JUDY AT CARNEGIE HALL | Judy Garland | CAPITOL | 1961 |
| 13 | HAIR | Original Cast | RCA | 1969 |
| 14 | PERSUASIVE PERCUSSION | Enoch Light | COMMAND | 1960 |
| 15 | BREAKFAST AT TIFFANY'S (SOUNDTRACK) | Henry Mancini | RCA | 1962 |
| 16 | SOLD OUT | Kingston Trio | CAPITOL | 1960 |
| 17 | THE FIRST FAMILY | Vaughn Meader | CADENCE | 1962 |
| 18 | CALCUTTA! | Lawrence Welk | DOT | 1961 |
| 19 | THE MONKEES | Monkees | COLGEMS | 1966 |
| 20 | ABBEY ROAD | Beatles | APPLE | 1969 |

## UK TOP ALBUMS OF THE '60s

| | Title | Artist | Label | Year |
|---|---|---|---|---|
| 1 | THE SOUND OF MUSIC | Soundtrack | RCA | 1965 |
| 2 | SOUTH PACIFIC | Soundtrack | RCA | 1958 |
| 3 | PLEASE PLEASE ME | Beatles | PARLOPHONE | 1963 |
| 4 | SERGEANT PEPPER'S LONELY HEARTS CLUB BAND | Beatles | PARLOPHONE | 1967 |
| 5 | WEST SIDE STORY | Soundtrack | PHILIPS | 1962 |
| 6 | G.I. BLUES | Elvis Presley | RCA | 1961 |
| 7 | WITH THE BEATLES | Beatles | PARLOPHONE | 1963 |
| 8 | A HARD DAY'S NIGHT | Beatles | PARLOPHONE | 1964 |
| 9 | BLUE HAWAII | Elvis Presley | RCA | 1962 |
| 10 | ABBEY ROAD | Beatles | APPLE | 1969 |
| 11 | SUMMER HOLIDAY (SOUNDTRACK) | Cliff Richard | COLUMBIA | 1963 |
| 12 | ROLLING STONES | Rolling Stones | DECCA | 1964 |
| 13 | THE BLACK AND WHITE MINSTREL SHOW | George Mitchell Minstrels | HMV | 1961 |
| 14 | JOHN WESLEY HARDING | Bob Dylan | CBS | 1968 |
| 15 | RUBBER SOUL | Beatles | PARLOPHONE | 1965 |
| 16 | HELP! | Beatles | PARLOPHONE | 1965 |
| 17 | BEATLES FOR SALE | Beatles | PARLOPHONE | 1965 |
| 18 | ANOTHER BLACK AND WHITE MINSTREL SHOW | George Mitchell Minstrels | HMV | 1961 |
| 19 | AFTERMATH | Rolling Stones | DECCA | 1966 |
| 20 | THE BEST OF THE SEEKERS | Seekers | COLUMBIA | 1969 |

## TOP ALBUM ACTS OF THE '60s

| | UK Charts | | US Charts |
|---|---|---|---|
| 1 | BEATLES | 1 | BEATLES |
| 2 | ELVIS PRESLEY | 2 | ELVIS PRESLEY |
| 3 | CLIFF RICHARD | 3 | FRANK SINATRA |
| 4 | FRANK SINATRA | 4 | ROLLING STONES |
| 5 | ROLLING STONES | 5 | KINGSTON TRIO |
| 6 | BOB DYLAN | 6 | HERB ALPERT & THE TIJUANA BRASS |
| 7 | JIM REEVES | 7 | ANDY WILLIAMS |
| 8 | BEACH BOYS | 8 | ENOCH LIGHT |
| 9 | SHADOWS | 9 | BARBRA STREISAND |
| 10 | GEORGE MITCHELL MINSTRELS | 10 | MONKEES |
| 11 | TOM JONES | 11 | BEACH BOYS |
| 12 | CREAM | 12 | DIANA ROSS & THE SUPREMES |
| 13 | MONKEES | 13 | MITCH MILLER |
| 14 | SUPREMES | 14 | RAY CHARLES |
| 15 | VAL DOONICAN | 15 | HENRY MANCINI |
| 16 | SEEKERS | 16 | LAURENCE WELK |
| 17 | ENGELBERT HUMPERDINCK | 17 | TEMPTATIONS |
| 18 | HOLLIES | 18 | PETER, PAUL & MARY |
| 19 | BUDDY HOLLY | 19 | RAY CONNIFF |
| 20 | KINKS | 20 | JOHNNY MATHIS |

## TOP SINGLES ACTS OF THE '60s

| | UK Charts | | US Charts |
|---|---|---|---|
| 1 | CLIFF RICHARD | 1 | BEATLES |
| 2 | ELVIS PRESLEY | 2 | ELVIS PRESLEY |
| 3 | BEATLES | 3 | SUPREMES |
| 4 | ROLLING STONES | 4 | BEACH BOYS |
| 5 | HOLLIES | 5 | FOUR SEASONS |
| 6 | SHADOWS | 6 | BRENDA LEE |
| 7 | MANFRED MANN | 7 | TEMPTATIONS |
| 8 | ROY ORBISON | 8 | ROLLING STONES |
| 9 | ADAM FAITH | 9 | HERMAN'S HERMITS |
| 10 | KINKS | 10 | CONNIE FRANCIS |
| 11 | EVERLY BROTHERS | 11 | RAY CHARLES |
| 12 | TOM JONES | 12 | CHUBBY CHECKER |
| 13 | BILLY FURY | 13 | MARVIN GAYE |
| 14 | HERMAN'S HERMITS | 14 | BOBBY VINTON |
| 15 | CILLA BLACK | 15 | DAVE CLARK FIVE |
| 16 | BEACH BOYS | 16 | ARETHA FRANKLIN |
| 17 | DUSTY SPRINGFIELD | 17 | ROY ORBISON |
| 18 | SUPREMES | 18 | STEVIE WONDER |
| 19 | ENGELBERT HUMPERDINCK | 19 | DION |
| 20 | SANDIE SHAW | 20 | MONKEES |

# INDEX

PICTURE ACKNOWLEDGMENTS

The Publishers gratefully acknowledge the tremendous assistance of London Features International in providing the majority of photographs for this book:

*London Features International:* Half title, Title, 6 TL&CL, 7 TR,CR&BR, 8 TR, 9 TL,TR&B, 10 BL&BR, 11 BL&BR, 13 L, 14 C, 15 T,C&B, 16 TL&TR, 17 L, 18 C, 19 L&TR, 20 T,C&B, 21 T,BC&BR, 22 R, 23 L,C&R, 24 TL,TR&BL, 25 T, 26 B, 32 B, 33 L, 35 TL,TR,C&B, 37 B, 38 T&C, 39 T, 41 BL&BR, 42 TL&B, 43 C, 44 TL,TR,BL&BR, 44-5 C, 45 TL, TR&BL, 46 T,C&B, 47 T&B, 48 TL,TR&BR, 49 TL,TR&B, 50 T&B, 51 TL&B, 52 C&R, 54 L&R, 55 R, 56 TR, 57 T, 58 ACL,BCR&BR, 60 T&B, 61 T&B, 62 T, 63 L, 64 T&BR, 66 B, 67 BL, 68 T, 69 B, 70 B, 72 T, 73 TL&BL, 74 BL&BR, 75 L,C&R, 76 T&B, 77 T&B, 78 T&B, 79 B, 80 T, 81 T,BL&BR, 82 T&B, 83 T,BC&B, 84 B, 85 T, C&B, 86 T,BL&BR, 87 T&B, 89 L&R, 90 T,BL&BR, 91 TR&B, 92 T,BL&BR, 93 T&B, 94 BL&BR, 95 L&R, 96, 97 TR&BR, 98 T&B, 99 T&B, 100 T,BL&BR, 101 B, 102 T&B, 103 R, 104 T&B, 105 TL,TR&B, 106 L&R, 107 L&R, 108 T&B, 109 T&B, 110 L&R, 111 B, 112 TL,TR,C&B, 113 T,BL,BC&B, 114 T&BR, 115 TR&B, 116 T&BR, 117 T,BL&BR, 118 T,C&B, 119 T,C&B, 120 T,C&B, 121 T,R&B, 122 B, 123 TR, 124 BC, 125 BC, 126 T,BL&BR, 127 L&R, 128 TL,R&BL, 129 TL,TR&B, 130 T,BL&BR, 131 TL,TR&B, 132 C, 133 T,BL&BR, 134, 135 L&R, 136 T,C,BL&BR, 137 T,C&B, 138 C, 139 T&B, 140.

*Michael Ochs Archive/LFI* 6 BL, 8 TL,BC&BR, 12 L&R, 13 R, 14 T&B, 16 B, 17 T, 18 T&B, 19 BR, 21 BL, 22 L, 24 BR, 25 B, 26 T, 27 T,C,BL&BR, 28 T,L&BR, 29 T, 30 TL,TR,C&B, 31 T&B, 32 T, 33 R, 34 T&C, 36 TL,TR&B, 37 T&C, 38 BL&BR, 40 T&B, 41 T, 42 TR, 43 T&B, 48 BL, 51 TR, 52 L, 53 T&B, 55 TL&BL, 56 TL&B, 57 C, 58 TL,BC,TR&TCR, 59, 60 C, 62 C, 63 R, 64 BL, 65 T,BL&BR, 66 T, 67 BR, 68 B, 69 T&L, 71 T&BR, 72 B, 73 R, 74 T, 79 T, 80 B, 83 AC, 88 B, 94 T, 101 T, 107 TR, 116 BL, 122 T, 123 C&B.

The publishers would like to thank the following organisations for their kind permission to reproduce additional photographs in this book: *Deram Records* (The Decca Record Co. Ltd); 99 C; *Ronald Grant Archive:* 70 T, 125 BR, 138 B; *The Hulton Picture Company:* 11 T, 29 B, 39 B, 97 TL, 103 L; *Jimi Hendrix Information Management Institute/Allan Koss:* 124 BL; *The Kobal Collection:* 34 B, 57 B, 62 B, 115 TL, 121 TL, 138 T; *Popperfoto:* 71 BL, 97 BL&BC; *Rex Features:* 58 BL, 84 T, 103 C,/Dezo Hoffman: 29 C.